Prais

"It's always darkest in the sh[...]d to prove itself along the wa[...]s story is a uniquely America.. one about a uniquely American sport. I highly recommend it."
—Jay Leno

"After all the things Kyle's done, I knew there had to be a book in there somewhere. Well, here it is. And I'll tell you what: Kyle doesn't believe in keeping secrets. Even I learned some things in here. And yeah, his mom deserves all the credit for how he turned out."
—Richard Petty

"He's lived through the worst possible scenario that could happen to anyone. Imagine going back to Loudon after that! You could throw haymakers at Kyle. He just rolls with it. He's like, 'I'm gonna walk around with a ponytail. . . . I'm gonna sing. . . . I'm gonna say whatever I wanna say on TV.' With that upbeat attitude of his and the way he grabs every opportunity, I do think Kyle has lived the lives of five people combined."
—Joey Logano

"For a guy that could be a prick because of who he is, he is just the greatest, most down-to-earth person I've ever met. Just like his dad. You gotta read Kyle's book. You gotta."
—Ric Flair

"As a competitor, broadcaster, family member, and dear friend, Kyle has lived through every era of our sport, impacting the lives of so many along the way. With a heartfelt gift for storytelling . . . his love for NASCAR and passion for the people in it make his firsthand account of motorsports history a must-read for racing fans everywhere."
—Lesa France Kennedy, executive vice chair of NASCAR

"An alternately entertaining and sobering look at the sport and big business of auto racing."
—*Kirkus Reviews*

"An intimate view inside one of NASCAR's foremost families."
—NASCAR.com

"A seemingly endless reel of NASCAR highlights."
—*The Daytona Beach News-Journal*

SWERVE OR DIE

Life at My Speed in the First Family of NASCAR Racing

KYLE PETTY
and ELLIS HENICAN

ST. MARTIN'S GRIFFIN
NEW YORK

Published in the United States by St. Martin's Griffin,
an imprint of St. Martin's Publishing Group

www.stmartins.com

Designed by Steven Seighman

The Library of Congress has cataloged the hardcover edition as follows:

Names: Petty, Kyle, author. | Henican, Ellis, author.
Title: Swerve or die : life at my speed in the first family of NASCAR racing /
    Kyle Petty and Ellis Henican.
Description: First edition. | New York : St. Martin's Press, 2022.
Identifiers: LCCN 2022007311 | ISBN 9781250277817 (hardcover) | ISBN
    9781250285553 (signed) | ISBN 9781250277824 (ebook)
Subjects: LCSH: Petty, Kyle. | Petty, Kyle—Family. | Stock car racing—United States. |
    NASCAR (Association) | Automobile racing drivers—United States—Biography.
Classification: LCC GV1032.P465 A3 2022 | DDC 796.72092 [B]—dc23/eng/20220321
LC record available at https://lccn.loc.gov/2022007311

ISBN 978-1-250-87564-8 (trade paperback)

First St. Martin's Griffin Edition: 2023

10 9 8 7 6 5 4 3 2 1

To my mom, who made me the person I am.

To my wife, Morgan, who showed me again
who that person was and who I could be.

CONTENTS

IV: THE ROAD AHEAD

INTRODUCTION

"Call Mike Helton."

I was in England with my daughter Montgomery Lee, looking at Welsh horses.

My son Adam was at the New Hampshire Motor Speedway with his red-and-black no. 45 Sprint PCS Chevrolet. His regular guys—Chris Hussey, Chris Martin, Scott Kuhn, Steve Mitchell, and Stephen Patseavouras—were at the track with him. A rising young racer and his crew, all good friends, doing exactly what they wanted to be doing with their lives. The Busch 200 was set for Saturday. Friday was for practice and qualifying. All of which just gave me another reason to smile.

The Cup teams had the weekend off. For us, it was a two-week breather between the Pontiac Excitement 400 in Richmond, which Dale Earnhardt, Jr., had won, becoming the first repeat winner of the season, and the Winston, the all-star race on May 20 in Charlotte. A perfect time for a father-daughter getaway!

The NASCAR world had been buzzing about Adam ever since he'd won an ARCA race (part of the NASCAR feeder series named for the Automobile Racing Club of America), his first ever, at eighteen years and three months old, the youngest driver to ever do that. You know whose record he broke? Mine. I was eighteen years and eight months old. There we were, Adam and I, already making our own family traditions! He was now in his second season as a Busch Series regular, itching to move up to Cup Series racing, NASCAR's main event. No one could say for sure how far Adam might go in racing. It was much too early to speculate. But when people asked me how I felt about my son's career choice, I always had the same answer: "Like any dad feels when his teenager leaves the driveway for the first time. I sure hope he makes it back safe."

I thought the line was funny. It almost always got a laugh.

It had been quite a spring for the Pettys. On April 5, my grandfather, Lee Petty, the patriarch of the Petty racing family, had died at eighty-six. What my grandfather started, my father, Richard Petty, and my uncle, Maurice Petty, carried on—it always felt more to me like a family business or a family farm than anything as grand as most people made it out to be. Stock car racing had supported our family for more than half a century, brought amazing joy into our lives, and gotten Adam labeled the first fourth-generation professional athlete in America. That sounded nice. But when you thought about it, it was also an awfully weighty legacy for a nineteen-year-old to haul around. Adam was just a kid, as anyone who knew him at all could plainly see.

And let's be honest, I wasn't exactly tearin' 'em up in my no. 44 Hot Wheels Pontiac. Just one top 10 finish so far that season, my twentieth as a Cup regular. But I wasn't sweating it. The season was just getting rolling, and I felt like I was starting to fall into a good rhythm. Plus, I had decided in my mind to step back from driving and move out of my son's way as my father, for personal and financial reasons, had been unable to move out of mine. My dad won his seventh NASCAR championship the year I started. He loved racing too much to quit. I didn't want to do that to Adam. I wanted him to have every chance to thrive. Once he was really up and running, he should be *the* Petty driver, I believed.

Montgomery Lee was fourteen and loved horses at least as much as her brother Adam loved race cars, which is to say she really, really loved them. She rode Western and seemed to have a knack for it. She had a beautiful bay mare named Dawn, and they'd been doing well together at some serious horse shows. Montgomery Lee wanted to see what showing horses was like in England. So, we were going to a show at a castle outside London. For me, it was that one week a year where it was just the two of us.

I didn't know much about horses, and what I did know was entirely from the dad's perspective. I knew it didn't make any difference whether your daughter had a $2 million horse or a $2 horse. It still ate the same amount of food. And I knew that, however much you thought your daughter's love of horses was going to cost you, you had no earthly idea. As I told my friend Jeff Burton when his daughter started riding: "Figure up how much that horse is gonna cost and multiply it by ten. Get the money in five-dollar bills, and go to the Bank of America building in Charlotte. Then, throw all that money off the roof. It'll be much cheaper that way." Jeff didn't believe me—until one day he did. "If only I had known," he said with a laugh. He wasn't complaining any more than I was. My daughter loved horses, and her daddy was along for the ride.

We had a magical Saturday at the horse show. The beautiful castle. The impressive animals. The talented riders. The look on Montgomery Lee's face as she took it all in. There was a message waiting for me in the lobby when we got back to the hotel.

"Call Mike Helton."

From the highest highs to the lowest lows, no one has lived the NASCAR life quite the way that I have. Thankfully, along with the worst nightmare any father can imagine, I've also been blessed with far more than my share of amazing experiences, special relationships, and thrilling race-day triumphs. I'll tell you this much, as NASCAR begins to reimagine its future and the sport confronts a whole new period of upheaval and change: It's been one hell of a ride so far—for me and for racing—and I can't wait to share with you exactly what I see up ahead!

Born into racing royalty. The only son of NASCAR's winningest driver ever. The grandson of one of the sport's true pioneers. The nephew of our very first Hall of Fame engine builder. It's quite a family to represent, and through it all, I've somehow managed to keep being Kyle.

I wouldn't attempt to tell the whole story of NASCAR entirely through people named Petty, but you almost could. My father, Richard, won two hundred races, a record that could easily hold forever, and seven Cup Series championships. Now well into his eighties, he remains NASCAR's undisputed King and still has his fingers in damn near everything, including the racial reexamination that has gripped our sport. When all that exploded, Bubba Wallace, the talented young African American driver who demanded the Confederate flag be banned, was part of Richard Petty Motorsports. And there was my father, in his signature black Charlie 1 Horse cowboy hat, standing right at Bubba's side. Whatever's happening in NASCAR, my dad's been at the center of the action for more than sixty years.

My Grandfather Petty was there at the start. He flipped his car in the very first NASCAR race ever and won the inaugural Daytona 500. His era began when stock car racing was little more than a bunch of country boys in the moonshine business trying to outrun each other and the tax man. It was Grandfather Petty who became NASCAR's first full-time driver and one of its earliest stars. Before him, driving a race car wasn't even considered a job. He finished top 5 in points every year from NASCAR's formation in 1949 until 1959 and won three national championships in those years. It should have been four. But he pissed off NASCAR founder Bill France, who docked him in points for driving in an unsanctioned but very well-paid race. Grandfather Petty didn't care. He always preferred the cash to the trophies.

My uncle Maurice, who passed in the summer of 2020, rarely got the credit that Richard and Lee have been given. I won't be making that mistake here. While the drivers soak up most of the attention, the cars wouldn't go anywhere without the hard work and the genius of the mechanics in the garages and the pits. That's something I figured out early, and I've never forgotten it. It's just one of many lessons you learn growing up Petty.

As for me, I was tossed into the family station wagon and dragged to the races even before I graduated from a bottle to a sippy cup. From the Allisons to the Earnhardts to the Waltrips, from the Cales to the Dales to the Jeffs and the Jimmies, my sisters and I got to know just about everyone who was anyone in racing, and I still know 'em all, along with their wives, ex-wives, aunts, uncles, children, cousins, grandchildren, and dogs. No, it wasn't your typical American upbringing. And, yes, it's fair to say that NASCAR is more than a little intertwined.

I was helping out at the Petty race shop in Level Cross, North Carolina, by the time I was in junior high school. I started racing professionally as soon as I turned eighteen. Somehow, I wore down my father's insistence that I wait until twenty-one, like his father had demanded that he wait. My own driving record never held a candle to my father's or my grandfather's—but, really, whose did? Across a long, action-packed career of 829 NASCAR Cup Series races, I won, lost, and crashed on some of the fastest, wildest, scariest, and most storied racetracks in America. And with Adam's entry into racing, the Petty tradition I had inherited was about to be passed on again.

I had known Mike Helton since he was sports director of a small AM radio station in Bristol, Tennessee, and worked public relations part-time at the Bristol Motor Speedway. After working at racetracks in Atlanta, Daytona Beach, and Talladega, Mike took a job with NASCAR, where he became the first person without the name France to run day-to-day operations. He would soon be appointed NASCAR's third president, replacing Bill France, Jr. I can and will say this about Mike: He was a racing guy through and through.

He skipped all the pleasantries and got right to the reason for his call.

"Adam's been in a bad wreck," he said to me. "He's been transported to the hospital."

You know that feeling you get when someone punches you in the stomach? This didn't feel like that at all. This was more like the air coming out of a balloon. I didn't feel pain. I just felt suddenly deflated.

Mike didn't seem to know much yet, but he promised: "I'll call the minute I know any more."

Montgomery Lee was up in the room. I stayed down in the lobby. Since I didn't know what to tell her yet, I didn't tell her anything. Mike was back on the phone maybe twenty minutes later.

Calling back so quickly, I knew it couldn't be good.

"Man," he said, reaching for the right words and realizing there weren't any, "I'm so sorry. He didn't make it."

Short and to the point.

I didn't ask Mike a lot of questions. I didn't really want to know every last detail. There'd be time for that later. All Mike said was that it was a single-car collision during a practice round. Nobody else was hurt. What else did I really need to know?

"Thank you for calling," I said to Mike before I headed upstairs to talk to my daughter and try to make sense of the two-by-four that had just been slammed against the side of my head.

There may be a couple of people who are more steeped in the world of NASCAR than I am, but I kinda doubt it. And no one can afford to speak any more freely than I can. Honestly, what's anyone gonna do to *me?*

In every role I've ever played—and by now I've played just about all of them: racer, car owner, motorcycle rider, country singer, songwriter, camp counselor, broadcaster, Christian, voice actor, body-art proponent, philanthropist, son, brother, husband, dad, and friend—I've come to be known as an outsider-insider, someone whose knowledge goes all the way back to the ancients and who isn't afraid to hang his opinions out to dry. I can get along with just about anybody, but I always say what I think. And I don't waste time worrying how others might respond.

"That's just Kyle," people have been saying for decades. And I don't suppose they'll be stopping any time soon. They may not always love my ponytail. But no one's ever accused me of being boring, dishonest, or shy. Or taking myself too seriously.

These days, I hang out on what some of my friends jokingly call *the dark side,* analyzing and commentating on NASCAR for NBC Sports. Then, I toss out a tweet or two, having jumped into social media in 2009 when most NASCAR people were still hesitant. I interview my friends on *Coffee with Kyle,* a digital series for NBC Sports focusing on the history of NASCAR, and *Dinner Drive with Kyle Petty,* a TV show on Circle Network that's all about cars, good food, and great conversations with notable names in sports and entertainment. And every chance I get, hang out with Morgan, Overton, and Cotten at home. Telling stories. Swapping gossip. Getting laughs. Getting more laughs. Solving all the world's problems whether anyone's asked me to or not. Sharing my feelings about the racing world in ways that hardly anyone else will dare to.

This book has been decades in the making. I am so excited to say, "Here it is."

You may be a lifelong NASCAR fan who craves to know the story behind the story behind the story. You may be itching for the inside version that only I can tell. Or you may be a curious newcomer, shaking your head and wondering, "What the heck is going on in there?" Whatever brought you, get ready for an eye-opening, nerve-racking, soul-bending romp through this crazy sport of ours, just as its future is being debated, defined, and declared.

For better or worse, NASCAR has never been more important in politics, culture, and business—not just of the American South but of the whole United States and, increasingly, beyond. You certainly can't understand America without understanding the people, places, and events that live in the pages to come.

I promise I won't shy away from the tough stuff. I never do. And that includes my own dark days after Adam's accident, my decision to keep driving longer than I probably should have, and the wonderful joy that is Victory Junction and the Kyle Petty Charity Ride Across America. Through it all and still today, I've never forgotten how blessed I am.

But I'm getting ahead of myself already. We'll get to all of it. The racing. The characters. The controversies. The big, sprawling, complicated family. The dramatic changes that are already shaking NASCAR and redefining this sport that we love and that also sometimes drives us crazy. NASCAR is finding its place in a rapidly changing world. So the sport is changing too. There are exciting possibilities and hidden obstacles ahead. We need to sort them out. It'll be an amazing journey for those who can handle the speed.

Come on. I'll show you. Let's take a ride.

Part I

DREAMER

1

UNIQUELY PETTY

"He thinks he's a cowboy."

Randolph County, smack in the middle of North Carolina, wasn't famous for much. But at one time, it was famous for having more dirt roads than any other county in the state. I grew up on one of them, Branson Mill Road, at a tiny X on the map called Level Cross. When I was a kid, they would cancel school if it rained too hard. The buses couldn't make it through all the muck. And this wasn't the Great Depression. It was the 1960s. Astronauts were zooming through space, and interstate highways were speeding car travel. A lot of things came to other places before they came to Randolph County.

Like paved roads.

The Piedmont—that's what folks called our part of North Carolina. The hills were rolling. The people were churchgoing, family-focused, and more than a little suspicious of outsiders. The land was ideal for cows, chickens, tobacco, and also buzzing past the neighbors' farms on a motorcycle. Sometimes, I would whine to my mother that I was bored, and she always had the same answer for me: If I was looking for fun, I'd darn well better go make some of my own. And she seemed to mean it. Greensboro, High Point, and Winston-Salem, actual cities, were all within a half-hour's drive of us. But Level Cross and the nearby town of Randleman might as well have been in a different state or a different century. Andy Griffith didn't come from Randolph County. He hailed from up the road in Mount Airy. But he might as well have. We had our very own versions of Andy, Barney, Opie, and Aunt Bea. Local boosters sometimes bragged that Randolph County was the original home of what became Duke University, and that's true. It was called Brown's Schoolhouse at the time. But the fast-growing institution packed up and moved to Durham in 1892, and there's never been any talk of moving back.

You want to know how crazy things were? When I was little, we still had a four-digit phone number. No area code. No prefix. Just four numbers. To call home when he was off somewhere racing, my dad would ring the hotel operator from his room. The hotel operator would call a long-distance operator. The long-distance operator would call a North Carolina long-distance operator, who would connect to North State, the independent telephone company in High Point, whose operator would connect to a North State operator in Randleman, who would connect the call to our house on Branson Hill Road. The hotel operator would ring my dad in the room as soon as my mom was on the line. It could take a good ten minutes for the call to go through. My dad's phone number still ends in the same four numbers, though now his friends have to remember six more digits before they ever get there or keep it programmed on their cell phones.

For a long time, I've been thinking about my family and where we come from and how we got to be the way that we are. I remember talking with Adam about that one day. He'd asked me about some of the weirdness that hovers over the Petty family and what being a Petty should mean to him. I answered the best way I knew how.

"I don't know whether you've noticed it or not," I said to him, "but your granddad is a little odd. We live in North Carolina. He wears dark sunglasses at night. He wears a cowboy hat and cowboy boots. He thinks he's a cowboy, and he's never even ridden a horse. Don't you think that's a little odd?"

Adam just laughed. He had to agree.

You know how it is: I could say those things because I was talking about my own family. If someone else had come along and started spouting off like that—well, there might have been a problem. But this was just us talking.

I offered Adam a second example, one that hit even closer to home.

"Now, you look at me," I said to my son. "I've got long hair in a pony-tail. I've got a couple of earrings. I'm a race car driver who also wants to sing at the Grand Ole Opry. That's probably a little odd too."

Adam laughed again.

"But you?" I said, getting around to the real point I was driving at with my son. "You don't need to be like your grandfather, and you don't need to be like me. Figure out who *you* are. Just be you and be happy about it. That's the main thing. Be you."

Nothing happens by accident. At least nothing in our family does.

Four generations of Pettys did not randomly decide that, instead of getting real jobs, they would spend their lives driving round and round in circles on Sunday afternoons, trying and often succeeding to do it faster than a couple of dozen other guys who decided to do the exact same thing that same day. What's the chance of that? What's the chance it would have been so successful? It had to come from somewhere.

That *somewhere* was Randolph County.

My mother's people were the Owenses. They came from around High Point, ground zero for the furniture industry, and then moved to Randle-man, which was more of a mill town. Granddaddy Owens, Leonard Gar-land Owens, had worked at a shipyard in Jacksonville, Florida, during World War II, where he breathed in the sharp fibers that would poison his lungs later in life. After the Army, he became a carpenter and a cabi-net maker, working for a small construction company and installing cab-inets in people's kitchens. Grandma Owens, Helen Louise Cable Owens, worked her whole life in a textile mill. There was nothing glamorous about any of that work. The mills were right out of the movie *Norma Rae*. You'd drag in every morning. You had your machine and your little clique of friends around you. And for most people, that was as far as you would ever expect to go. Grandma Owens was one of thirteen children. Not a lot of them survived. Infant mortality was still rampant in the Piedmont. She learned to deal with a lot of loss when she was small. She did it by trusting in Jesus and being the nicest, kindest, sweetest, most generous person you could ever meet. If she saw a man begging in the street, she'd give him something, even if she didn't have anything herself. You could tell her, "That man's gonna take that five dollars and buy a fifth." She would say, "That's between him and God. That's not between him and me." She'd say, "God put it on my heart to give to this man. I'm blessed I gave. What he does with it, that's no concern of mine." And she believed it. She and Granddaddy Owens, they were just special, real down-home North Carolina people, not an ounce of pretension between them. All they did was be nice to people and try to make the world a better place. They had three children, two daughters and a son.

My mom, Lynda Gayle Owens, was born in 1942 while her dad was in the Army. She was a popular girl with tons of friends and loads of energy. She had a sister named Rebecca, almost seven years older, who everyone called Tootsie, and a younger brother, Randy, who was thirteen years behind. By the time my mom got to Randleman High School, she was helping to raise her little brother while her parents were off at work. Even at an early age, this was a girl who could take care of things. To her closest girlfriends—Martha Jane, Betty Jo, a tight-knit group of others—she was Lynda Gayle. Both names. But with everyone else, including her family, she went by her first name alone.

She was a perky freshman cheerleader and future homecoming queen when she caught the eye of a lanky, dark-haired boy almost five years her senior. His name was Richard Petty. He'd been an All-Conference guard on the Randleman football team and dreamed of becoming a race car driver like his father, Lee Petty. After a quick *hi-bye* at Greensboro Junior College, young Richard was helping out in his father's garage and plotting his own racing career. Suddenly, he was showing up again at high-school sporting events ("Go, Tigers!") and volunteering to be the official transportation director of the cheerleading squad, driving the young ladies to away games.

That's when Richard and Lynda officially started dating.

He picked her up for their first date in a car with no passenger seat. She tolerated it for a time or two, then put her foot down. She wasn't getting back in until he gave her something to sit on. The next time he drove up to the high school, he had a tire where the passenger seat belonged and a rope for a seat belt. And their wild ride had only begun. They went to movies at the Rand Theater in Randleman. They went to more movies at the Rand. There weren't all that many places for a young couple to court in greater Randleman. They drove to Greensboro to pick up auto parts. She could tell he loved her because some weekends, when he could have been off racing with his father, he hung around to be with her.

In that part of Randolph County, there were 1,300, maybe 1,400 people. The whole high school had maybe one hundred students. This wasn't Atlanta or Charlotte or even Greensboro. In those days, people from Randolph County didn't travel very much. Most of them didn't go *anywhere*. Once the teenage pairing off began, everybody was swimming in a fairly shallow dating pool. But these two spending so much time together did raise some eyebrows, and not just because of the five years between them. In those days, folks didn't talk much about social class. Not in so many words, they didn't. Outsiders might have looked at Randolph County and thought, *All those people are pretty much the same.* But this speck of North Carolina had a pecking order just as sure as feudal England or imperial Japan. And everybody knew where everybody else fit in.

At the top were the "city people" who lived right in Randleman. Having moved from High Point, the *big city,* my mother's family, the Owenses, were even a step up on that. They weren't rich, obviously. But both parents had regular jobs and a house in town, and they came from somewhere bigger. All that stuff mattered.

Just below the city people were the farmers outside town. They had land. That also meant something. You could live in a shack, but if you had fifty acres, you were a rich man. You weren't a sharecropper like your ancestors most likely were. You owned something God wasn't making any more of, something your neighbor almost certainly coveted—to grow more crops on or to graze his animals. (No one was thinking about subdivisions yet or condos.) The children or grandchildren might not want to make their lives there. The next generations might see the land as just a commodity, not understanding that once it was gone it would be gone forever. But that land gave farmers a certain status in Randolph County that went beyond how much money they almost certainly did not have.

On the bottom were the country people who didn't have land. The Pettys, for example. Sitting out there in Level Cross. Working on cars in that garage of theirs. Driving like hellions on the dirt country roads. How did they even make a living? Sometimes, my grandfather would weld a farmer's tractor in exchange for a bushel of corn.

A suspicion of outsiders was one thing that was shared by all these different groups.

Neighbors were helping neighbors all the time. Getting up hay, returning missing livestock, helping with repairs, whatever it took. And if an outsider wandered by, everyone would be cordial, up to a point. But there was a strong suspicion too. The message to strangers, unspoken or not, was, "You need to get gone as soon as you can get gone."

Especially if an outsider acted like he knew better than the locals did, that cold shoulder would come right out. The idea was, *We've been getting along OK without you so far.* There was a strong feeling of, *You may think you know better, but you don't know us.*

That resentment of people who think they know better—that's always been a part of the American character, right up to the politics of today. Well, that was never far below the surface in Randolph County.

When Lynda Owens was seventeen and Richard Petty was twenty-two and just beginning to drive his own race car, he proposed marriage, and she agreed. Imagining the reaction they would get from their families, they decided they should probably elope. They didn't tell anybody. They drove across the state line to Chesterfield, South Carolina, where the town clerk took one look at the girl standing in front of him and announced that she was too young to marry without her parents' permission. The young couple thought about asking but decided that was hopeless. Instead, they returned the next day with Lynda's birth certificate, altered to show that she was already eighteen.

So there it was: Some time in 1959, my parents got married. You read that right. I don't know when their anniversary is. No one does. It's a bit of a family mystery, but it's true. Just know that young love triumphed over age and the social divide!

My father didn't have money for a ring. It took him three months to save up. But once he did, he and his teenage bride broke the news to both their families and moved into his parents' stone house on Branson Mill Road. When they'd saved a few more dollars, Richard and Lynda moved out—and into a trailer in his parents' side yard, eventually to be replaced by a small house of their own.

Despite the social distinctions of Randolph County and the young couple's decision to elope, Granddaddy and Grandma Owens accepted their new son-in-law with open arms, even if he did come from a family of racers outside town. They just loved him. If their daughter had gotten hitched to a man with three heads, I'm sure they would have found something to love in him too. Grandma Owens, especially. That's just how she was. The ones who looked askance were my father's parents, Grandmother and Grandfather Petty, as I would always call them—formal like that. With them, there was a feeling of, *You don't need to be marrying yet. You're twenty-two. That'll be a distraction, for sure.* But married he was, and there wasn't much his parents could do about it, except to let their feelings be known in their own awkward ways.

It was mainly Grandfather Petty.

From all I've heard and seen, I don't think he had anything particular against his new daughter-in-law. She was supportive and cheerful and pregnant in a hurry with me. But just to tick her off, a lot of the time he would call her *Brenda*. He knew her name was Lynda. But Brenda sounded a little like Lynda, and I guess he thought it was funny to mess with her that way. (Later, he'd take similar little digs, equally pointless, at Patsy, the wife of his younger son, Maurice.) That's just how he was. Ornery is a good word for it. I don't doubt for a minute he loved his family, including his two daughters-in-law. He felt a keen responsibility as a breadwinner, that's for sure. But he certainly had a self-centered way of carrying himself.

Coming from nothing, Grandfather Petty never pulled a punch in his life. He was honest and straightforward in everything he did, but I wouldn't call him charming or fun. He said what he was thinking, and he meant what he said. The last thing he cared about was other people's opinions. Whatever it was, it was just what he felt. It was your job to deal with it.

His phone used to ring at his house, and he'd let it ring and ring and ring. This was long before answering machines or, God knows, voice mail. When the phone would finally quit ringing, I remember asking him, "Why didn't you answer that?"

"I didn't need to talk to whoever it was," he told me. "If I needed to talk to them, I would have called them."

"You don't even know who it is," I reminded him.

"That's my point," he said.

Thank goodness he had a wife to soften the edges.

Grandmother Petty was easily the warmer one. She was involved with everything and everyone. Born Elizabeth Toomes, one of eight children of Robert and Allie Hodgin Toomes, she married my grandfather when she was twenty and he was twenty-three, which wasn't so young for the time. Though her husband could obviously be difficult, it never seemed to rattle her. She walked what in hindsight must have been a difficult line, recognizing that her husband could be a handful but treasuring his admirable qualities and loving him for who he was. I've never seen two people more in love than Grandmother and Grandfather Petty.

She took almost full responsibility for the child-rearing, looking after Richard and Maurice while Grandfather Petty was driving trucks and then racing cars and making a living. But she was also involved in running the business too.

I don't think she considered any of that remarkable. She'd been around farm wives. The same way they kept things running on the farm, that's how she juggled the bills, wrote the checks, weighed the big decisions, and smoothed out the hurt feelings my grandfather left in his wake. Actually, she did pretty much everything besides driving and fixing the cars, and she didn't seek a crumb of credit for any of it. It was exactly like when the farmer said to his wife, "The tractor's broke. Do we have enough in the account to buy the part?" And the wife said, "Yeah, we have enough" or "No, we don't."

That was Grandmother Petty.

Without her, Grandfather Petty would not have been half the success he was.

2

FAMILY BUSINESS

"It's the money, man."

No one can say for sure when stock car racing began. No plaque marks the exact location. No green flag was waved that day. Probably it was a couple of guys on a backroad somewhere throwing shade on each other's rides.

"Look at that junk you're drivin'!"

"Wanna race?"

People like to trace our sport's nativity to the Prohibition days of the 1920s and early 1930s. You've heard this version of the story, I'm sure. It features a bunch of thrill-seeking hillbillies spinning out on sharp mountain passes and busting their axles on bumpy dirt roads. With booze suddenly illegal, the country boys had an extra incentive to drive like maniacs. They had to outrun the federal agents who wanted to seize the local moonshine—and, once Prohibition ended in 1933, tax it beyond the reach of regular working folks. I love a good story, especially one that pits clever working people against the big, bad government. And this story does have some truth in it. No doubt those country boys did hate taxes and did learn a driving trick or two outrunning the revenuers. But stock car racing really didn't blossom as a sport until the 1940s. That's when soldiers were coming home from World War II and looking for something fun to do. The options were thin, in the South especially. We didn't have the Yankees and the Cubs and the Red Sox to root for. It wasn't until 1966 that the Braves hightailed it out of Milwaukee for Atlanta. The NFL, the NBA, and the NHL—those teams couldn't find their way South with an Esso map and a Trailways bus ticket! But we did have a couple of things going for us in this part of the country. We had plenty of pasture space and no shortage of good ol' boys who were willing to go out on a Sunday after church and race each other—and even more people who were willing to watch.

Pretty soon, guys were driving fast cars all over the Carolinas, Virginia, Tennessee, Georgia, Alabama, northern Florida—the whole core of the rural South. A farmer would cut a circle in his pasture. Then, some promoter would come to town and say, "We're having a race out here." But when the tickets had all been sold and the race was underway and everybody was watching from the little grandstand or lounging on the hoods of their cars, something sneaky would frequently occur. The promoter would slip out of town with the prize money and nobody would get paid. That kept happening until a man in Daytona Beach, Florida, named Bill France said, "If we all come together under one umbrella, we can fix that."

France, who was a mechanic and a driver, had moved down from Washington, D.C. He'd been promoting races on Daytona's hard-packed beach sand and running a course where the drivers had broken some land speed records. People were skeptical of him at first. How did they know he wasn't just another smooth-talking promoter looking to fleece the decent folks? But he seemed to have it all thought out. On December 14, 1947, he called a meeting at the Ebony Club bar on the roof of Daytona's Streamline Hotel. A couple of dozen drivers, car owners, and mechanics showed up. Which led, a little more than two months later, to the creation of NASCAR, the National Association for Stock Car Auto Racing.

I should probably point out here that *Car* and *Auto* are the same thing. They really didn't need to say it twice. People have been laughing about that for three-quarters of a century now. The group was originally going to be the National Stock Car Racing Association, which would have been NSCRA. But that didn't sound as good and another organization was already using that name. It was a long-forgotten mechanic, not an English major, who suggested *NASCAR*, repetition and all. And so the future was born.

Not surprisingly, things got off to a bit of a rocky start.

France planned for three distinct racing divisions: Modified, Roadster, and one he called Strictly Stock. His highest hopes were for the first two. But the fans turned up their noses at the roadsters, which they considered overly precious or, even worse, too northern. That division was quickly abandoned. The Modified division got rolling, but the stock car racing had to be put on hold. Detroit just couldn't produce enough family sedans to keep up with the roaring postwar demand, much less supply a new racing industry. So NASCAR's first stock car race wasn't held until June 19, 1949, eighteen months after the glasses were clinked in celebration at the rooftop Ebony Club.

That first race was held on a three-quarter-mile red-dirt track a few miles southwest of Charlotte, just beside what is now Charlotte Douglas International Airport, where some of the rental car places are located. And from that very first day of racing, the name Petty was in the mix. Joining the crowded field was a flinty Carolinian from Randolph County's Level Cross: my grandfather, Lee Petty, who hadn't even begun racing until he was thirty-five years old. That race would mark the earliest official connection between NASCAR and the Petty family, the very Sunday afternoon that NASCAR stock car racing was born.

It was an appropriately seat-of-the-pants operation for both the Pettys and for NASCAR.

Before he started racing, Grandfather Petty had a small trucking company with a couple of his brothers. Whether they were actually running moonshine, I'll leave that to your imagination and just explain it like I've been explaining it for years: *He was in beverage transportation before he was in racing.* He drove a 1948 Buick Roadmaster for that first race in Charlotte, though the car wasn't his. He borrowed it from a neighbor with the assurance that the prize money would certainly pay off any potential damages to the car.

"I listened in on Daddy's half of that conversation when he was on the phone with the guy, Gilmer Goode," my dad told me many years later. "It was the greatest sales job I've ever heard."

By all accounts, the racetrack was more like a disaster zone. With my dad and his younger brother, Maurice, watching from the weed-infested pits, the thirty-three cars funneled into turn 1 with so much force, red dust was flying like a tornado, blinding the drivers, choking the fans, turning the track surface into a pot-holed obstacle course, as the cars bounced and boogied along. Breaking suspensions. Tossing off parts. Exhausting the drivers. Half the field was out by the midway point.

That's about where my grandfather lost control of his borrowed Buick and barrel-rolled through the third turn. Said my father, "My first thought was, 'I hope Daddy's OK.' My second thought was, 'Oh, man, how are we gonna get home?'"

Grandfather Petty was fine, but the Buick was totaled.

My grandfather wasn't the least bit discouraged by all the mayhem that day, even after breaking the unfortunate news to Gilmer Goode. My grandfather entered a couple more races and he won them. That's all it took for him to say goodbye to the trucking business and make racing his full-time job, a distinction that remained quite rare for the first eight or ten years of the sport. Everybody else, they were carpenters or roofers or drove a truck for a liquor company or they had a farm. Buck Baker and Joe Weatherly and the Flocks—they all had other jobs Monday to Friday. They just showed up at the track and drove. That would remain true for some highly successful drivers into the early 1960s. When Ned Jarrett was about to win the championship in 1961, he was still in the sawmill business. Even later, Harry Gant was putting roofs on houses during the week, then wiping the tar off his hands and heading to the track. I remember being surprised when I heard that Franco Harris, the four-time Super Bowl–champion Pittsburgh Steelers fullback, worked as a baker during the off-season. Well, he had nothing on those early NASCAR guys.

There was no starry-eyed reason for my grandfather's decision to jump into racing with both feet. It wasn't the thrill of competition or the love of speed or the quest for trophies or the thirst for fame or a desire to bring pleasure to the cheering fans or anything remotely like that. His interest was far more practical. He saw racing as a way to earn a buck—a better way to make money and put food on the table for his young family. Nothing more, nothing less. That's what racing was all about for him.

His two sons, Richard and Maurice, were twelve and ten years old by then, and Maurice had battled a tough bout of childhood polio. He was a strong, strapping kid with extraordinary determination, who figured he could do anything any of his friends could. He wouldn't let a limp keep him from following in his older brother's cleat-steps and making the football team at Randleman High. Of the boys, gritty Maurice seemed to take more after his father, while Richard's friendly, sunny demeanor was far closer to his mom's. But both his sons were top of mind as Grandfather Petty threw himself into his new racing career. He would go on to finish top 5 in each of NASCAR's first eleven seasons, winning three championships, and would become one of stock car racing's earliest stars. He'd grown up in a hardworking family in a quiet corner of the country at a time when the opportunities for social betterment were few and far between. Through his drive and his talent, if not his cheerful personality, he'd found a way to provide for himself and especially for his family. He was a practical man. He knew what he wanted, and he got busy achieving it.

And if you ever asked him why he did it, he wouldn't hesitate to tell you.

"It's the money, man."

My father drove his first race on July 18, 1958, sixteen days after his twenty-first birthday. Back then, NASCAR didn't have an official minimum age for drivers, but Lee Petty did. "You can drive a race car when you're twenty-one," he'd been telling his impatient son for years, almost always adding, "And not a day sooner."

My grandfather had been running the no. 42. So when my father came along, he ran the no. 43.

That first race was the Jim Mideon 500 at Exhibition Stadium in Toronto, Ontario, Canada. So Richard Petty, who'd go on to be America's greatest stock car racer ever, began his professional driving career on Canadian soil. He didn't care. He was so excited to begin his racing, he'd have done it anywhere, anyhow, anytime.

Canada had a law at the time that allowed only team sports to be played professionally on Sundays, and the Canadians didn't consider stock car racing a team sport, even after NASCAR officials pointed out the pit crews that accompanied each driver. So the race was held on Friday night. One hundred laps, 33.3 miles, and nineteen drivers, including Lee and Richard Petty.

Just because his son was racing, my grandfather felt no compunction to get out of the way. My grandfather, driving a 1957 Oldsmobile 88, took the lead from Rex White in lap 72 and held it until the end. He won with an average speed of 43.184 miles an hour. But that's not what would be remembered by any of the 9,700 racing fans in attendance. What they'd all recall—or pretend to, anyway—was the kid in the no. 142 car, another 1957 Olds, whose minor crash on lap 55 put him out of the race, leaving him with a seventeenth-place finish and a $115 check.

They couldn't say he looked like much that night in Toronto. But for decades to come, they could all brag that they were present when a future legend started his engine on a racetrack for the very first time. In fact, so many people have claimed they were there that night, forget the official crowd count of 9,700. Two and a half million race fans must have somehow squeezed into Exhibition Stadium for my father's first run.

3

FAST START

"I had Beauchamp by a good two feet."

It took a solid decade for Bill France to give his racing dream a proper home. But he finally got it done, chasing off hundreds of unhappy alligators and snakes, filling in a rugged patch of Florida swampland and constructing a modern racetrack four miles west of the Streamline Hotel. All these years later, his Daytona International Speedway is still the sport's premiere venue and its holiest shrine. And since the very first running of the Daytona 500, February 22, 1959, the fundamentals have hardly changed at all. Same basic layout. Same banked design. Same twenty-nine-acre lake in the middle, dredged to fill in the swamp. Same 2.5-mile, four-turn track configuration (with a couple of possible alternates, a 3.56-mile road course and a 2.95-mile motorcycle circuit). Most of the alligators are gone. Most of them. One occasionally waddles across the concrete just for old times' sake. But all these years later at Daytona, everything is still the same. That's vision for what a sport, a facility, and a business can be. And to think: All the drivers were hoping for at the start was less sand in the carburetors once the races in Daytona finally got off the beach.

The Pettys were well represented that first day at Daytona. My dad qualified to race in the convertible division, driving an open-top 1957 Oldsmobile, the no. 43 car. My grandfather had a hardtop 1959 Olds Super 88, no. 42. My uncle Maurice was in the pit. Racing in two divisions on the same track at the same time was certainly unusual—and not something that would be repeated very often in the years to come. The convertibles would race the other convertibles. The hardtops would race the other hardtops. A winner from each division would be named. The field was huge that day, twenty convertibles and thirty-nine hardtops.

But it wasn't traffic jams the drivers and crew members were worried about. It was Daytona's potential for speed. Before the race, they all sat together in the garage area and stared up at France's enormous, banked track. No one had ever seen anything like it before. Everyone knew the steep design would make the cars go faster and give the fans a clearer view of the race. But how much faster and what else would that mean? Some of the drivers were convinced that a car could run down the backstretch so fast, it might actually take off like an airplane. A few other drivers were sure they'd slip straight off the bank and into the lake with the remaining snakes and gators. All the drivers were anxious. But they weren't about to say, "No, thank you, Mr. France." Not with $19,050 waiting for the winner, the richest purse an official NASCAR race had ever seen. So they did the only thing they knew how to: They took a deep breath, started their engines, and hoped for the best.

"We popped through that concrete tunnel," my dad recalled, "and it was like, 'Oh, my gosh, what do we do now?'"

None of the cars actually got airborne, though the average speed, 135.5 miles an hour, was a shocking pace to maintain for more than three and a half hours, the second-fastest 500-mile race ever recorded. At various points in the race, seven different drivers held the lead. It all came down to the final lap, when things got confusing really fast.

Here's what happened: Three drivers were side by side by side roaring toward the finish line. One was Grandfather Petty. The second, a gentleman from Iowa named Johnny Beauchamp, was a typical racer for that time. Just a regular guy who hung out in local garages and was good with a screwdriver and a wrench. Johnny had been racing unmodified stock cars on dirt tracks since World War II. A mechanic friend of his bought a 1959 T-Bird for $5,500, car no. 73, and asked Johnny to drive it at Daytona. And damned if Johnny wasn't side by side with Grandfather Petty, battling for the lead. Right there with them was Joe Weatherly, a wild man from Norfolk, Virginia, in the no. 48, a 1959 Chevy. Joe had a reputation as a late-night drinker and was a great showman who had once taken practice laps in a Peter Pan suit and, another day, came across the finish line standing in an open convertible with flames shooting out the back, his very own "chariot of fire." But at Daytona that day, as the checkered flag flew, the fans who were paying attention knew that Joe was actually a lap behind Lee and Johnny, just trying to get out of the way.

So who won the race as the two of them roared across the start-finish line?

It was hard to tell from the grandstand or the pits.

Johnny Beauchamp pulled his car out in the grass. My grandfather pulled his car out in the grass. There was no Victory Lane at Daytona back then. Exactly 41,921 race fans were standing and squinting at the two top drivers and their dirty cars. Bill France arrived.

"I'm sorry, Lee," he said to my grandfather. "Johnny won the race."

"No, he did not," my grandfather responded. "I beat him to the line. I won this race, and you're gonna pay me my money." My grandfather knew why he was there. To get paid.

"I'm sorry, Lee," France told him.

"I won the race," my grandfather insisted.

"I'm sorry, Lee."

They went back and forth like that a few more rounds with neither man budging. As things got testier, some men in uniform escorted my grandfather away a little bit. The disagreement spilled into the local papers.

"I had Beauchamp by a good two feet," my grandfather told the *Daytona Beach Morning Journal*. "In my own mind, I know I won."

Johnny agreed on the two-foot part but insisted those two feet were his. "I glanced over to Lee Petty's car as I crossed the finish line, and I could see his headlight slightly back of my car," he told the paper's afternoon edition. "It was so close I didn't know how they would call it, but I thought I won."

Driver Fireball Roberts, who'd led the race at one point before dropping out with engine trouble, had been standing by the finish line. "There's no doubt about it," he said. "Petty won." But it wasn't Fireball's decision. It was Bill France's, and he was sticking with Johnny Beauchamp.

My grandfather went back to the hotel and called France in the morning.

"As soon as we get a photo and look at it," the NASCAR chief said, "we'll know for sure. Somebody has to have a photo."

This was half a century before every man, woman, and dog showed up at the racetrack with a cell phone camera. Race photos were fewer and farther between, and they all had to be developed. NASCAR put an ad in the newspapers, asking for photos. None of that was quick. And my grandfather called every morning and every afternoon.

Finally, France said, "You can come by, Lee. You're right. We have a photo of it. You won the race."

You can see that photo today at the NASCAR Hall of Fame in Charlotte. They have a big, blown-up version. It's clear as day. The white no. 42 car is two feet in front of the no. 73 car, just like my grandfather said it would be.

"I do have to tell you," France said to my grandfather before he hung up the phone, "Johnny has already gone back to Iowa, and he has the trophy."

My grandfather did not miss a beat. "I don't give a shit about the trophy," he answered. "You got the check? I'll be there in thirty minutes."

Twenty-nine minutes later, that check was in my grandfather's pocket. He and my grandmother, along with my dad and Maurice, were driving out of Daytona and home to North Carolina.

From then until the day he died in 2000, three weeks after his eighty-sixth birthday, my grandfather would remain convinced that France knew all along who really won that race. He purposely handed the victory to Johnny Beauchamp to stir up controversy. As my grandfather told me: "France would have done anything to generate publicity for his racetrack. Not that I blame him. If I was in his shoes, I might have done the same thing."

Most parents today will bend over backwards to give their children every last opportunity, even the occasional undeserved leg up in life. I get it. It's only natural. I feel that way about my kids. But that was definitely *not*

Lee Petty's child-rearing approach. I know he loved his sons. He wanted them both to do well. But that didn't mean Grandfather Petty would ever go easy on my uncle or my dad.

If there was ever doubt, it was shattered on June 14, 1959, when my father took the checkered flag at Atlanta's Lakewood Speedway in the 150-mile Sweepstakes race, signaling his first-ever NASCAR Grand Nationals win.

What a great achievement a month before the young driver's twenty-second birthday!

Or not.

The time trials were rained out that morning. So the forty drivers drew their places by lot. Grandfather Petty started way back at thirty-seventh. My dad was twenty-seventh. But as the laps ticked by, the pack thinned out, accidents forcing Bob Burdick, Ken Rush, Johnny Allen, Mike Price, Gene White, and Harlan Richardson out of the race. The dirt track was a sloppy mess. Meanwhile, father and son Petty kept moving up the field. And it was my dad in a 1957 Oldsmobile convertible who finished first beneath the flying checkered flag.

He was standing in Victory Lane, pulling off his dirt-caked jersey, mopping the sweat off his lanky frame, and celebrating with his crew when my grandfather marched up.

"He didn't win this race," the older man announced to everyone who was standing there. "I won this race."

My grandmother was right there with them. She shot her husband the dirtiest look. "Lee!" she snapped. "Richard won this race!"

But my grandfather wasn't having any of it. "No! I won!"

Was this Daytona all over again? Yes, but even more so! This time the driver on the other side of my grandfather's adamance was his own race car–driver son, who was just then celebrating the very first victory of his professional driving career.

My grandfather filed a formal protest. He deserved the $2,200 first prize, he said—not the $1,400 for second. The NASCAR officials did what the rules required. They went and reviewed the score cards. To score the race, they'd had people noting each time each car passed. Somehow, my grandfather passed one time and the people who were scoring didn't see it. When the officials went back to check, they discovered the error. My grandfather was right. He'd won the race.

My father was furious at his father. My grandmother was even madder. Did he really have to do that? In the postrace interview with the *Atlanta Constitution,* Grandfather Petty insisted that he did.

"Either way you look at it, we're 1–2," he said. "But I won the race. I lapped Richard twice when he was in the pits. He's my boy, and I'd love to see him win a race. But when he wins one, I want him to earn it. This wouldn't be the right way for him to get his first victory."

I think the term for that is *tough love.*

Very, very tough love.

It always seemed a little harsh to me. But till the day he passed away, my grandfather swore he'd made the right decision, and I think he truly believed it. He said, "Nobody's going to give you anything. And if they do it's not worth having." He was not going to give Richard Petty his first win, even if Richard Petty was his son.

There was one other reason I think my grandfather was sure he'd done right. It had to do with the money, as things with my grandfather often did. Father and son were teammates, so it shouldn't have mattered which one came in first and which one came in second. The first- and second-place prizes were going into the same pot. But bonuses were also dangled that day, and things got a little more complicated there. If the winning car was an open-air convertible, *boom!* The driver would get an extra $250. My dad's car was a convertible. Grandfather Petty's 1959 Plymouth was not. So considering that, Lee would have cost the team money if his hardtop was declared the winner. But that wasn't the only bonus on the line that day. There was a $450 bonus paid to the winner if his car was a new-model 1959. Since my grandfather's was and my father's wasn't, flipping the finish with Lee in first did mean $200 extra for the Petty team.

Got it? Follow all that? Grandfather Petty certainly did.

In Grandfather Petty's mind, that $200 nailed it. That's the way he looked at things. And he could calculate those numbers like lightning in his head. It wasn't that he was greedy. It wasn't that he wanted the win more than anybody else did. To him, racing was all about making a living. That's what he was there for. He had come through the Great Depression. He had come through the Second World War. He wasn't about to let $200 slip through his hands.

"I would have protested even if it was my mother," he told reporters after the race that day. And you know what? Everyone believed him.

Must have been a fun ride home to Level Cross after the race!

Family was everything with the Pettys, just not in the way most people mean that.

My dad didn't get his NASCAR Grand Nationals victory until the following year. But in that first full year of competition, he had nine top 10 finishes including six top 5s, and he was named NASCAR Rookie of the Year. Maybe more important to my father, people started referring to him as *Richard Petty,* not just *Lee Petty's son.*

All these years later, I have no trouble understanding how relieved that made him feel.

My dad's first win finally came on February 28, 1960, at the Southern States Fairgrounds, a half-mile dirt track in Charlotte. My mom was not quite six months pregnant with me. The race was so minor, it didn't even have a name. But the record book says it was Richard Petty's thirty-fifth start, and the prize money was $800.

And once my father started winning, it would be a good long while until he stopped.

Six weeks after the first win, on April 10, he won again, this time on asphalt at Martinsville Speedway in a race with an actual name, the Virginia 500. A driver named Jimmy Massey gave him a pretty good run that day, but my dad pulled past him in the later going. The story was all but forgotten until 2013 when the Nashville group Wild Ponies released a song called "Massey's Run." Songwriters Doug and Telisha Williams, who come originally from Martinsville, tell the story from the runner-up's perspective.

He was behind me
Right there in my mirror
That red, white, and blue STP
If it hadn't been for the number 43
I coulda been the King

Well, I crossed the line in second place
The day Petty won his second race
Since then, he's won a hundred ninety-eight more

If two Petty drivers were good, wouldn't three be even better? My dad's younger brother, my uncle Maurice, decided that year to test that proposition. The same way he had followed his big brother onto the Randleman High football team, now Maurice could see himself behind the wheel of a race car. He'd been helping around the Petty garage since he was barely in his teens, just as his older brother had. And now that he'd reached Grandfather Petty's magic age of twenty-one, Maurice didn't see why he shouldn't be the next Petty driver. He knew a lot about cars. He certainly didn't lack the grit or the competitive spirit. And he wasn't about to let the lingering effects of his childhood polio stand in the way. Since Grandfather Petty had car no. 42 and my father had car no. 43, it was decided that Maurice would extend the family's growing monopoly on the low forties and slap a no. 44 on the side of his inaugural ride, a 1960 hardtop Plymouth. Those car numbers would stay in the Petty fold for decades to come.

So would a certain shade of blue.

Just about the time Maurice was getting ready for his big debut—race 28 at the Dixie Speedway in Birmingham, Alabama—a man gave Grandfather Petty some navy-blue paint and some white paint. My grandfather always liked getting free stuff. As far as he was concerned, saving money was just as good as making it. But there wasn't enough in those two cans to paint two cars blue or two cars white, much less three cars. And Grandfather Petty figured that if the Pettys' fleet was growing again, shouldn't their cars all be the same color? "What sense does it make having all the colors in the rainbow out there running around?" he asked my dad.

I don't think my dad cared one way or the other, just so he was driving one of those cars.

The answer was obvious. Mix the paint together. So that's what they did.

Once the white paint and the navy-blue paint were blended into one, they produced a distinct shade of their own. It wasn't light blue exactly. It certainly wasn't dark. It was almost like a robin's egg, but not quite. It wouldn't be long before fans started calling the color Petty blue.

Ned Jarrett won the race that first day Maurice joined the field, having led every single lap. Good for him. But the day was still historic. For the first time ever, there were three drivers named Petty on the track, all gunning for the win. They certainly made their presence felt. My dad came in second, just behind Ned. Grandfather Petty came in third, just behind my dad. In his NASCAR Cup debut, Maurice Petty finished a respectable eighth out of sixteen cars.

And there was no shortage of blue out there.

Maurice was a good race car driver. He was not a great race car driver, as he would eventually come to recognize. The difference between the two is one of the eternal mysteries of NASCAR, what it is exactly that lifts a precious few into the stratosphere.

Talent is clearly part of it. So are hunger and drive. Having a really fast car obviously helps. Then, there is a magic something that is almost impossible to define. But the fans can see it and, eventually, many drivers see its absence in themselves.

The difference between good and great is only an inch or two—and also a million miles.

Uncle Maurice would end up starting twenty-six Cup Series races over the next four years, running various low-40s numbers, no. 41, no. 42, no. 43, and no. 44. Though he would never find himself stepping into Victory Lane as a driver, he had seven top 5 finishes and sixteen top 10s. His best was third at Piedmont Interstate Fairgrounds in Spartanburg, South Carolina, in 1961. His best year in points, 1962, he came in fifty-seventh.

But it wasn't in the driver's seat where my uncle would find his true calling. It was underneath the hood. He'd always been a good mechanic. Better than good. Great. And he gradually turned more and more of his attention to building and messing around with the engines of race cars, especially race cars driven by his older brother. His last race as a driver was the 1964 Joe Weatherly 150 at Orange Speedway, just outside Hillsborough, North Carolina, a 0.9-mile dirt track Bill France built two months before NASCAR was organized. Maurice and his no. 41 Plymouth came in twenty-second that day out of twenty-seven cars on the track. That was enough for him.

He recognized his true calling, engine building, and vowed to make that his life's work.

Occoneechee didn't last much longer. The final race there, before the track closed for good, was a Richard Petty victory on September 15, 1968. The pressure to close that track—local church people objected to the Sunday racing—led France to look for alternate sites in North Carolina and South Carolina. But he eventually settled on a spot in Alabama, fifty miles east of Birmingham, where he built what became known as Talladega Superspeedway, which grabbed Occoneechee's date on the race schedule.

Yes, everything in NASCAR is connected somehow.

As for Uncle Maurice, he would have an extraordinary run on the mechanical side of our family race team. In 1970, he would become crew chief for Petty Enterprises driver Pete Hamilton, who won that year's Daytona 500 and both races at Talladega. But it was as his older brother's engine builder that Maurice would really leave his mark. That's what would eventually earn him a place in NASCAR history that no engine builder had ever achieved before.

So a good driver settled into the role that would make him great.

4

JUST KYLE

"Kyle is Kyle."

My whole life, people have been asking me: What was it like growing up with Richard Petty? Only now, all these years later, can I see how truly unusual my upbringing was. It all seemed so normal at the time. What else did I know? It wasn't until I was seven or eight that I began to grasp that my family was maybe a little different from most other people's families. One weekend, a kid in my second-grade class came with us to Greenville-Pickens Speedway in upstate South Carolina. His daddy was a race fan, and this kid was one of the few race fans in our class. He could hardly believe where he was, going down to the garage area and talking to guys in the pits. He was fascinated by everything. Before the race, we waxed Jabe Thomas's car. My dad wouldn't let me near his car yet. But Jabe was always happy to have me roll tires for him and help with the waxing. My friend from school was sure we were going to get in big trouble. There didn't seem to be any other kids hanging around down there before the race, talking to the drivers and their crews like they were regular people.

I was like, "It's just a race car."

That was the first time I think I actually realized: *Not everybody's daddy drives a race car.* And that made all the difference in the world. To me, having a father who worked 9-to-5, now that would have been *weird*! I'm not sure I could have lived in that house. But my world back then was made up of the things I saw and the people I had around me. I knew nothing else. How could I? From the day I arrived, kicking and screaming, at High Point Memorial Hospital, June 2, 1960, the rhythms of our lives were the rhythms of the only life I knew.

It was my mom who settled on *Kyle*. There was a boy with that name at her church, Mount Lebanon United Methodist, and she liked the way the name sounded. As it turned out, the boy was named after Kyle Rote, Sr., who'd been an All-American running back and wide receiver at Southern Methodist University and the overall first-round pick in the 1951 NFL draft. Rote went on to play eleven seasons with the New York Giants, making the Pro Bowl four times. My mother didn't care about any of that. She just liked the name. It also met a requirement my dad had. He didn't want to saddle his son with a name that could easily be turned into a nickname. He'd had some sour experience with that. He was always Richard. At least he wanted to be. His family called him Richard. His friends called him Richard. He was happy being Richard. But when he started racing, some of the sports writers, up north especially, decided for some reason to call him Dick. So there he'd be racing at Islip on Long Island or Fonda in Upstate New York—and showing up in the local papers as Dick Petty.

"Dick Petty?" he'd bellow to my mom as he read the racing report to her. *"Dick Petty?!?"* He was double-down P.O.'ed at that.

"There's no nickname for Kyle," he told my mom, immediately blessing her choice. "No way to shorten it. Kyle is Kyle."

My middle name didn't come from anywhere, other than my mom's rushed imagination. "I had to come up with something quick for the birth certificate," she told me many years later. "I thought, 'How 'bout Eugene? That sounds nice.'" It's just what popped into my mom's head.

Given the shape she was in after giving birth to me, it's lucky she could come up with anything at all. When she came out of the delivery room, my mother had a big black eye. I swear I didn't give it to her. The way she told the story, she had a female doctor, which was unusual in our part of North Carolina. "The doctor kept telling me to quit screaming," my mother said. "But I couldn't. The delivery hurt so bad. To quiet me down, the doctor finally popped me in the eye."

You never know with these family stories, but every word of that is true, my mother always swore.

By the time they had me, my parents were still newlyweds. They'd moved from my dad's parents' house into a trailer beside the house and then finally into a small house of their own next door, maybe two thousand square feet. The race shop was on one side of my grandparents' house. Our house was on the other side.

Like most kids, I would have my bratty stages, my awkward stages, and my stages of conflict with my folks. But I never, ever, ever—not once—doubted I was loved. My dad deserves some of the credit for this. Despite his intensity on the racetrack, he was a fairly laid-back father. Until he wasn't, I should probably add. But my mom deserves most of the credit for child-rearing. She was the one, while my dad was off racing and supporting the family, who would handle all the heavy lifting at home.

My dad was the first to give credit where credit was due. As he often said, "Your mom's the boss around here."

The first big development in my life occurred when I was one year and twenty-eight days old. That's when my sister Sharon was born. We shared a nursery and then a bedroom for the next five or six years and did almost everything together until my middle sister, Lisa, was born three years behind Sharon. Then it was the three of us on a team. Lisa got the nursery. Sharon and I shared the bedroom, and the three of us were never far apart. No one thought anything about the boy-girl room sharing, which continued until I was in second grade, I believe. That's just what people did back then. The same way we played outside together, rode the school bus together, went to races together, hung around with our parents together, and made up little games together at night. We were the kids in the house, and we always had each other.

Everything was right there for us. Everyone was going back and forth between our house, my grandparents' house, and the race shop. And what wasn't there was accessible enough. The dirt road out front ran two or three miles across the county. Every weekend of the year—most of them, anyway—my father went somewhere to race. That was his job, and that's what he did. If it was some place close by, he'd spend the rest of the week with us at home, though sometimes when the races were far away, he'd string a few stops together and be gone for several weeks at a time. To Michigan. To Texas. Even all the way to California. To wherever the schedule happened to send him. In the summertime, my mom, my sisters, and I would all pile into whatever car or station wagon we had at the time and hit the road with Daddy. That was the fun part of the year. There was a whole other life out there, including the kids of other drivers—the Allisons, the Bakers, the Pearsons, and a few others—joining their fathers on these summer racing swings. The way some children go to sleepaway camp, psyched to see everyone from last summer, that's how it was for us once the weather turned warm. But from September to June, with one big exception, we stayed home with our mom and lived a whole lot more like normal kids do.

As the oldest child and the only brother to three sisters, I didn't have much trouble establishing my own identity. I was curious. I was boisterous. I hated to sit still. After a moment of suspicious reflection, I was up for just about anything. My dad used to laugh that I always started out leery before I tried something new. Climbing on a hobby horse. Going off a diving board. Riding a two-wheel bike. "You like to think about it, analyze it, weigh it," he marveled. "But once you see somebody else doing something, there's no holding you back."

He got that right.

One day, the United States Army came to town. They had a trampoline troupe that put on demonstrations, one of those goodwill publicity tours. This was the 1960s, Vietnam days. Not everybody was loving the military. The soldiers were bouncing way up in the air, hopping from one trampoline to another and doing flips. They seemed like fun guys. It was a really cool show. When they asked for volunteers, my hand shot up.

I jumped on the trampoline and did a flip of my own.

One of the soldiers looked shocked. "Have you ever been on a trampoline before?" he asked me.

"No," I said. "But I just saw you do it."

That's the kind of kid I was. If I saw somebody do something, I was just arrogant enough to figure I could do it too. Maybe not as well as you could, but I was willing to give it a try. I'm still that way. I'd rather look back and say, "I tried" than look back and say, "I had the chance and I didn't take it."

All kinds of things become possible when you are willing to fall on your face. I rode a bull one time. They opened the gate. We both went up. We both came down. We both went up again. He came down, and I stayed up. I started down, he started up, and then, *boom!* That was the most violent collision I'd ever experienced in my life, and I can say that after thirty years as a race car driver. But I tried, and the winding road that got me there began when I was just a little kid.

I wasn't much of a student. Which isn't the same thing as saying I didn't like school. I *loved* school.

They didn't have kindergarten yet in our part of North Carolina. You went straight into first grade, and it was all day long. *You signed up, didn't you? Might as well make a day of it!* Grandmother Petty's younger sister Gail had a son named Rodney who was a year ahead of me. Rodney was already in Miss Morgan's first-grade class at Randleman Elementary School when I was getting ready to start. They had a thing where the first-graders could bring a younger friend on a certain day, and I went to school with Rodney.

"Oh, my God!" I said to myself as soon as I got there. "This is going to be the greatest! There are kids everywhere!" We lived in the country. I knew the kids who lived near us, the kids I was related to, and the kids we saw when we traveled with my dad. But I'd never seen so many kids in one place before. School for me was one giant social event. I went to school to see people. I went to school to hang out. I went to school to be part of what was happening. I went to school for everything but the schooling.

I did OK in first grade, not as well in second, and by third, I was having trouble paying attention to the teacher and staying quiet in class. When my mom came to the PTA open house—as usual, my dad was off racing—she was shocked by what she saw in Mrs. Goodrum's classroom.

All the student desks were pointing forward except for mine. My desk was in the corner facing the back wall.

"It's better if I give him the lessons individually," Mrs. Goodrum explained patiently. "If he faces the same way as the other students, he'll never stop talking to his friends."

Goodness knows, Mrs. Goodrum tried. During recess, she made me sit in the classroom and copy words from the dictionary. She opened a page at random. I copied each word and one definition for it. I put a pretty good dent in Webster's by the time I was sprung. In my late twenties, I would wake up and begin to read everything I should have been reading in school. I'd even start collecting first editions of Ernest Hemingway and Graham Greene. But none of that happened when it was supposed to. I could kick myself for that now.

Meanwhile, as I was goofing off in the classroom, my sister Sharon was taking the opposite approach. Even before she started school, she knew she was going to be a teacher. She just knew. She had an easel with a chalkboard on one side and magnetic letters on the other. She set her dolls up and taught them lessons before the bus came in the morning. In fact, she would grow up and make a long career as a dedicated kindergarten and first-grade teacher. Some forty-year-olds still have no idea what they want to do with their lives. Sharon knew at four. Too bad she didn't make me sit down with her dolls in the bedroom. I might have actually learned something from my younger sister.

When I was in fourth grade, my school started a chess club. I was fascinated. I checked a chess book out of the library, devoured it, and joined the chess club. Chess came easier to me than I thought it would. I won a couple of matches right away, and then I quit. I certainly couldn't say I had mastered the game of chess. But I could beat the people around me, and it just didn't seem like all that much fun anymore. My lack of focus was really starting to alarm my teachers. My fifth-grade teacher, Mrs. Toomes, was the wife of one of Grandmother Petty's brothers. Yes, everyone was related to everyone, and all of them seemed to know my mom's phone number by heart. Mrs. Toomes called my mom one day and said, "He's not going to make it. He won't read anything we give him."

My mother certainly didn't like the thought of me repeating fifth grade. "What am I supposed to do?" she asked.

Mrs. Toomes, excellent teacher that she was, had an idea. "Does he read anything at home?" she asked my mom.

"He reads stock car racing magazines and *Speed Sport* news. That's about it."

A week later, Mrs. Toomes came in with a stock car racing magazine and a *Speed Sport* newspaper. She'd drawn circles around some of the articles. "You're going to read these stories," she said to me. "And you're going to write a report for me on what you've read."

That didn't turn me into a voracious reader overnight. It didn't even catch me up with my classmates. But at least I was reading something in school and really digesting it. It did plant the idea in my head somewhere that reading could actually be fun. It just had to be something I was interested in. As my mother put it when I told her about the racing magazines that Mrs. Toomes brought in: "There are things you like and things you don't. The things you don't like, you won't even give 'em the time of day."

The only time my sisters and I were pulled out of school was for the Daytona 500, a trip to Florida that kept us away from home for three weeks every winter. Our teachers piled us up with homework, and my mom made sure we completed every last assignment. Before we went to the pool. Before we went to the beach. Before we went to the racetrack. Sometimes instead of all those things. I could snow some of my teachers, but Lynda Petty didn't mess around.

In the same way, when we traveled with my dad in the summer, it wasn't just for fun. My mom made sure of that. Wherever we went, she tried to make our visits educational. While my dad was at the racetrack in Michigan, we spent two days at the Henry Ford Museum. When he was busy at the fairgrounds in Nashville, she drove us out to the Hermitage, the plantation owned by Andrew Jackson, so we could learn that history. From Riverside, we went to the San Diego Zoo. We didn't realize that last one was educational, but they had a good way of sneaking the knowledge in with the fun.

"There's a museum I want to take the kids to," I can still hear my mom saying to a hotel desk clerk.

"That's two hours from here," he warned her.

She didn't care. "We drove fourteen hours yesterday, so two hours is nothing for us," she said with a shrug. And then to us kids: "Pile in! Let's go!"

Those cross-country station wagon journeys of ours could turn into real marathons. We might drive from Level Cross to Michigan then to Los Angeles, stopping in Texas on the way back. Then, we'd swing back home before heading down to Daytona for the Fourth of July race. All summer, we'd be gone like that two or three weeks at a stretch. Because my dad was a race car driver, I got to go to a lot of places that none of my classmates had ever been to. That definitely opened my eyes to the fact there was a whole big world out there beyond Randolph County. Some of the kids I went to school with had never even seen the Atlantic Ocean, and it was only three hours away.

My sisters and I were just about the only people in our school whose family had anything to do with racing. There were a couple of short tracks in the area. A few people we knew raced at Caraway down in Asheboro. Junior Johnson was in Wilkesboro. Holman and Moody, whose car-building genius was later celebrated in the movie Ford v. Ferrari, were working out of a World War II Air National Guard hangar at the Charlotte Airport, where nobody complained about all the noise they made. But in those days, racing didn't play such a prominent role in the life of North Carolina. You were into it or you weren't. Hardly any of my friends in school knew about any of that or cared. And I never saw much reason to bring it up.

When my dad won the 1971 Dixie 500 at the Atlanta International Raceway, his two-car-length victory over Bobby Allison made him an official millionaire, meaning he'd won just over $1 million in his driving career. Someone in Washington must have heard about that because, right after the race, he and my mom were invited to the White House along with some other drivers and their wives.

I knew my parents had gone to Washington. I heard something about them seeing President Nixon. But, again, I didn't have the perspective yet to recognize that as anything special. *Didn't lots of people go see the president in Washington?* And I saw no reason to make a big deal of it in school. But the *Greensboro Daily News* ran a photo of President Nixon and the drivers standing together in the White House driveway around my dad's no. 43 Petty blue car. My dad was in front of everyone.

The teacher called my mom. "I saw the picture in the paper," she said. "You were at the White House! How exciting! We've been studying the three branches of government, but Kyle never mentioned a thing!"

Was I supposed to?

When I got home from school that day, my mom asked me: "Why didn't you say anything?"

I had a perfect answer: "You're always telling us, 'Don't be bragging about the places you go and the people you see and the things your family does. That's not polite.' Should I start now?"

I think I had her with that one.

The same way I once thought everybody's dad had a race car, I still didn't fully grasp what was normal and what wasn't. No, most people's parents didn't drop by the White House with a bunch of their friends. That said, my mom should have been happy my teacher didn't look any more closely at the picture in the paper. Through the open front window of my dad's car, you could see that the driver's headrest was shaped like a peace sign.

Instead of wearing his politics on his sleeve, he wore it on his headrest.

I'm not sure my teacher would have appreciated that, any more than President Nixon would have if he'd noticed that small detail!

5

LOVING SPEED

"A motorcycle will teach you some respect."

Unlike a lot of future racers, I never had a go-kart when I was a kid.

My dad wouldn't let me. His theory was, "You can get hurt on a go-kart and hurt bad." But he was totally fine with motorcycles. "A motorcycle will teach you some respect for speed," he said. "Just when you think you understand how to ride it, it'll put your butt on the ground." He could have found no better proof of that than me.

I got my first motorcycle when I was six years old, a Yamaha 80 dirt bike, and every time I took a spill, which was often, I developed a little more respect for speed, though not quite in the way my father imagined. I developed so much respect for speed, I'd keep chasing it for the rest of my life.

My cousin Rodney, who'd taken me to school with him, and his older brother Randy had little Hondas. So did a lot of kids in our area, the farm kids especially. When we rode to the Little League park, there'd be six or seven motorcycles parked next to the field. The farm kids had all been operating tractors and other machinery since their feet could barely reach the pedals. To them, motorcycles were just an extension of that. Growing up in the country, there were so many places to ride. Farmers let you cut across their land as long as you didn't tear up their crops or run their cows off—and you closed the gate on the other side. They didn't care. They had kids too. Weekends, mostly what we did was ride.

Accidents were always part of the mix, just as my dad predicted.

It was almost dusk as I rode up to our house one day, late as usual, following my favorite shortcut home: bearing off the road and down through a ditch and up a little hump across the parking lot of the race shop. Right past the parking lot was a telephone pole with a guide wire. I knew the wire was there. I'd avoided it a thousand times. But in the falling darkness and my rush to get home, I wasn't paying careful attention and rode straight into that wire. Since my dirt bike didn't have a headlight, I never saw the wire coming at me. And then . . . *wham!* I got thrown off the bike, lost one of my boots, and had to crawl all the way across my grandfather's front yard to our house and up the steps onto the front porch. When I banged on the door, my mom came out. She took one glance at me and didn't even look surprised. All she said was, "I'll call Doctor Sue and pull the car around." Dr. Samuel Sue was an orthopedic specialist. He and I were well acquainted.

My mom piled me into the car, and we headed over to the hospital, where Dr. Sue snapped my leg back together and threw on a plaster cast for what was either the third or fourth time. To me, the cast was a badge of honor more than a source of embarrassment, though it was hard to imagine what more could have happened to me on a go-kart. Over the years, I would break my leg, break my wrist, dislocate several collarbones, and bang up various other parts of my anatomy—all riding motorcycles.

Over the years, motorcycles would mean independence to me, being inside a helmet and feeling like I was the only person in the world. I never raced motorcycles in any organized way. My friends and I would race each other for little stretches down the power lines, but mainly we went exploring, seeing where and how far we could go. Kids and their bicycles are the same way, I know. It's just that on a motorcycle we could go a whole lot farther. I'd leave the house on a Saturday morning by eight or nine and not show back up until seven or eight in the evening. My parents never worried. I might come back sometimes in the middle of the day if I ran out of gas or I'd stop at Whit's store. He'd fill the tank, and we'd pay later.

One day, when I was nine, I stayed too late at Rodney and Randy's. I was definitely going to miss supper. So I decided to take the fast way home. Normally, I followed the power line that ran through the woods. The rule was: *Don't ride your motorcycle on the highway! You're nine years old!* But this time, I decided to take the highway and get home as quickly as I could.

I was cruising along on my little Yamaha when I spotted a state patrolman sitting in his car. I saw him before he saw me, and I quickly veered onto a dirt road, figuring I could loop back to the path beneath the power line. Unfortunately, a second state patrolman was sitting right where I turned. The two of them were waiting for somebody. Not me. But, apparently, I would do under the circumstances.

The second cop waved me over, and I stopped.

It didn't take much detective work to see I wasn't anywhere close to legal.

"You're going to have to leave your motorcycle here," one of the patrolmen said to me. "We'll drive you home."

That didn't sound like a very good idea. "I'm not leaving my motorcycle," I said. "It won't be here when I come back to get it."

The two of them whispered back and forth, then relented. "Okay," one of them said. "Get back on the bike. Ride slow. We'll give you an escort."

I climbed back on my motorcycle. With one state patrol car in front of me and one state patrol car behind me, I began the slowest motorcycle ride I'd ever taken in my short life. A mile and a half—and what felt like four hours—later, I turned onto the circle driveway, stopped the bike, and climbed off.

"We need to talk to your parents," one of the patrolmen said.

I went inside. My dad was sitting on the couch with the TV on. It was after six by then. My mom had held up supper. "There's two guys out there that want to talk to you," I said to my dad, motioning toward the screen door.

Nothing unusual about that. A lot of people knew where Richard Petty lived. Racing fans were always stopping by the house wanting autographs. My dad would go out and talk to them. But as soon as he got to the door, he saw those two state patrolmen standing there in their uniforms. He glanced at me and stepped outside.

They were really nice, and he was really nice in front of them. Everybody appreciated what everybody said. But I knew not to take all that cheeriness as the end of the story. My mother usually took care of family discipline. But my dad stepped in that time, suggesting that thirty days without my motorcycle might help me remember what the rules were.

Playing sports. Playing guitar. And riding motorcycles. As a boy in Level Cross, those were the things I loved doing most.

We played pickup football and basketball in the front yard, but baseball was our first organized sport. My mom signed me up to play in the Randleman Southern Little League. It would take me a good, long time to realize the true importance of the lessons I learned from being a part of a team. The Little League ballpark was right up the road from us, maybe a five-minute motorcycle ride. When my dad was in school, he spent baseball season at first base. So I naturally gravitated to that position. But my uncle Randy, my mother's little brother, had been a catcher. He used to tell stories about being a catcher, and that's where I ended up. I liked to catch because you were always doing something, not just standing around wondering if the ball would ever be hit your way. People talk about shortstop. But catcher is baseball's perfect short-attention-span position and definitely its most injury prone. I got hit in the chest. I got hit in the throat. I got my mask knocked off with the bat because I was too close to the hitter. Whatever falling off a motorcycle didn't do to me, a baseball or a bat could fill in for.

Eventually, I would trade traditional team sports for a unique one, joining a group of guys who liked working together to make a race car go fast. Nothing teaches the importance of teamwork, the thrill of competition, and the meaning of sportsmanship like getting at it with your friends when you're young.

I stumbled into guitar in a more haphazard way, and it happened at the racetrack, not a venue that is generally known for launching musical careers. There was a preacher named Bill Frazier who came to the track on Sundays, and that was a bold move right there. Everyone knew that if you worked on Sundays—especially if you were in the racing community— you were probably a heathen and most likely on the slippery slope to hell.

So Bill certainly had his work cut out. He was a wonderful guy. He held worship services in the garage area and worked to save all of us.

Bill played the guitar. He preached every Sunday and then played a song or two. At the time, the country singer Marty Robbins drove a race car, which even as a kid I thought was pretty cool. We'd be at Talladega hanging around the hotel lobby or sitting beside the swimming pool, and Marty would be there with his guitar. He'd start singing. I could hardly believe it. Friggin' Marty Robbins! Sitting right there! I knew him from the radio, and I'd seen him on *Hee Haw*. But there was Marty on the couch at the Ramada Inn in Talladega singing "El Paso." How could you be eleven or twelve years old and not be blown away? I'd seen people play guitar on TV. But outside of Bill and Marty, I had never seen a person play a guitar right in front of me. I was mesmerized watching their fingers dance across the strings. It really seemed like magic.

Bill loaned me his guitar, and my mom found a man in Randleman who agreed to give me lessons. She drove me to his house for thirty minutes on Tuesdays after school. He taught me the C chord and the G chord and the minor chords, and then he taught me how to fingerpick "House of the Rising Sun." I took lessons with him for three or four months, at which point he said to me, "I've taught you what you need to know."

How could that be? I had only begun to learn. I didn't sound anything like Marty Robbins or even Brother Bill.

"If you really want to learn to play guitar," the teacher said, "you'll learn it yourself, and you'll keep playing. I could teach you a lot of other stuff, but you would just be doing it because I told you to. You have to explore the instrument on your own."

And here's the part that surprised even me: I started exploring, and I did not stop. I'd finally found something that could grab—*and hold!*—my imagination, other than motorcycles and baseball. There was no band program at Randleman Junior High School, but they started one when I was in the seventh grade. I joined immediately and started playing the saxophone. I'd stay in the band all through junior high and high school. The concert band, the marching band, any kind of band they had. I played the saxophone. I learned to read music. Some people, when they heard I was in the marching band, they'd say, "Only geeks are in the marching band." I didn't care. I told them straight out, "I love band." Music to me was a whole other language, and it was constantly changing. Just when you learned something, your mind opened to something else you could learn. I know mine did. Even back then, I knew: Whatever else I did with the rest of my life, I would never stop learning and loving music.

6

TEAM SPORT

"Don't just say it's broke."

There was never a time in my life when I didn't go to the race shop almost every day, even if I only stayed fifteen minutes and got a Coke. I knew everyone there from the time I was six or seven, and they got used to me being constantly underfoot. Today, some race teams have hundreds of employees and dozens of cars. But in the 1960s and 1970s, Petty Enterprises was a one-car team, then a two-car team, then a one-car team, and by the late 1970s when I started driving, a two-car team again. The whole workforce fluctuated between ten and thirty. That included everyone from the maintenance man who cleaned up around the garage and looked after the putting green in my grandfather's backyard all the way to my dad, grandfather, Uncle Maurice, and Dale Inman, my dad's cousin (either first or second, I could never get that part straight) who was also the race team's crew chief. The lineup also included my grandmother, who looked after the finances, wrote the checks, and did the books, along with Martha Jane Bonkemeyer, my dad's secretary and my mom's best friend, who was also like a second mom to me. No, Petty Enterprises never had an antinepotism policy—thank God, I guess I should add.

It was an amazing operation they had there.

They would bring the car in on Monday morning. Put it up on jack stands. Take it apart. The engine would go back to the engine room. They'd pull the front end out from under it and the rear end out from under it. All that had to be sandblasted, Magnafluxed, and repainted by Tuesday to get to the next race in time. They only had a couple of sets of spindles and two rear-end houses. So the timing was tight. They couldn't afford to waste a minute. And while all that was happening, the car would go to the body shop because my dad would not show up at the racetrack without his car being touched up, painted, smoothed out, and looking good.

They had an intricate system for getting everything done, and everyone played a role. Working together, this small crew of people would turn a car around in a couple of days and take that same car back to the racetrack.

It was probably inevitable, raised the way that I was raised, by the family who raised me, that people would start asking me from a very young age:

So what about you and racing?

Well, the truth is I did not come into this world intent on being a race car driver. That was something that grew up over time, and it didn't happen because anyone pressured me into it. Yes, I was Lee Petty's grandson and Maurice Petty's nephew and Richard Petty's son and Dale Inman's whatever-I-was. But that didn't mean I was required to join the family business or follow a preordained path. My mom and dad never once acted like I had a responsibility to carry on anyone's legacy, no matter how powerful that legacy had become over the years. They just never talked that way to me or sent that message in my direction, however many people outside the family might have begun to speculate. What I remember is being eleven or twelve and telling my dad that I might want to be a race car driver someday and him telling me, "If you really want to drive, you need to know how to work on cars."

He let me sweep the shop and acted like he was doing me a favor. That bit of child psychology, if that's what it was, was effective, I suppose. I swept every inch of that place and was ready to do it again. Then, I started sandblasting. Dale taught me. I'd stand at the sandblaster with my arms in big rubber gloves and sandblast all day long. And then I was allowed to start painting. That's when Dale showed me how to Magnaflux and make sure there were no cracks in the car body.

I'd circle a spot and say, "Hey, Dale. Is there a crack right here? It looks like a crack."

He'd wipe that Magnaflux fluid off and say, "Nah, that's not a crack. Don't worry about it. You can paint that one."

That's what I started doing after school, my very own, never-ending, one-man Petty Enterprises internship program. If I wanted to be a race car driver, the deal was I would have to work one year everywhere. A year as a mechanic. A year in the engine shop. A year in the body shop. And I began to learn the special weekly rhythm of repairing and maintaining a race car.

The people who worked at Petty Enterprises loved three things. They loved cars. They loved racing. And they loved Richard Petty.

Though not always in that order.

Some of them may have loved Richard Petty before they loved cars and racing, while others might have had a different one-two-three. But their love for all three was what drove them. I won't even call it love. Passion is probably a better word for it. That's how deep their commitment ran. You wouldn't believe how bad those guys hurt when they got beat at the racetrack, and that's exactly how they looked at it. Richard Petty didn't get beat. They *all* got beat. They could not stand to lose. Ever. Racing wasn't a game to them. It was what and who they were. Luckily, they did a lot of winning together. These guys were loyal to Richard Petty.

By this point, my dad had become known not just as a winning driver but as the winningest driver in NASCAR. *Winningest.* I didn't even know that was a word until people started saying it about my father. I certainly liked the way it sounded, as did everyone else in the race shop, and I think he did too, though I never remember him saying so directly. That wouldn't have fit with his laconic style. In the summer of 1969, he and his no. 43 Ford crossed that 100-win mark close to home at the Myers Brothers 250 at Winston-Salem's Bowman Gray Stadium, a quarter-mile asphalt oval that now calls itself "NASCAR's longest-running weekly racetrack."

And now that local track had NASCAR's winningest driver.

Nothing like this had ever been achieved before. Race fans everywhere couldn't get enough of it. For them, it was a thrill just arriving at the track and catching a glimpse of that pretty Petty blue no. 43 sitting on the pole, a position my dad and his race team had also earned a hundred times. Racing and motor magazines kept putting him on their covers, and one time even Elvis Presley came around. He was filming a movie called *Speedway* at the track in Charlotte. My dad ended up all over the film's opening credits. What could be bigger than that? The King and the King, sharing the same movie screen.

It wasn't all high fives and Victory Lanes on the road to all those wins. Stock car racing is a dangerous sport, and that danger never fully disappears, no matter how many checkered flags a driver might be greeted by. Occasionally, that danger presented itself in a truly heart-stopping way. On May 9, 1970, fans at Darlington and all across America got to see just how dangerous racing could be. My dad was cruising along in his 1970 Plymouth Road Runner, having wrecked his Superbird earlier that week in practice. Now on race day, he brushed the wall going into turn 1, knocking his front end out of line. But he pressed on, and within a few laps he had the car back up to speed. But as he came off turn 4 at lap 174, something broke. Was it a ball joint? Hard to say. But suddenly, the car seemed to have a mind of its own, pulling so hard to the left, my dad was just along for the ride. This time, he slammed into the concrete wall so hard, the car flipped five—count 'em, five—times before landing upside down, though my dad would have no recollection of anything after the first tumble.

It just so happened that the race was being carried by ABC's *Wide World of Sports,* giving the crash a mammoth audience. Thanks to the miracle of instant replay, those dramatic car flips were shown over and over again, scaring a whole lot of folks including any of our family who hadn't driven to South Carolina for the race. I swear, it seemed to take a good fifteen minutes for that car to land. Then, all the world got to watch as my dad hung upside down in the driver's seat, his left arm and what turned out to be his broken shoulder dangling out the car window, just blowing in the Darlington breeze.

Pulled unconscious from the car, my dad was thrown on a stretcher and rushed by ambulance to the hospital. He was OK, thank God, and the crew had a busy week at the race shop in Level Cross figuring out what exactly went wrong. But it was Grandmother Petty who came up with the best idea. She couldn't stand the sight of her son upside down like that, his twisted arm flopping outside the car.

When she got home to Level Cross, she sat down at her Singer sewing machine. From an old uniform, she sewed the first window net that anyone ever used in NASCAR. Nothing fancy. Just something to keep the driver's limbs inside the vehicle. Simple but obvious and long overdue. Right away, other drivers picked up on the idea. And pretty soon, NASCAR had a new rule. Window nets. The original net my grandmother sewed is now on display in the NASCAR Hall of Fame. Creative and forward thinking! It was nice seeing a woman get at least a piece of the credit she deserved!

When you have a passion for something the way the Petty crew did, it ceases to be a game. What happened in the race shop and at the racetrack, that was their lives. They almost all had wives and children. I don't want to say they put racing above their families. But I will say that all of them missed a lot of family events and obligations, and I will say almost every one of them had some making up to do at home.

Of the crew that worked in the race shop, probably a third of them went on the road every week. Everyone was back at the shop on Monday morning, getting that car ready for the following weekend. But whether they traveled or not, this was more than a full-time job. Whenever something happened, in the shop or at the track, no one gave a rat's rear end if you were an engine builder or a regular mechanic or what you thought your job was. You'd better be jumping in there and fixing the problem the best way you knew how. That car had to get going again. It was one for all and all for one. And everyone there worked long hours. Seven to five. Seven to seven. Seven to midnight. All that was normal. Whatever it took to get that car ready to go. It wasn't a 9-to-5 cubicle job, ever.

I've never played on a professional sports team, outside of auto racing. But this is what I imagine it's like. You have offensive players and defensive players and maybe some specialty players too. Well, we had mechanics and fabricators and engine builders and people who took care of various other jobs. And just like in football or basketball or hockey, they all still played for the same team. Their real job, whatever their specialty happened to be, was to jump in any way they were needed and help the team win. That's how it was with the Petty crew.

Many of the people who worked there came from right down the road, and more than a few of those were related to us. Others arrived from all over the country. Level Cross and Randleman were not in the top 5 tourist destinations in North Carolina. Or the top 100. This wasn't somewhere you'd hit by throwing a dart at a map. You had to want to be there. And they did. Some hugely talented people were happy to plant their lives in this tiny community in the middle of the state for a chance to work on my dad's car. They wanted to be in NASCAR and wanted to be with the team that they perceived to be *the team*.

Things didn't always work for everyone.

You had some guys who started working there and thought, *Yeah, man, I'm gonna work on a race car!* They thought all the job entailed was putting a cool car out at the racetrack and saying, "Let's go race it!" It didn't take long till they discovered, *Holy crap, this is work!* Guys like that usually lasted about a week and a half. But the ones who stayed, they really stayed. Richie Barsz came to work in 1969, and he never left. Dale Inman was there, and then he went to work with Billy Hagan, but he came back. Wade Thornburg was still there when he passed away. It was not a place that you came and worked for a year and went somewhere else.

Among those who lasted, the garage was filled with talented characters and wonderful guys.

Wade Thornburg built all the rear-end housings. Danny Holiday was the paint-and-body man extraordinaire. We had savvy crew chief Barry Dodson. There was Stafford Wood, one of the best machinists in the business, and the iron-focused Richie Barsz, the genius fabricator who taught me how to weld. Frank Ruth was Dale Inman's brother-in-law. He worked in the engine room with Uncle Maurice. There was Joe Millikan, who was cousin to my cousins Randy and Rodney and made his own run for Rookie of the Year in 1979 against Earnhardt, Labonte, Harry Gant, and that crowd. John Coble wasn't related to us, but he might as well have been. He was Uncle Maurice's right-hand man.

Richie came from Chicago. Steve Hmiel, who was Richie's number two, came down from Syracuse, New York, showing up in September 1975 just after my dad's comeback victory at Dover. Roger Wasson was from just outside St. Joseph, Missouri. He also was in the engine room with Uncle Maurice.

My dad, uncle, and grandfather's name was on the door. But watching over everyone and everything, right in there with the three of them, was the all-knowing and never resting Dale Inman. Like me, Dale had been hanging around that garage since he was a kid, helping Grandfather Petty even before my dad was allowed to climb behind the wheel. After graduating from Randleman High School in 1954, a year before my dad, Dale went into the Army for a couple of years and then went to work at Western Electric, still dropping into the garage in his spare time. I don't think corporate life was the right fit for him. In 1963, my dad's fifth year as a racer, cousin Dale quit the day job to become my dad's crew chief. And that's when my dad's racing career really took off. Those two were totally simpatico. That first season together, they won fourteen races, leading in Cup Series wins. The next year, they won their first Daytona 500 and their first NASCAR championship. Four years later, in 1967, they really showed the racing world what the two of them were capable of, grabbing twenty-seven victories with an incredible ten in a row, a feat that would never be matched by anyone again. It was an awesome run they had together, five championships in nine years.

Dale didn't believe in waiting for something to break. He was a stickler for prerace preparation and detail. They all learned that from my grandfather. It was Dale who oversaw the complete disassembling of the no. 43 car every week. He knew every inch of that car, its history, its strengths, its weaknesses, and the tweaks it might at some point in the future benefit from. He had confidence in the people who worked for him and confidence in the car he was sending out to the track. He was a master strategist on race day, especially when the no. 43 was pulling into the pit. And when time was especially precious late in a race, he knew when *not* to act, one of the first crew chiefs to make "gas and go" a regular part of his race-day repertoire. Sometimes, all the car needs is gas! Why waste time, even a few extra seconds, giving it anything else?

Dale was a master at making tough calls and keeping my dad's car on the track. You had to make decisions like that when your car total was one or two, and you had to run whatever you had week after week after week.

Uncle Maurice and Dale believed that what they needed was a specialty speedway car, but even that wasn't always possible in the 1960s and 1970s, before they went up to three or four cars in the race shop. A lot of teams just had one car. But once our guys got their routine down, juggling and prepping the best cars for each week's unique conditions, we did the best we could. Much better than most teams. We had a car for Daytona, Talladega, Charlotte, Atlanta, speedway stuff. And then we had a car to run at Martinsville, Bristol, Wilkesboro, and short tracks, which was a little bit different car. And that was about it. What we didn't have was a road-course car for tracks like Riverside. But we had the best of the best talent in the garage to improvise. So what we did was change the filler neck at the back of the car because road courses are run in the opposite direction. Running oval, when you go into turn 1 and come down pit road, you gas it on the left side. At Riverside, you gas on the right side. Before a race like that, all we did was take the fuel cell out, turn it around, and put the filter neck out the other side and just cover it up. It was simple, but it worked.

Once I started working seriously in the shop at the ripe old age of thirteen or fourteen, shifting over time from one area to the next, I was happy to see that none of those guys babied me in the slightest. Holy crap, no! Anything but! Somehow, they managed to make me feel welcome without ever quite treating me like the boss's son. They expected me to work hard and stay focused and get things right, just like they did, even if I didn't have their experience yet. They definitely expected me to demonstrate knowledge and common sense. It was like they were running the NASA space program in there, and no one could afford to screw up. That's how they looked at it. To be an astronaut, you didn't have to be a rocket scientist. But you needed to know when the vehicle was out of gas. You had to have some working mechanical knowledge, and you had to speak up. My dad was big on the speaking-up part.

"Don't just say, 'It's broke,'" he warned me more than once. "That doesn't help anybody. Try to diagnose what broke. Try to say where it's broke. And try to say why you think that's what it is. That'll speed up the process. You wouldn't go to a doctor and just say, 'I'm sick.' Do you have an ingrown toenail or a brain tumor? Tell the man!"

So I learned to say, "I think it spun a bearing" or "I think it dropped a valve" or "I think maybe the alternator is gone and the battery's dead." If I could point the other crew members in some direction, that would help to diagnose the problem more quickly. In a race, I didn't have to be told, those seconds could be critical.

I never saw Dale or Maurice or any of those guys walk in that shop and ask someone to do something they hadn't done a hundred times before. And they could probably do it better than you could. That wasn't the point. The point was that I always knew when I did something, the guy looking at my work would have an opinion. It was going to be a knowledgeable opinion, and it was going to be an opinion that mattered.

Over the years, those guys, especially the younger ones, would become some of my closest friends in the world. They had a decade or more on me. But they didn't seem to feel like I was slowing them down. You get a very different perspective on reality when you're a teenager and a twenty-eight-year-old is having a cocktail and telling you all about life. I could relate to some of that stuff when I first heard it, though some of it sailed right over my head. But those guys are who I grew up with. They didn't just open my eyes. They opened my mind and also taught me everything I know about cars. When I was fifteen or sixteen, they were the people I spent the most time with just because I was at the shop every day. After I turned eighteen, some of them would play the same role for me they had for my father and grandfather, helping me to launch my own driving career. I am grateful to all of them. They taught me so much and influenced me in ways large and small.

The part I liked the most was working with Richie Barsz. Being a fabricator just appealed to me. I loved to bend and weld metal and try to make something out of it. Part of that, I guess, came from being Richard Petty's son, and part of it probably came from being the grandson of Granddaddy Owens, who could take a flat piece of wood and make it into the most perfect cabinet you've ever seen. It didn't matter how much schooling any of those people had. They were creative geniuses. People like that, when they see something, they see it more deeply than other people do. It's like the rest of us are drawing stick figures and they're painting beautiful portraits. They capture all the nuances that other people miss. All you can do is look at what they've created and go, *Wow!*

There was nothing Richie couldn't do with a piece of metal and a welding torch. If you could say it, he could make it—whatever *it* was. You could say to Richie, "I need an oil tank. I need a baffle about two-thirds of the way up. I need it about this tall. I need two vents, one that leads out into the right rear and one that leads out toward the right front, but I need a 90-degree fitting in it to take it to the left side of the car."

When Richie came back, damned if he wasn't holding an oil tank exactly like the one you had described!

Oh, my God! How did you do that? My reaction was the same every time. He couldn't have been a more generous teacher!

"There's two types of welding," Richie explained to me soon after I started working in the shop. "There's TIG and MIG." I'd never heard of either one of them. They sounded like cartoon characters to me. But Richie explained patiently, and I was fascinated watching him and his guys go to work. Once they started welding, they were totally in the zone. Then, all of a sudden, just to mess with you, they would hit the welding table with a broom handle, and see if you flinched. If you flinched, you failed the test. You were supposed to remain so focused that the building could fall down around you and you'd just keep welding, not even thinking maybe you had to stop.

Richie had a crazy saying. I think he got it from the man who came to fix the welders. The welder repair guy used to compliment Richie, telling him he was the greatest welder in the world.

"Richie," he would say, "you could weld a broken heart to the crack of dawn."

And you know what? I think Richie probably could.

Before I started working at the race shop, I called my father *Daddy*. Isn't that what kids do? But once I went from hanging around to working, I began referring to him the way everyone else in the race shop did. He was the King. "The King wants this. . . . Oh, the King's not gonna like that. . . . Just wait until the King gets here." That's always how they referred to him. *The King.* Dale and Uncle Maurice were about the only ones who called him *Richard*. They'd all grown up in Level Cross together. So my dad was still Richard to them. But everyone else in the race shop, at whatever level, called him *the King*. And even though he was my dad, I picked it up too. I didn't really think about it. I guess I did it to fit in with the guys or to make me feel like one of them. I certainly didn't want them thinking, *The only reason you've got a job is because he's your dad,* which of course was the only reason I had a job. But in a funny way, that put more pressure on me and made me work harder. I didn't think of it as an opportunity to coast. The King wouldn't have stood for that anyway, even if that's how I was inclined. But that little world inside that race shop launched me on a lifelong quest to prove I deserved to be there, blood and all.

In rare, private moments, when we were having conversations at home, my dad and mom and me, I would quietly refer to them as Daddy and Mama, and that didn't feel unnatural or anything. But as soon as I was back in the race shop, my dad was the King again.

What can I tell you? Families are complicated things.

7

REAL LIFE

"Someone in the Petty crew."

"When can I go racing?" I asked my dad, before I asked him again.

And asked him again.

The answer was always the same.

"Twenty-one."

That's all he would say: "Twenty-one."

Keep working in the race shop, I kept thinking, *and keep your eye on the calendar.*

"Twenty-one."

I didn't mind the first part. I liked the guys in the shop, and I liked working on race cars. But even as I inched through my teen years, twenty-one felt like nine centuries away. In the meantime, I still had my motorcycle. For now, that would have to do.

I rode that motorcycle and pretended I was Bobby Allison in a race car. But Charlie Glotzbach was my man. That purple wing car in the 1970s? Oh, my God, man! Purple! When my dad won Daytona in 1971, he was given a brand-new Plymouth Road Runner. Metallic purple. Half-white vinyl top. White leather interior. That thing was bad to the bone. I was allowed to drive it to the end of the driveway in the morning and sit in it, waiting for the school bus to come. In the afternoon, the bus dropped us home. I got to drive the Road Runner back up the driveway. I drove it all the time, if you can call that driving.

For a while there, I dreamed I was Evel Knievel.

I dragged the dog house from the backyard and set it next to the Road

Runner. I put a piece of plywood up against it and that was my ramp. I jumped my little Yamaha 80 and—*whoom!*—sailed over the hood of that thing, too scared to go front to back or over the roof.

I might not have officially been flying, but this would do OK until I had an actual plane.

But my dad and Dale and the rest of them, they would not let me get in a race car. Not in the driver's seat. They would not let me do that.

I'd get off the bus from school, and if I heard that race car running—*boom!*—I'd run straight across my grandfather's front yard and right into the race shop. There was always a chance, a good chance, that before they all went home from work, Dale was going to get in that car or my dad was going to get in that car and they might let me come along for a test ride. They weren't only going to drive it to the end of the driveway. They were gonna head three and a half miles to the county line, turn around in a certain farmer's driveway, and drive that car back to the garage, where they'd jack it up and make sure nothing was leaking and everything was ready to go and then load it up on the truck and head off to the next race.

I can only imagine what the kind citizens of Randolph County must have thought when they looked up from their own family sedans and caught sight of that winged Superbird roaring down the highway toward them.

Oh, my God! Aliens have landed in Level Cross!

But at the time, I wasn't thinking about other people's reactions. I just knew that one day I wanted to be the one behind the wheel of that race car.

When I was thirteen years old, I got a new little sister. I loved Rebecca. Everybody in our family did. She was the surprise we never expected. We all figured our parents had stopped at three—me, Sharon, and Lisa, one boy and two girls. But no. They and God had other ideas. It was almost like a new generation of our family. I was in junior high school. Sharon and Lisa were close behind, while Rebecca was at home playing in her crib and crawling around on the floor. She brought a new excitement to our everyday lives. Then again, this wasn't the first time the generations bumped into each other in our family.

My uncle Randy Owens, my mother's much younger brother, was only five years ahead of me. To me, he was more like an older brother than an uncle. When you put us together as a family, you certainly couldn't fill out a family tree just by looking at everybody and guessing their ages.

I didn't call Uncle Randy *Uncle Randy,* except when we were around outsiders or I needed to distinguish him from my cousin Randy, Rodney's older brother. The rest of the time, he was just *Randy* to me. He and I always had a blast together. He rode motorcycles just like I did and had an old Suzuki. We'd go to a place called Chestnut Oaks, a little dirt track up the road. Nothing was more fun than riding dirt bikes in the woods with Randy.

One Saturday morning, he showed up at our house in his car and said to me, "You wanna take a ride with me to Charlotte?" My mom had gone to the grocery store, and she had a couple of other stops to make. She mentioned that Dale's wife, Mary, would be coming by with their two children, Tina and Jeffrey, to use the swimming pool. That was a regular thing on the weekends, different relatives or friends of ours coming by to swim.

"Shoot, yeah!" I said to Randy. "Nothing's happenin' around here. What are we gonna do?"

"I need to pick up a sprocket and some other stuff for the Suzuki," Randy said. "They don't have it at the Greensboro store. I need to go to Charlotte."

"Sure, I'll ride with you," I said.

So I jumped in the car with Randy, and we headed off to Charlotte. Rode all the way there, an hour and twenty minutes. Went to the Suzuki shop. Hung out. Looked at all the new motorcycles. Talked to the people there. This was my idea of a Saturday. Hanging out with Randy. Looking at motorcycles. When we were finished at the shop, we got back in the car and drove home to Level Cross. We parked in the circle driveway, and the two of us went inside, where my mother was standing in the kitchen with a fierce look on her face.

She was livid. There was no mistaking that.

This was all before cell phones. I didn't call home from Charlotte. I didn't leave a note on the kitchen table. I didn't do anything. Randy came over, and then we left. I had no idea why my mother would be angry. But I knew that frosty glare.

"Where you all been?" she said in that nice Southern way of hers.

"Is everything all right?" I asked.

"Yeah," she said. "Where you all been?"

"Went to Charlotte," I said. "I went with Randy. He had to pick up some motorcycle parts. It was cool."

"Did you get everything?"

"I think we did."

"Did you forget anything?"

"Not that I can think of."

I turned to Randy, who hadn't said a word yet. He could see his older sister fuming just as well as I could. Heck, he'd known her five years longer than I had. "Did we get everything, Randy?" I asked.

"I think so," he said.

"Did we forget anything?"

"Not that I can think of, Kyle."

That's when my mother turned her gaze back to me.

"Did you forget you had a baby sister, and you were babysitting her, and she's only two months old?"

Gulp!

"You know what?" I admitted, my eyes narrowing with guilt and maybe a touch of fear. "I did forget that."

When I left the house that morning, little Rebecca was in her crib in my parents' bedroom. Nobody else was home. I had told my mom, no problem, I'd keep an eye on my baby sister while she ran her errands. But then Randy showed up, and I totally forgot. I jumped in the car and took off with him. Totally forgot I had a little sister in the crib in my parents' bedroom.

What happened was that Mary arrived with her children for their swim. At some point, she came in the back door to use the restroom and heard what sounded like a crying baby, coming from my parents' bedroom. Sure enough, there was Rebecca, all by herself in the crib.

Rebecca was fine, thank God. Nothing terrible had happened. But when my mom got home, Mary told her everything. "Isn't two months a little young to be staying home alone?" Mary asked my mom.

What I couldn't help but notice was how my mother wasn't mad at Randy. Randy wasn't the one who had totally forgotten about his little sister. That would be me.

Sometime in 1974, after I turned fourteen, my dad let me start carrying tires for him at the races. I loved being included, no matter what the role. This was against the rules of NASCAR, which prohibited anyone so young from "going over the wall." But things were a whole lot looser in those years than they are today, and I don't ever remember anyone checking IDs. As far as I was aware, nobody complained. Racing brought amazing thrills, that was for sure. But racing could also bring stunning tragedy. I came face-to-face with that reality a month before I turned fifteen.

The date was May 4, 1975. My dad was racing at Talladega, the Winston 500. My uncle Randy was also part of the crew. Randy was twenty by then. He already had a wife and two children. He certainly idolized my father, and there was nothing he treasured any more than being part of Richard Petty's pit crew under crew chief Dale Inman.

It was quite a sloppy duel on the track that day. Twelve drivers swapped the lead fifty-one times. The race was slowed by five cautions for forty-five laps. Buddy Baker dominated in terms of laps led. Cale Yarborough rocketed through the field from his sixteenth starting spot until his windshield kept breaking, forcing him out. Donnie Allison blew his engine leading lap 11, crashing fresh Daytona winner Benny Parsons. Cecil "Flash" Gordon's good run ended in a blown engine that spun him in his own oil and slid him into the infield off turn 4. Marty Robbins was involved in a fiery crash with Ramo Stott and James Hylton. But it was my dad and his crew who had the worst day of all.

He was in front on lap 141 with 125 miles to go. That's when his left front wheel bearing caught fire. As he steered the ailing Dodge into the pits, smoke was shooting out behind him. Randy and I and the other crew members sprung into action just like we were trained to.

Randy and I ran over to the pressurized water tank at the back of the pit box. Randy handed me the water hose. I ran toward the pit wall, which was maybe fifteen feet away. My dad was already out of the car, looking back at us. With an air hose, Randy began to pressurize the tank. Suddenly, we all heard an explosion.

Felt it, really. That's how ferocious it was. I spun around just in time to see Randy, who was bending over the tank, get slammed in the chest and under the neck with the powerful force of the explosion. He went flying into the air, crushing his chest and breaking his neck.

I loved Randy. Just loved him. Looked up to him. Idolized him. Loved spending time with him. I treasured our closeness and the way he treated me, five years younger, like his friend, his brother, his peer.

It was a horrible thing to witness. I was standing right there. I was in shock. It happened so quickly there was nothing I or anyone could do to stop it. It was over before we even realized it had begun.

My mom wasn't with us in Talladega that weekend. She was home in Level Cross, listening to the race on the radio. A pit reporter announced that a Petty crew member was down. But the report didn't have a name—just "someone in the Petty crew"—and no other details.

My mom was thrown into a panic. Was it her son? Was it her little brother? Was it her brother-in-law? She could only imagine. Pretty much everyone in the crew was kin to us somehow. And those who weren't were close enough that they might as well have been.

Her mind rushing everywhere, she did the only thing she could think of to do. She got on the phone and called the track switchboard in Talladega. She told the operator who she was and asked to be connected to the infield hospital. A doctor there told her that her baby brother was dead.

It was just a freak accident, like many racing accidents are. But her beloved little brother, working with her husband and her son, had woken up that morning lively and happy and feeling secure. Now, he was gone. My dad was crushed. So was I. I was standing right there when it happened. All these years later, I still can't get that image out of my head. It is forever etched in my mind.

I will never forget, ever. Dale and Wade and Wayne Dalton and Barry Dodson loaded up everything. My dad flew home, but the rest of us climbed into the van and rode all the way back to North Carolina, nobody saying a word. I was not quite fifteen years old, sitting in the van with a bunch of men, waiting for somebody to say something, and for six and a half hours, nobody ever did. There was nothing to stop me from thinking, over and over again.

Dang, that's my mom's only brother.
He was only five years older than me.
I grew up with Randy.
I went places with him.
He was like my brother. He was my best friend.

It was the first time in my life that I truly remember thinking that something had happened that could never be undone. I couldn't go back to the morning and get a second chance on the day. *You can't fix this. You just have to go forward. How do you go forward? What's it going to be like when I get home? What's my mom going to be like?* She practically raised Randy. Her parents were always working. She was often the one looking after him.

That was the longest car ride of my life.

I couldn't imagine my dad going home and having to talk to my mother. Was she going to blame him? Was she going to say, "I thought you were looking after my brother! How could this happen? How?"

I don't think she said any of that, but I could sure hear it in my head.

Randy's death was especially hard on my grandparents. Granddaddy Owens never recovered. Never. *Ever.* For the rest of his life, losing a son changed him. He was just different. That's all.

8

SPEED RACER

"If you can get that car ready, we can go test it."

I graduated from high school in 1978. Maybe I should say they *let me out of high school* that year. There was some confusion my final semester about how many phys-ed credits I'd earned. I guess the guidance counselor had miscounted. The bottom line was that, all that winter and spring, I went to homeroom every morning to be marked *present.* Then, I drove over to Holiday Lanes and bowled for an hour with my first-period class. I'd have a snack and then bowl for another hour with my second-period class, before I headed over to the race shop for the rest of the day.

No, not your normal senior year. But after more strikes, spares, and gutter balls than any seventeen-year-old should have to endure, I'd earned my phys-ed credits and was allowed to walk across the stage with the other proud graduates of Randleman High, following in my father's and mother's footsteps and in the footsteps of a huge percentage of the people I knew.

Like most of the other boys in my senior class, I had a girlfriend. Her name was Pattie Huffman. I'd met her one day at a track, where I was part of my dad's pit crew and she was a Miss Winston. Jeff Byrd, who worked for the tobacco company R.J. Reynolds and hired most of the young women, once said, "You had to be attractive enough for everyone to pay attention, but wholesome enough not to make any wife or girlfriend mad."

The Winston girls also had to be intelligent. There were three rules the company had for their Miss Winstons: Be on time. Don't miss your plane. And don't date anyone inside the sport.

"Most didn't have any trouble with the first two," Byrd told an interviewer years later. "Most of them got fired with the third."

Pattie was about ten years older than me, but what can I say? She liked me, and I liked her, and we didn't care what anyone else's opinion was.

I'd been working with my dad, my grandfather, my uncle Randy, Dale, and the rest of the Petty crew for a long time by then, and I had finally graduated to the body shop. I hated the body shop. Hated the smell of lacquer paint. Hated Bondo. Hated just being in there. But I stuck with it. For a while there, I swear I was coughing up Petty blue phlegm, while I kept finding excuses to ask my father when I could start driving a race car and my father kept saying, *Twenty-one. Twenty-one. Twenty-one.*

My mother had her own dreams for my future. She wanted me to go to college. She thought I should be a pharmacist. But I had no intention of becoming a pharmacist. So I offered her a compromise.

"OK," I finally said in response to her relentless hints, suggestions, urgings, prayers, and pleas. "I'll take night classes at Asheboro Business College. And I'll keep working with Daddy at the race shop during the day."

I went to the night classes at Asheboro for two full weeks. Then, my mom got a call from the dean.

"If he's not going to take a bath, he can't come back to campus," the dean said, adding she would happily return every penny of my tuition.

In my defense, it wasn't that I never took a bath. It was that I was rushing to class straight from the body shop, still covered in Bondo dust and reeking of lacquer thinner and other aromas that my classmates apparently found just as disgusting as I did. In my mind, college wasn't a beauty contest. We weren't there to smell sweet. I was mainly there to appease my mother—and if I learned something, *great!* But I couldn't deny the dean kind of had a point. And suddenly, I saw the escape hatch I was looking for.

"I tried the college thing," I told my mom. "But I really want to be a race car driver."

My dad wasn't winning a lot of races that year. Luckily, he had something along with racing to focus his passion on. He loved North Carolina and loved Randolph County. Always had and always would. He was concerned about some of the development that was coming into the area and some of the local Democratic politicians who were running things. An election was coming up, and to almost everyone's surprise, one of the biggest names in NASCAR decided to run for the Randolph County Board of Commissioners. He figured he should do something more than complain.

He was one of the few Republicans campaigning that year. He didn't stop racing. He wouldn't think of doing that. But he won the seat anyway, and he would go on to serve for the next sixteen years.

Things at the race shop were just beginning to change for the better. We were switching from Dodge to Chevy. We still had a huge 1978 Dodge Magnum sitting in the garage. I swear that thing must have been twice the size of the Magnum station wagons Dodge made in later years. Just a big, ugly car, when compared to its predecessor, the Dodge Charger. Not long after the dean called my mom, my dad said to me at the race shop, "You see that ol' Dodge sittin' over there? If you can get that car ready, we can go test it."

Are you kiddin'? Absolutely! I could hardly believe it! *I'm gonna get in a race car!*

I'm not sure what made my dad adjust his ironclad timetable for when I should be allowed on a racetrack, the same one he'd suffered at the hands of his father and had seemed perfectly content to impose on me. But I didn't want to ask too many questions and risk him changing his mind. All I said was, "Yeah. OK."

I got busy on the Dodge. I worked nights sometimes getting that car ready. Most of the time, Steve Hmiel or one of the other guys in the shop would help me. We had to do it on the side when our other work was finished. It took most of the fall and into the winter. We did everything we could think of to that car, using all I had learned during my never-ending one-man Petty Enterprises internship.

"Looks bad," my dad said when I finally called him over to look at the Dodge.

In King-speak, that was a big compliment. "Okay," he said, "let's take it to Daytona and test it." I could hardly believe this was actually going to happen.

Eighteen years old!

Heading to the track in Daytona!

Oh, my God!

We loaded the Dodge onto Clyde, a double-cab, roll-back truck we used for trips like this one. I don't know why that truck was called Clyde. That's just what they called it.

Daytona International Speedway might not have been the ideal track for my maiden trip behind the wheel. Home of the Great American Race, the Super Bowl of Stock Car Racing. With its high banks and speed, Daytona isn't generally thought of as a starter track. But that was my dad. If something was worth doing, it was worth doing at the most famous track in all of NASCAR. We pointed Clyde south from Level Cross: U.S. Highway 220 South to Asheboro. Highway 1 from Rockingham to Cheraw, South Carolina, then Route 52 to just past Darlington Raceway onto I-95 South into Daytona.

I'd been to Daytona dozens of times by then. But arriving at the track this time felt totally different than it had ever felt before and not just because no big race was set for that weekend. In all my trips to Daytona, I never remembered a knot in my stomach like this one. Rolling the Dodge off Clyde and knowing I was the driver—this was as different as chalk and cheese. I'll admit this was a little nerve-racking. We had the track for the next three days, us and Goodyear Tire. They were out testing motorcycle tires with Kenny Roberts, who was fresh from winning the Grand Prix motorcycle racing world championship, the first American racer ever to do that. All we had was one big, used Dodge.

Over the years, I'd seen a lot of racers on that track. All those drivers went out and did it and came home alive. Some of them even made it look easy. I used that to psych myself up. *If those old guys can drive this track,* I told myself as I stood there with my dad and the Dodge, *shouldn't I be able to?*

"Let's go around," my dad said with no particular buildup. "I'll show you Daytona."

We took off the car cover, bunched it up and set it where the front passenger seat would normally go. My dad got in and put on his helmet. He strapped in and told me to climb in too. My seat was the car cover. With him at the wheel, I should have known the kind of ride I was in for.

He eased the car into gear, lifted his foot from the brake, and stepped on the accelerator in a single, smooth movement. After that, it was one turn, then another, with a couple of straightaways and some steep banks in between. On the second lap, we ran 193 miles an hour. I know I'd supposedly learned to respect speed by riding motorcycles. But speed, I discovered right then and there, is a whole different experience from the floor of a race car. And I wasn't exactly strapped down. I was hunched on top of the car cover, hanging onto the roll bars for dear life, while my dad pushed the Dodge across every rise, dip, crack, gouge, and bubble along the two and a half miles of Daytona asphalt.

And my dad was talking all the way:

"OK, there's a big bump right here. You don't want to hit this."

"Don't come down this low. Stay up."

"Look how the track flattens as you come off the corner."

"You can see all the way over to turn 4 as soon as you come off two."

In another second, we were right up against the wall, putting the Dodge within a few inches of concrete. And he just kept talking.

Strange as it seems, that part didn't feel so odd to me. It was just, *OK. It's my dad. Telling me what I'm supposed to do. And I'm trying to remember.*

The Dodge ran well, and so did he. When he was done, he stopped the car and climbed out, still calm and matter-of-fact, no fuss at all, like he'd just gotten home from another day at the office. Which he kind of had. And now it was my turn.

I strapped myself into the seat where my dad had just been. I adjusted my helmet and goggles. And out I went.

I eased my right foot onto the accelerator, not as smooth as my father had. From that instant forward, everything that looked easy every other time I'd seen it, everything my dad and all those other drivers had done, suddenly felt almost impossible.

I was thinking to myself, *You're the one who said you wanted to do this!*

It all happened so quickly and from so many different directions, I really can't detail the order of things. I just know that my mind was flying, my heart was pounding, and I felt like I was slipping and sliding and bouncing along.

The stopwatch said 151. *One hundred fifty-one?* I swear I thought I was running 6,000 miles an hour. I didn't know whether I was coming or going. I didn't know where the straightaways were. I didn't know where the turns were. I didn't know where anything was. I was all over the race-track. I looked like an eight-year-old behind the wheel, just stabbin' and steerin'.

We stayed in Daytona for the full three days. I watched Kenny Roberts run his motorcycle like a two-wheel rocket. I watched my dad run the banks and hug the wall as casually as if he were driving to the grocery store. Then, I'd go out and drive another couple of laps. I didn't hit anything. I'll say that much. Actually, I'll say more than that. With every lap I made, I got a little bit better and a little bit more confident. It wasn't an instant success story. I don't want to oversell this. But it's good news for anyone who's ever dreamed of driving a race car. Even though you'll almost certainly suck the first time out, you're almost as certain to get better. And if you get to do it a whole bunch of times like I did on that trip to Daytona with my dad, who knows? Eventually, you might even show some promise.

With me, things slowly began to click. I started to settle down. My mind adjusted to how fast everything was flying at me. Whatever I was learning—and it's hard to put my finger on it exactly—it began to set in.

The way I like to explain it is like this: We all live in a world of 70 miles an hour. We've all learned to process things at highway speed. That's the top speed we're used to. When you double that, your mind doesn't process as quickly as you're asking it to. That's why, when people get in an accident, everything seems to slow down. How many people have you ever heard who've wrecked on the highway and they say, "Everything just slowed down"? It slows down, I believe, because your mind is having trouble processing. It hasn't clicked in. Probably, back in ancient times, cave dwellers processed things at 5 miles an hour or however fast they could run through the forest. So if one of their friends invented the wheel and suddenly they were going 10 or 15 miles an hour, they'd probably feel the way I felt when I first hit the track at Daytona.

Damn, stuff's coming at me so fast!

As the test ended, my dad said, "It's been a pretty good three days. Now, let's take it home and get it ready to race."

The car might have been ready. But was the driver?

It was the Daytona ARCA 200. February 11, 1979. A week before the 500. Hey, at least I had experience on that track!

I have to admit the ARCA race wasn't the only thing on my mind. A week before, I married Pattie. Our nuptials were big news in Randolph County. I don't want to call our wedding the social event of the season, but tons of guests celebrated at Kepley's Barn. I asked my dad to be my best man. We wore identical tuxes with tails, gray gloves, and top hats. I was just eighteen and marrying a girl who'd been picking out her wedding gown even before I'd been sprung from high school.

The place was packed with just about everyone from town. Lots of Dad's NASCAR friends. Even Bill Hobbs, the president of R.J. Reynolds. When Pattie and I said our thank-yous and our goodbyes, we walked outside to a $66,000, dark-blue Rolls Royce Silver Shadow II. It was time for our honeymoon.

And where did we go? The obvious place. Daytona Beach, the only place I wanted to be. The driver took us to the Greensboro–High Point–Winston-Salem airport, where we boarded a Florida-bound plane.

Once we got to the track, I have to say my dad's hand-me-down Dodge

Magnum looked pretty sharp sitting in the garage area. It was the no. 44. The paint scheme had some dashes of white, but it was mostly Petty blue. Even the Valvoline decals seemed to glisten. Though ARCA was a lower division that attracted younger drivers, some established pros also dipped in and out. The competition on this particular Sunday was real, including five or six pretty good drivers and cars, guys that didn't normally run the ARCA schedule: Billy Hagan, John Rezek, Phil Finney, and a couple of others. Then you had Moose Myers, Bill Green, Marvin Smith, and some other regulars who were going for the ARCA championship. I started second. Rezek, in a 1976 Chevrolet Laguna, was on the pole.

John Marcum ran ARCA, the Automobile Racing Club of America. He was a great character from Toledo, Ohio, who'd been around the sport since the 1930s as a driver, a car owner, a NASCAR official, and a track operator. He started racing the family car at fourteen after lying about his age, and he ran open roadsters in the 1940s against NASCAR founder Bill France.

"OK," Marcum told us in the drivers' meetings before the race. "We are here for one reason and one reason only, to put on a show for these fans who have come to see the Cup stars qualify right after we race. We have a limited amount of time. We need to get in, get it done, and get outta the way. We need to do this." The main thing he wanted, it seemed, was for the competition to stay tight. "If you stink up my show and pull away and we get too big a gap, there is gonna be a caution. We're not gonna let somebody get away."

My dad didn't have much advice for me before the race. All he said was, "Just kinda fall in line and figure this out."

What did that mean? I didn't know.

When they dropped the green flag, I don't know if it was nerves or strategy or confidence, but I went out fast. I don't know. My mind was moving so fast, I didn't know what I was feeling. All I know is that when I came around the first time, I was six car lengths ahead. Completely ignoring what John Marcum had just told us and my dad had just told me. All I could think was: *I don't know how to follow, so I might as well lead!* When I came down pit road for the first stop I was met by the best crew in all of

NASCAR and, on this day, ARCA—my dad's, these guys who had taught me everything! They were fast, really fast. After everyone else had made their pit stops, I was eighteen seconds ahead.

Boom! Caution!

Clearly, Marcum didn't like what he was seeing out there.

On that first pit stop, when they dropped the jack, I dropped the clutch. Man, it looked like a pro stock with the rear end up in the air as I was going away. Uncle Maurice was so mad at me, he threw his stopwatch at the car. It ricocheted off the back and went over the hood while I was still sitting there.

We ran pretty decent the whole way. Second, third, fourth. We led for a bunch of laps. And little by little, the other drivers started having issues and dropping out. Not my fault. I couldn't help that.

Finney, Rezek, and I traded the lead a few times, but the driver who should have won the race was Phil Finney. He had the best car. Finney's team put themselves in a position to win, to just outrun everybody. At lap 71 of 80, in the middle of the backstretch, he hit a seagull and his windshield caved in. Back then, everybody ran glass windshields as opposed to the Lexan windshield everyone runs today. People used to hit seagulls all the time in practice. The birds usually headed off once the racing started. But every now and then at Daytona, you'd have that seagull with a death wish. Or maybe he was curious. Whatever. He'd come flying back to see what was happening on the track.

It was Rezek and me at the end. We went into turn 3. He got to my outside but I beat him across the start-finish line. We ended up giving the people a show, after all.

You're welcome, John Marcum.

It was the first race I ever ran, and I won it. It also made me, at eighteen years, eight months, and nine days, the youngest driver ever to win an ARCA race. One hour, thirty minutes, fifty-five seconds. Average speed: 131.964 miles an hour. Margin of victory: less than half a second. I led the pack for forty-nine of those eighty laps. I can still quote most of those numbers without even looking them up.

There were some press people in Daytona who knew I'd just gotten married, and they asked me how I had time for the race, the wedding, and the honeymoon. I just told them, "Might as well get everything done at once."

How did my father respond to my first-race victory? Exactly like he would always respond when I or anyone else he cared about won a race. He was happy. There was nothing he loved more than winning or helping someone he cared about be successful. But that didn't mean he wasted a lot on praise or enthusiasm.

"Hey, that's great. You did good." I think those were his exact words.

Once we got home, I am sure he had some criticisms, constructive criticisms, to pass along, though I have to say I have crowded them out of my mind. His tendency, like his own father's, was to mention the things that needed improving and to gloss over the things that went right. Like the time my dad won by seven laps. All my grandfather said to him was, "Why didn't you win by eight or nine? You coulda won by two more laps if you really drove."

My dad didn't grow up in a family where people often told you, "Good job!" And neither did I. We were all expected to do a good job. And the truth was, I did have some advantages in the ARCA race that day. I had a Cup car. I had a Cup crew. At the same time, it was a race. It was my first race. I won it, and I was eighteen years old.

I got a real nice trophy and a check for $4,150. Did that make me a professional racer? I guess it did.

Which is proof, I suppose, that miracles do happen, after all.

Part II

DRIVER

9

FLAG WAVER

"He's Richard Petty's son, and he won a race!"

Suddenly, everybody wanted a piece of Kyle Petty.

For one brief, shining moment after I won the ARCA race at Daytona, I was a full-fledged media darling. The race fans were talking about me. Everyone in the racing media wanted to interview me, and so did a lot of people in the mainstream media. That's how it seemed, anyway.

"He's Richard Petty's son, and he won a race!" they said.

You'd be surprised how quickly something like that can explode.

A week before Daytona, I was just a kid on a pit crew. A week after the win, they made me the grand marshal at Rockingham for the Carolina 500. I was the official starter, waving the green flag to Richard Petty, Bobby Allison, Richard Childress, David Pearson, Terry Labonte, and all my racing idols. How quickly things had changed!

All I could think was, *What? What am I doing up here? I'm just a kid who wants to drive a race car.*

If my name was Joe Smith or Johnny Racer and I showed up and won my very first ARCA race, I think that would have provoked a totally different kind of publicity. "So cool!" people would have said. "He came out of an Iowa cornfield or the Mississippi Delta or the Okefenokee Swamp, and good for him—he won." Then, they'd have gone right back to whatever they were doing before the race began and forgotten entirely about the unknown winner until he won again.

My win provoked a whole multigenerational storyline.

"Young Petty wins first race! NASCAR's first third-generation driver!"

The media couldn't get enough of it. From their way of looking at things, this was way better than some winner they'd never heard of. I'd lived up to what was perceived to be my destiny and made us all look good.

Apparently, there's nothing the media likes more than when you confirm what they already want to believe. It was almost preordained. Because of who I was—or more precisely, who I came from—I went to the racetrack and carried on the legendary Petty name.

They even convinced *me* for a minute.

"Oh, my gosh! I'm on my way!" I said to myself. "This is going to be great!"

On some level, I understood a lot of this was hype and I wasn't really a race car driver. Not yet, anyway. Not a real one. That would take years of practice, experience, and motivation. There was also the question of how much talent I really had. But I was just young and arrogant enough to believe that I was the next big thing in NASCAR and my winning days had only begun. Why *couldn't* I beat a bunch of thirty- or forty-year-olds every Sunday? I was eighteen. I knew I could outrun those old guys.

If we're playing one on one, I gotcha!

I had seen ten million races in my life and not just on TV. I wasn't some clueless Cole Trickle, the Tom Cruise character in *Days of Thunder*, when he's asked, "What do you know about stock car racing?"

He replies, "Well, watched it on television, of course . . . The coverage is excellent. You'd be surprised at how much you can pick up."

I'd actually seen the races in person and from the pits of tracks all across the country. I'd worked on race cars that competed at the highest levels of the sport. And now I'd won a race of my own.

All that attention did teach me one thing, and I'm glad I learned it early: You need to be skeptical about anything you see in the media, especially when you and your family are the ones they are focusing on. Don't let it go to your head . . . good or bad. People will heap praise on you that is totally unjustified, and people will talk trash about you that is equally uncalled for. Exaggeration is easy every which way, especially when the media's all hyped about a prepackaged storyline. In the middle somewhere—that's where the truth usually lies. But as the person being talked and written about, you've got to grow thick skin from the beginning or you'll be miserable. Don't take anything too personally because, really, it's not personal at all. These are just stories someone's building an audience off of or making a buck on. Your opinion of what I do and what I say, that's your opinion. And my opinion of you is my opinion. That doesn't make either of us right or wrong. But when you show up with a name that people already recognize and therefore are already interested in—you'd better be ready! The one thing you won't be is anonymous anymore.

Others have been down this road before. I'm not the first race car driver with a famous last name. Dale Earnhardt, Jr., got pretty much the same attention when he did well early in his career. So did the various Allisons, Jarretts, Pearsons, and Parsonses. So did Michael Waltrip, even though Darrell was his much older brother, not his dad.

I suppose the descendants of successful people experience some version of this in all different fields. It's an expectations game that can also be a double-edged sword. Yes, there are advantages to growing up with successful relatives. You can learn from them. They can open doors early on. They can make people pay attention to you. But one thing you learn in racing—it's probably true in other fields, as well: Soon enough, you'll be judged by your own performance. So you'd better perform.

OK, so what was the plan?

Prior to winning the ARCA race, we'd thought about one race and one race only. But now that I'd won it, where would we go from here?

It was only then that we laid out a plan.

I probably shouldn't say we. *They* laid out a plan—my father and my grandfather and Uncle Maurice—to start my driving career. "We've gotta get him some Cup races," my father said. My grandfather said exactly what was always on his mind: "We need to get a sponsor and get some money. End of discussion." And that was the plan.

They came up with a list of five Cup races for me to run in the 1979 season. They saw no reason to delay. My first race was going to be May 27 just down the road in Charlotte, the World 600. As the name suggests, the race was 600 miles long, and I didn't even have a car or a number yet!

Numbers are a funny thing in NASCAR, the question of which driver gets which number on the side of their car. I wouldn't call it a *big deal*, but sometimes maneuvering goes on behind closed doors. The hard-core fans can sometimes be obsessed with the subject. But usually, it's something they only see from the outside.

Because many drivers keep the same number year after year, some people assume that the drivers or the car owners *own* those numbers. Not true. The first thing to understand is that the numbers belong to NASCAR. As a driver, you run the number you run only if NASCAR agrees to let your owner run it. At any given time, NASCAR could take that number back and give it to somebody else. They probably won't do that. What would be the point? NASCAR would never take no. 43 from Richard Petty or no. 24 from Jeff Gordon. There's too much tradition and too much emotion wrapped up in those numbers. The fans would be in an uproar if the race teams weren't. That's how much a part of the sport those familiar numbers became over the years. But that door was always opened a crack. A big sponsor might come along and want a certain number. NASCAR might get it for 'em. Anything's possible, right?

To explain how I got no. 42, I need to drag you down a bit of a rabbit hole. There are rabbit holes all over NASCAR.

Numbers in the low forties had history with the Pettys. That started, like most things Petty, with Grandfather Petty. From the earliest days of stock car racing, he ran no. 42. So when my dad came along in the late 1950s, it was only natural that he would run no. 43. The number was available. No one else was using it. He took it, and that was his number for his entire career. Uncle Maurice, he ran four different numbers, everything from no. 41 to no. 44.

Which, honestly, wasn't that strange in those days. But he always stayed right in those low forties.

As we plotted my future in Cup racing, things got a little complicated. The natural thing for me to do would have been to run no. 44. That would have kept the Petty line going, neat and clean: no. 42, no. 43, and no. 44. Unfortunately, no. 44 wasn't available at the time. Billy Hagan, who'd run in that first ARCA race that I won, also owned a Cup car. His driver was twenty-two-year-old rookie Terry Labonte. Stratagraph, Billy's oilfield service company, sponsored the car, the no. 44 Chevrolet. And Terry was doing great that year, giving Dale Earnhardt, Harry Gant, and Joe Millikan a strong run for 1979 Rookie of the Year. Dale would end up with the title, but Terry would be one of three rookies to finish top 10 in points—with thirteen top 10 finishes. He wasn't about to give up no. 44, and neither was his owner, Billy.

I understood why, and I never would have even asked.

The next idea we came up with was for me to run the no. 42, which had been my grandfather's number. He hadn't used it in eighteen years (not since the Daytona Qualifying Race in 1961), and now in his midseventies, he didn't seem likely to need it again. That was good with me. A nice tribute to Grandfather Petty. But hold on! Someone else also had the no. 42.

Cotton Owens was the car owner. His driver was Marty Robbins. Yes, *that* Marty Robbins. The full-time country-music superstar and part-time race car driver whose guitar playing beside hotel swimming pools had sparked my boyhood interest in taking up music. And 42 was the number he and Cotton had chosen, and that's the number they were running. It had nothing to do with Lee Petty or anything else.

Marty had been racing in Cup since 1972. He didn't race a full season. But he showed up with his magenta-and-chartreuse car at Talladega, Daytona, and Charlotte every year and ran a few smaller venues too. His personal best top 5 finish came at the 1974 Motor State 360 in Michigan. That year marked his highest season finish, forty-eighth. So he wasn't at any risk of becoming a champion, but he was a pretty good race car driver.

Marty had some memorable moments on the track. He got credit for saving Richard Childress's life at the 1974 Charlotte 500 by deliberately crashing into the wall instead of T-boning Richard. Two years before that, at the Winston 500, Marty stunned everyone when he ran a lap 15 miles an hour faster than his qualifying time. After the race, NASCAR officials tried to name him Rookie of the Race. But Marty wouldn't have it. Sheepishly, he admitted that he had taken the mandatory restrictor plate out from under his carburetor and "just wanted to see what it was like to run up front for once."

Everyone loved Marty so much, no one seemed to mind.

I called Marty.

"Hey, I know you've seen me around the racetrack," I said. "I'm Richard's son. You won't remember this, but back when I was about eleven years old I used to watch you play the guitar by the hotel pool on racing weekends. As you know, I've started driving, and I would like . . ." I had to catch my breath. I was trying to get the words out, making sure I did my asking right. "Is there any chance that I could have the no. 42 and run my grandfather's number? If not, I completely understand."

Marty could not have been nicer.

"Listen," he said, "that's family. It's your number. I've just been keeping it warm. It's your number. You take it back. I'll make sure Cotton knows. We'll find another number."

Marty ended up with no. 6.

Really, he didn't have to do that. No one would have pressured him in any way. He was just that kinda guy. First, he inspired me to learn how to play the guitar. Then, he let me have his number without a second thought.

All class.

I went to Charlotte Motor Speedway a few weeks before the race so we'd have time to test the car, a 1979 Dodge Magnum, just like the one I drove in Daytona but this time with a no. 42 on the doors. As soon as we got to the racetrack and unloaded the Dodge, my dad took it out . . . because that's what he does. I was standing with Dale Inman and the same group of guys that had been with me in Daytona. As my dad was running around the track, I paid about as much attention as I'd paid in my fifth-grade reading class. There were a couple of other guys out there too. Harry Gant was testing a Modified or a Sportsman car, I'm not sure which. I didn't pay any more attention to Harry than I did to my dad.

Then, it was my turn.

My dad had already shook the car down and warmed it up. Everything seemed normal. I was having fun. I came off of turn 2 and ran down the backstretch into turn 3. Shifted into fourth. Came off turn 4, flatfooted all the way down to the front stretch.

Hauling the mail!

I got off in the first corner and went right down to the line.

I turned the wheel, and the Dodge kept going straight. I turned the wheel harder, and the car kept going straight. I turned the wheel a little bit more, and the car kept going straight. Then, somewhere between turn 1 and turn 2, over in that direction, more over toward two, I bounced off the wall.

I heard it, and I felt it.

Damn! That wasn't good!

The car was still moving. I was able to steer it back in. But as soon as I stepped out of the car, I could see the right front fender was torn up. The car wasn't totaled, but it had taken a pretty good beating against the concrete wall.

You might ask, was this embarrassing? No, it wasn't embarrassing to eighteen-year-old me. I didn't know enough about driving at that time to be embarrassed. Write that down. That, right there, was quickly becoming my lot in life: *You can't embarrass me.*

Dale and the others were all waiting for me in the garage area.

"What happened?" Dale asked.

"It wouldn't turn," I said.

"What do you mean it wouldn't turn? Your dad just went out there and ran it."

So what if he did? "I'm just telling you. I got to the corner. And I turned, and it wouldn't turn."

Dale looked straight at me like he was drilling a hole in my forehead. "Do you know *why* it wouldn't turn?"

"I don't have a clue why it wouldn't turn," I said. "You tell me."

Every bit of my teenage arrogance was on display in that tense exchange. I was pretty sure everyone was an idiot but me.

"You tell me why it wouldn't turn," I said again.

"Because you have to let off the gas. You can't run around this place wide open."

"Well," I said, "I ran around Daytona wide open."

"That's right," Dale answered. "And you can run around Talladega wide open. But there's not another racetrack in this country that you can run around wide open."

It had never occurred to me, I guess, that the Charlotte track was a mile and a half and Daytona was two and a half miles and what difference that might make.

"Did you not watch your dad?" Dale asked.

"No, I didn't."

"Have you never seen a race at Charlotte?"

"I guess not," I mumbled.

How was I supposed to know that, when you got to the corner in Charlotte, you had to let off the gas? Maybe I should have, but I didn't. Otherwise, it would be like running down a side street and turning in your driveway but not hitting the brakes and letting off the gas. You're just gonna overrun the driveway and run out through the neighbor's yard. Basically, that's what I did. Anyway, we put the car back together, and I took it out again that afternoon.

Slowly, I improved. Mostly from repetition, I guess. That and understanding a little better where I *was*. And the better I got, the more they would free the car up. And the better I got, the more I understood what I was supposed to be doing out there. Feeling the car out. Learning what it could and couldn't do. Driving for the track I was on. But there was no disguising the fact that I was still very much a work in progress. And it didn't take long to prove just how far I had to go.

When we came back the second day, I promptly spun out coming out of turn 2, all the way down the backstretch. There was a metal crossover gate toward the end of the inside backstretch wall. As the car rotated around, I backed into the metal gate. I knocked the gate down and slammed into the concrete wall it was connected to. This was no fender bender. It almost cut the car in two. The wreck sliced about a quarter of the car—the fuel cell and everything—off the rear. Now, the thing was totaled. I had managed to total the car even before I made it to my first Cup race.

Officially, that was my third time in a race car, counting my test at Daytona, and I'd already experienced the ecstasy and the agony of stock car racing. I had been to Daytona and won a race, and I had been to Charlotte and totaled a race car. One win and one wreck! That was my driving record up to that time.

It was not a happy ride back to Level Cross.

10

MEASURING UP

"Tougher than it looks, ain't it?"

I'd like to say Charlotte was a fluke, just a bad day for a guy who'd already shown he had some talent. I'd like to say that, but I can't. Because in early July, we took a Cup car to Daytona for the Firecracker 400. That seemed like a sensible thing for me to do. I had already run that racetrack. That was the scene of my biggest (and only) triumph. But this time, I crashed the car in qualifying. All by myself on the racetrack. I spun coming out of turn 2.

That was embarrassing!

So at that point, when it came to Cup racing, I had already crashed twice before the race had even begun. Two failed attempts. A real failure to launch if there ever was one.

And that's how my first Cup race ended up being at Talladega. August 5, 1979. The Talladega 500. This time, my Dodge and I got off to a far more promising start. No bent fenders. No metal gates. No wrecked cars. I qualified eighteenth. They had two rounds of qualifying. They took the top twenty the first day and then the next twenty the second day. I made it on the first day. And not only that. I out-qualified Bobby Allison, who was nineteenth. I thought I'd really done something.

This is huge, I thought. *I just out-qualified Bobby Allison in my first Cup race!*

When they dropped the green flag on that race, it was my dad and Bobby and Donnie and Darrell and Pearson and Cale and Buddy—and that was the last time I got a good look at any of them. It seemed like the only time I saw them at all was when I looked in the rearview mirror and they'd be coming up behind me and I'd pull out of the way. I never gave up, but that whole group was flying!

Holy cow, I thought. *How are they going that fast for that long? Five hundred miles! This is friggin' amazing.* I mean, I had watched them do it. I'd been on my dad's pit crew. I'd stood right there on pit wall and watched 'em come by again and again. And still I couldn't believe it. *How are they doing this?*

The race ended. Darrell Waltrip had won. I got out of the car. I could barely stand on my own two legs. Eighteen years old, and I was physically exhausted. I was born in 1960. Pearson was born in 1934. He was twenty-six years older than me.

I took my helmet off. Set it in the seat of the car. I poured water down my back. I put a rag on top of my head. And I lay down like an old dog on the cold concrete.

You know how cold concrete is? On a hot day, that feels *good.* Lying down on that cold, hard concrete. I shut my eyes, and I was just lying there when I thought I felt something touching my ribs.

It was just a nudge. Then, I felt it again. I opened my eyes, and standing there was David Pearson. He had a beer in one hand and a cigarette in the other.

"Tougher than it looks, ain't it?" he said.

"Yes, sir."

"You're gonna have to get a hell of a lot tougher if you're gonna run with us." And off he walked.

And I thought, *Holy crap, these are the toughest men I have ever seen in my life.* I mean, I never thought about it being that hard. Even though I'd watched my dad do it all my life and I knew all his friends, I just never thought about the physical effort they put into driving those cars. What I realized that day was these drivers were physically tough. What I would come to realize over the next seven or eight years running with most of them was just how mentally tough they were too. I have never run across, anywhere, a group of men who could will themselves to sit in a car in 140-degree temperature with broken ribs and broken arms and dislocated shoulders and drive the crap out of that car. Because that part was all mental. In my mind, they were the toughest guys to ever drive a race car. Period.

In the race that day at Talladega, I actually did better than I felt like I had done watching those guys fly past me. I ran ninth. A top 10 finish wasn't so shabby for my first time out with the big boys in Cup. Forty-one drivers started. Twenty finished. For what it's worth, Bobby Allison left the race after ninety laps with engine trouble. Did I mention I came in ninth? I went home to North Carolina with a check for $3,315 for Petty Enterprises and a smile on my face.

My dad bought a dirt car from Hoss Ellington. Hoss owned the no. 1 car that Donnie Allison drove. My dad thought it was important. "You're not gonna get enough experience just driving Cup," he said.

So we ran a few dirt races too. They took this dirt car and painted it up. It looked just like my dad's car. It was Day-Glo orange and Petty blue with no. 44 on it. We started dragging that car to dirt tracks, and Grandfather Petty went with me sometimes. Me and a couple of other guys and my grandfather. We'd get paid to come because I was Richard Petty's son. It boosted the attendance.

Show money, *they* called it. Money just for showing up.

One of those races was at a dirt track in Pender County near the North Carolina coast. The track was run by Richard Brickhouse, who is famous for having won the very first race at Talladega, that crazy Boycott Race, the one my dad and the majority of other top drivers skipped in a tire-safety dispute with Bill France, Sr. All these years later, Brickhouse agreed to pay $10,000 for me to come to Pender County.

Cash. In a bag. Those deals were always paid in cash.

We had a pickup truck and an enclosed trailer, which was a step up from the open trailers most other drivers used at local tracks at the time. So we stood out as soon as we rolled in. We pulled down in the pits and parked. There were fans everywhere. As we unloaded, my grandfather was walking around smoking his pipe.

"Did you get your money from Brickhouse?" he asked me.

"I haven't seen him yet," I said.

My grandfather turned to the guys we'd come up with. "Load it back up," he said. "We ain't unloading till we get our money."

So, we pushed that car back up in the trailer. The fans were staring at us, wondering what was happening. One of Brickhouse's guys came over.

"Are you all gonna unload?" he asked.

I wasn't quite nineteen years old. I had absolutely no experience at this. I had hardly driven a race car. But the man asked a question, and I figured I'd better answer it. "My grandfather said we're not gonna unload till we get our money," I said.

"I'll go tell Richard," the man said before walking away.

Figuring we were good, the guys and I started unloading again.

A minute later, my grandfather and his pipe returned.

"Did he bring you your money?" he said, smoke rising from his pipe.

"No, he didn't bring the money yet," I explained. "But the guy came down here, and I told him, and he went back to get it."

Grandfather Petty did not look pleased. And now some of his legendary scowl seemed to be aimed at me.

"I told you. Load it back up."

So we loaded the car back on the trailer.

Now the fans were really confused and ticked off. They didn't know if we were coming or going. I wasn't sure either.

There were some who'd been drinking since midafternoon. That's how they seemed, anyway. And I don't think they were enjoying all the up-and-down, back-and-forth. They were getting mad and impatient, never a good combination. They had all bought tickets expecting Richard Petty's son to race.

We were in their backyard, and I couldn't count the numbers the way everyone was spread out. But there were a whole lot more of them than there were of us.

They knew we were getting money to be there.

Finally, Richard came down. This time, he talked to my grandfather directly, which was better than me being in the middle. He told my grandfather he'd be back in a minute. Grandfather Petty still wasn't impressed.

"Don't unload it till he comes back," my grandfather said for about the tenth time.

We'd been at the racetrack nearly two hours by then. We'd unloaded twice, and twice we'd pushed the car back onto the trailer. Other drivers were practicing on the track already, and our car wasn't even out on the ground.

That's when a very large man stepped forward.

Larger than my grandfather.

By a lot.

He seemed to grasp exactly what was going on.

The man got right in Grandfather Petty's face. He was seething. I could see little specks of spittle flying as he spoke.

"We work all week long to come out here and have a good time on a Saturday night," he said. "We come to see a damn race, and we're gonna see one tonight. We come to see that Petty boy run, and we're gonna see him tonight. You best tell him to unload that car and get out there right now."

He stood six or eight inches taller than Grandfather Petty. He was twenty years younger at least. My grandfather stood there with his pipe in his mouth. He took a slow breath. He spit on the ground. And then he spoke.

"Lemme tell ya somethin', *pard-ner,*" he said. That's how he said it, *pard-ner,* right up in the man's face. "I don't really give a shit how much you work. All I can tell you is we're gonna make more money here tonight than you're gonna make all year long, and we'll unload it when we damn well please."

With that, my grandfather turned and walked away.

The big man just stood there. My grandfather didn't lift a finger. All he did was talk and puff on his pipe. But the way the man was flinching, it was like he'd just been popped between the eyes.

All I could think was, *We'll never get outta here alive.*

Richard came back with the money. Grandfather Petty took it and counted out the bills. We unloaded the trailer, and I raced.

It was a good run. I'm not really sure where we finished. But I think the people got their money's worth. But even so, the second the race was over, I pulled the car up in the trailer. We jumped into the truck and locked the doors and got the hell out of there, not slowing down until we had Pender County safely in the rearview mirror.

You could call 1979 a sporadic year for me. You could call it stop-and-start. Some weeks I raced. Some weeks I didn't. But as far as I was concerned, it was still one helluva ride.

11

ROOKIE MOVES

"We're gonna be about 350 pounds light."

The summer of 1980 brought some exciting news at home. I became a dad. Adam Kyler Petty arrived at High Point Hospital on July 10. He was perfect, and I was thrilled.

We didn't run for Rookie of the Year that season because we still didn't have the money to cover the full thirty-one-race season. But with the support of Petty Enterprises and Greg Barnicle as my crew chief, I ran fourteen races in the no. 42 Chevrolet after getting in a crash and using up the last of my dad's Dodge Magnums trying to qualify for Daytona. We had some respectable runs that year. Nothing spectacular. But six top 10 finishes and twenty-eighth place in points. Not too shabby for my first half-season out.

Did I have the equipment I needed to win?

That's a question drivers are always asking . . . themselves, their owners, and anyone they happen to run into in the parking lot at the Food Lion in Randleman on Monday afternoon.

Win or lose, "Was it me or the car?"

With better equipment, I was sure I could have done better. That seemed obvious to me. But that was only half my answer to that eternal question. I also had to admit that, for my level of experience, I had more than adequate equipment. Frankly, I had better equipment than I deserved. Even at the time, I was smart enough to recognize that.

The cars I had were cars my dad had run or would run. There were a couple of cars we shared. He would run one for two or three races, and then I would end up with it. Then, he would take it back and run it for two or three races. So, my being there allowed the race team to add a car to the fleet. Same with the engines. My dad would run an engine one race and take it out. And if I was running the next week, I would get the engine that he just ran. Very rarely did those engines make it to the end of the second race. In fifteen races that season, I blew a whole bunch of tires and had more than my fair share of mechanical issues. But I didn't look at any of this as something bad. I was racing. I was getting experience. I didn't think, "Aw, man, you're giving me junk! Why are you giving me junk?" I was out there driving a race car. That's all that mattered.

I can look back now and say, "Y'all gave me some crap at the beginning!"—and, yeah, that's true. But at the time, I could also say to anyone inside Petty Enterprises, "Thank you very much" because what they were giving me was so much better than anything I had earned at that point in my career.

And the fun had only begun.

NASCAR made a big rule change in time for my first full season of Cup Series racing, 1981: a mandatory shift to what was known at the time as the *small car*, dropping down from a 115-inch wheelbase with a 64-inch tread width to a 110-inch wheelbase with a 52-inch tread width. Those six inches might not sound like much, but believe me, the difference was huge. For the race teams, the change meant swapping out the familiar Dodge Magnums, Oldsmobile 442s, and Chevy Monte Carlos of the late 1970s. That Monte Carlo, by the way, was quite possibly one of the greatest all-around race cars that ever came to NASCAR. Even in my short career, I'd already seen the rear ends of too many of them with Darrell, Cale, and those guys behind the wheel. Inexperienced as I was, I could tell: Those were *bad* cars! Really good!

In their place, we shifted to one of the most famous muscle cars of all time—*as if!*—the Buick Regal. I mean, really! Who races a Buick Regal? But that was going to be my new ride. And the new, smaller car was an entirely different animal. It drove different, and it looked different, but it sounded the same. It was a race car, and I knew we could make it work.

Everyone was driving the same stuff, rookies and veterans alike.

All of us had to figure it out together. In that respect at least, even the champions had nothing on me. And I was loving racing so much, it was easy to forget how new I still was. By the start of the 1981 season, I'd run a total of twenty Cup races—five the first year, fifteen the second—plus the ARCA race, plus six or seven dirt races and a couple of late-model races. A grand total of fewer than thirty starts if you counted everything. There's a word for a résumé like that one. The word is *thin*. But Mike Beam, just a couple of years older than me, had signed on as my new crew chief. We had a small team of other enthusiastic young guys in the Petty garage. Brad Hall. Tony Glover. Mike's brother Scott. A couple of others. And all of us were thrilled to go racing—thirty-one of thirty-one races that year. And you know what? For our first full season, we didn't do half bad. We had back-of-the-pack finishes. But we also had ten top 10s and a fifth place at the World 600 in Charlotte, the very same race I'd crashed during a test two years before.

STP was a solid sponsor for me. They were all about Petty in those years. My dad and Dale and Uncle Maurice and the other Petty Enterprises guys were in the race shop and at the racetrack, ready to help whenever our young crew needed them. Even our prize money shot up, to $117,433 from $36,045 the previous year. We ended the 1981 season ranked twelfth.

The next year, 1982, promised more of the same. We switched to Pontiac over the winter and had high hopes for the new year. But this one was getting off to a sluggish start. In the first twenty-three weeks of the season, we had just two top 10 finishes, a fourth-place at Talladega, and a sixth at Michigan. So starting at Daytona in July, I began dividing my racing time between two Cup cars, my no. 42 Petty Enterprises Pontiac and the no. 1 UNO/STP Buick owned by Hoss Ellington, my father's old buddy who'd sold us my first dirt car. But hope springs eternal in racing. And for a driver, some racetracks are like a good T-shirt. You pull it on and you say, "This is gonna be my favorite T-shirt . . . *forever*!" The first time I ever drove the one-mile track at Dover Downs International Speedway in Delaware, I thought to myself, "I'm gonna like this place."

A lot of people didn't like Dover. For whatever reason, it just felt right to me. On this topic, my dad agreed with me. He'd won there the year the track opened in 1969. There are other tracks I've never liked. But this one slid on me as comfortably as my favorite T-shirt ever. So I felt good when we showed up in Dover for the CRC Chemicals 500, the twenty-fourth race of the 1982 season, on September 19. As we both rolled in for inspection, what a different impression the two teams made!

My dad had his regular crew members. Then he had guys who were such huge Richard Petty fans, they would come on the weekends on their own dime and help. He'd give them uniforms. So there in Dover, his regular crew was pushing the car through inspection plus five or six of these other guys. There had to be twelve of them all together pushing his car through the garage area.

We had three or four pushing our stuff, including me.

We had the same uniforms they had. We had a Petty Enterprises car. But you'd never see my dad pushing his own car through inspection, I promise you that. We were not in that circle. We were outsiders. We didn't have a lot of volunteers wanting to be around us. We were just young and hungry and doing things our way.

My dad and Dale Inman and their team, they had won what seemed like a million races in their careers. They were all aggressive competitors. I will say they might lean on a rule. They might bend a rule. But they were sticklers for not straight-out breaking a rule. They'd been at this long enough to know where NASCAR drew the lines.

Me and my team? By contrast, we were a bunch of reckless kids.

Mike, Scott, Brad, Tony, and me, I'll admit it: We were prepared to blatantly break a rule. Not just lean on it. Not just bend it. Break that sucker right in two. Of all of us who worked on that car, Mike, the crew chief, was the oldest. He was twenty-six that year. I was twenty-two. We really were a generation unto ourselves.

I was never much of a qualifier. I always struggled qualifying. I struggle going fast by myself. You give me someone to race, and I will run my guts out chasing them down. But I needed somebody else to chase sometimes. I never mastered the art of qualifying. So I almost always started back of the pack. At Dover that day, I qualified eighteenth.

When they lined the cars up on pit road before the race, the pole guy would be first and everyone else would be in line in the order they had qualified. A single file, before they ever pull off pit road onto the race-track, all in order from the first qualifier to the last. One, two, three, four, all the way to however many cars there were.

Well, unlike today, NASCAR only had a limited number of officials. Today, it seems like there are as many officials as drivers, owners, and crew members. Back then, one official may look after six or seven pits. So as you would line up, most of the officials would be up front, focusing on the people who were gonna win the race. Back where we were, the officials never got back there.

That gave young guys like us certain ideas.

At the time, a car had to weigh 3,700 pounds. Without the driver. You'd roll it up on the scale. It had to weigh 3,700 pounds. That meant if you were under, you had to add lead to the car. Ballast. Just like a ship needs ballast to keep it steady. You had to add weight to a race car.

There was a crazy saying I had heard for years: "The best place for weight is in the truck, not the car." Well, we might have taken that saying a little too much to heart. As our season had ground on, we'd figured out a way to take 350 pounds out of the car. We'd take the car through inspection, and it would weigh 3,700 pounds, just as the rule required. But by the time we put the car in line to go racing, we were at 3,350 pounds.

And where did all that weight go?

It was magic. Almost.

Let me explain. If I step onto a scale, say I weigh 200 pounds. But then if I take off my jacket and I take off my shoes and I walk across the room and get on a scale, now you'd think I'd weigh a little less than 200, maybe 195 pounds. Right? Well, what if, when I got over there, instead of weighing 195, I weighed 150?

Maybe my jackets had weights in the pockets.

Maybe my shoes were packed with lead.

Well, we followed that very same logic and applied it to a race car.

We had a spare helmet sitting on the car seat as we rolled through inspection. That helmet weighed forty-five pounds. We had goggle boxes, three of them on the dash—a clear pair, a smoked pair, and a blue pair. None of those goggle boxes actually had goggles in it. Each of them was packed with eight or nine pounds of lead.

You getting the idea?

Every team had a wagon. And when I got ready to climb into the car, we would take the goggle boxes and throw them in the wagon. The same with the heavy helmet and the other hidden ballast we had on board.

We weren't the only people doing this. I know that for a fact. That doesn't make it right, I understand. But other people were doing it too. We knew we were breaking the rules, but in our youth and competitiveness we justified it. We felt bad, but we didn't feel *that bad*. And we told ourselves we were just trying to get to the top 10 or the top 15. "We're not being greedy," we said. "And who's gonna find out, anyway? The NASCAR inspectors don't pay any attention to the cars way back here."

When they dropped the green flag at Dover that day, we just took off. We ran, and we ran, and we ran, ticking off those five hundred laps, one mile at a time. And look at us: As we got down to the end of the race, we were running second to Darrell Waltrip in the no. 11 Mountain Dew Buick he was driving for Junior Johnson. I was inside. I was outside. I was right behind him, crowding his rear. I swear I was wearing Darrell out. At one point, according to what Darrell said later, he got on the radio with Junior and demanded to know: "Did Richard get in that car? Is Richard in that 42 car?" He thought maybe my dad had gotten in during one of our pit stops.

Truth is it was not uncommon for a driver to fall out and be replaced by a relief driver. That happened sometimes. But not this time.

"No," Junior radioed back. "That's Kyle."

And if I had been a real race car driver, not an inexperienced kid, I probably could have won that race. I would have figured out a way around Darrell. I just didn't know what I was doing. I had no clue.

It's a simple mathematical formula. Six hundred horsepower can push 3,700 pounds so fast. But if I have 600 horsepower pushing 3,350 pounds, it's gonna go faster. That's just physics. And by lightening up the way we did, it's easier on the tires and a lot of other parts of the car.

So we ran second.

People were thrilled for us. Hugs and high fives all around! It was, "Oh, my gosh! Y'all ran second! How did that happen?"

All these people had watched us grow up and be there and start to compete against the previous generation. They were all just pulling for us. That's about the time our predicament sunk in.

I looked at Mike, and he looked at me, and we realized we were busted.

Because both of us knew: If you run in the top three or four, you'll have to go back through inspection again. That had not been an issue for us lately. But it was about to become a big one.

One of the first rules anyone should know about bending the rules is, if you're gonna bend one, you'd better be able to bend it back again. Think twice before breaking it because you may not be able to put that broken rule back together again.

The point was, if we could get to 3,350 pounds, we had to figure out a way to put the missing 350 pounds back in that car before we went back through inspection at the end of the day. And here we were in that situation. We couldn't imagine how to get it done.

In Dover, they had what they call a grain scale right in the middle of the garage area. A grain scale is just a big pad. You roll up on it. It weighs the whole car. And you roll off the other side. Connected to the pad was an old-time Toledo scale with a big needle that swings around.

We rolled that car up on that scale. Mike and I standing there. I looked at Mike. He looked at me.

"Let me take this one," I said.

"OK," he agreed, sounding more than a little relieved to let me handle whatever was coming next. So I walked over to stand beside Dick Beatty.

Dick was NASCAR's chief inspector who looked after all this stuff. Like the others, he was so happy for us. We were the kids in the garage area. Everybody else was Richard Petty and David Pearson and Darrell Waltrip. They were the old guys. Everybody was just thrilled we had run so well.

The grain scale had a release knob on it, which turned like a door handle. Once the car was on the platform, Dick reached and turned the knob, and the needle made its first long sweep to the right.

I don't believe that needle made any noise at all. But to me it sounded exactly like the falling blade of a guillotine.

I was standing right beside Dick. Just looking at him. Waiting for that needle to land where it shouldn't and my entire future to darken in front of my eyes. Yes, he had just pulled the cord on my guillotine. And that needle went, *whew, whew, whew,* back and forth across the large round face of that Toledo scale. As the needle was bouncing back and forth, that's when I spoke up.

"Dick?" I said.

"Yeah?" he answered, glancing my way.

"We're gonna be about 350 pounds light."

He looked at me like he was sure he hadn't heard me right.

"What?" he asked.

The needle was still dancing on the scale. But I could see the movements were getting slower and narrower with every swing.

"Three hundred and fifty pounds light," I said again.

Dick still had his hand on the knob.

In one swift twist of his wrist, he gave that knob a hard turn to the left. Instantly, the needle stopped swaying and immediately went back to zero.

"Come see me in the trailer," he said sharply.

"Yes, sir."

That's all I said: "Yes, sir."

Dick Beatty had just saved my life.

There were other people who were watching all this. Other crews and officials. Maybe they were paying attention. Maybe they weren't. I don't know if anyone noticed or anyone suspected or anyone thought anything. There's a big difference between a needle that's supposed to land on 3,700 and one that's about to stop at 3,350, a long way from where it would stop for everyone else. But no one said anything. That needle was back at zero. And just like that, the car was being pushed off the grain scale.

I went straight to the NASCAR trailer. I was scared to death. Scared to death because I'd never been called to the trailer before. Scared to death that my dad and Dale were gonna kill me.

"I am . . . I am so sorry," I said to Dick when he shut the door.

He didn't yell. He just spoke to me.

"I appreciate you telling me," he said, "'cause that woulda made me look really bad, you know? It's bad enough that you did it. But it would have made us all look bad."

But what did he intend to do about it? Thankfully, Dick didn't leave me in suspense for very long.

"I'm not gonna do anything," he said. "But we'll be incredibly strict going forward. We'll be on you guys. Remember that, OK?"

"Yes, sir. Yes, sir." All I could say was, "Yes, sir."

At that point in time, they didn't fine people the way they do today in NASCAR. But they certainly could have made a stink out of it and fined us something. Even worse would have been the embarrassment once the whole world knew what we did. It would have been embarrassing to my dad. It would have been embarrassing to Dale. It would have been embarrassing to Petty Enterprises. The car came out of their shop. It would have been embarrassing to NASCAR.

Let's be frank. If you give a bunch of kids access to a car that'll run 200 miles an hour, they're going to experiment. They just are. They're going to try some things because they think they're smarter than everybody else. Trying some of those things, of course, could very well prove just how wrong they are.

Our second-place finish was a happy story at the time. Here was Richard Petty's son. He ran second at Dover to Darrell Waltrip, one of the greatest race car drivers of all time. That happy story could have turned ugly fast.

In the end, I chalked it up to immaturity. My team, myself included—we just weren't mature enough to handle the equipment we'd been given. Everything Dale and my dad and those guys had done was totally straight up because they were straight up. But by then my dad's crew wasn't looking over our shoulders as closely as they had been for the two or three years prior. They couldn't babysit us forever. We knew that. We realized we would have to maintain standards on our own.

We got off much easier than we ever deserved. But I guess the whole experience still had the effect it was supposed to. We never did anything quite like that again.

Plenty of other crazy stuff. But not that again.

12

SURROGATE FAMILY

"OK, but let's stay friends."

Southland Corporation, the owner of 7-Eleven, wanted to get into NAS-CAR. Ralph Seagraves, who ran the motorsports program for R.J. Reynolds, brought them to us. Big Tobacco would eventually be chased out of NASCAR as society got more focused on the health risks of cigarettes. But as the title sponsor of what was still known as the Winston Cup Series, Ralph and his people were really good at helping teams be competitive and move forward, trying to make the sport work for everyone.

7-Eleven sold truckloads of Winstons, Newports, Camels, Lucky Strikes, and other Reynolds brands. All the executives knew each other, even though Southland was based in Dallas and Reynolds was headquartered just up the road from us in Winston-Salem. That's just the way business got done. (As anyone in the Carolinas will tell you, the cigarettes were named for the city, not the other way around.)

Starting with the 1983 season, I said goodbye to STP as my primary sponsor and welcomed the world's largest chain of convenience stores, running the Pontiac Grand Prix at Petty Enterprises.

The 7-Eleven people had only one real demand, and it wasn't hard to guess what that might be. They wanted me to switch my number to 7.

I get it, guys! Consider it done!

Prior to 7-Eleven coming on board, my Cup car had always carried the logo of STP, just like my dad's had since he first signed on with the motor oil and additives company in 1972. It was Cup racing's first nation-wide sponsorship deal. They stayed with my father, a relationship that would ultimately run for forty-seven years. But 7-Eleven would turn out to be a great sponsor for me.

They were learning about racing as we were learning about them. And we finished the 1983 season thirteenth in points. But by the time we got to 1984, we were not in the best place at Petty Enterprises. My dad, who turned forty-seven that year, had been struggling since 1981–82. STP was struggling too. And even though I'd been in Cup for most of four years by then, you still couldn't say I had a lot of experience as a race car driver, not compared to the people I was racing against. I had driven probably 130 races altogether. As a company, it wasn't hard to see where we were headed. We were running out of money. That was just a fact. My dad decided that, to keep Petty Enterprises alive, one of us had to step away for a while. And then he announced he would be the one.

First, he decided to go drive for Rick Hendrick. Then, he changed his mind and decided he didn't want to join Rick's team, after all. Instead, he signed on to drive for Mike Curb, the mega-rich musician, record producer, and former lieutenant governor of California who also owned a race team. Driving the no. 43 car for Curb Racing, my dad would celebrate his two-hundredth Cup victory that July 4 at Daytona. It was an incredibly emotional day for our family and a record that hasn't been broken since. It may never be. President Ronald Reagan was among the eighty thousand fans who turned up to watch the race, a fact that many commentators saw as proof that NASCAR had become a genuine force in American sports and politics.

Meanwhile, I was toiling away in Level Cross, racing each weekend and trying to run a race team. The last part of that equation wasn't turning out to be much fun at all. I was twenty-four years old and had never had to run the business before. I had no business experience other than pitching sponsors. But I recognized immediately that, with just one car in the fleet now and my dad gone, there was no way that Petty Enterprises could possibly afford to keep all its employees on the payroll.

Was I really going to have to make the toughest decision of my life, letting people go to save Petty Enterprises? These were *people,* after all, who'd been part of my life since I was a baby. They knew and had worked for my father and grandfather. Level Cross and Randleman being such tight-knit communities, they might as well be related to me, if they weren't already. Wasn't being a race car driver supposed to be fun? Suddenly, it didn't feel any fun at all. I had to make some tough decisions or else Petty Enterprises wasn't going to survive. There was simply no way we could afford to pay the salaries of a two-car team, especially when the driver who left was a NASCAR legend and the one who stayed was pretty much just starting. I had some good runs but was still waiting for my first Cup win.

When I called everyone together on a Friday afternoon, I think they all knew what was coming. They could look around the half-empty race shop as well as I could. "The ones that will have jobs," I said, "I will call you over the weekend."

Oh, man! I loved all these people.

I went through the entire workforce and picked out people who could do multiple jobs. If you could weld and do bodywork and you were also a great mechanic, chances are I called you back in. If you could just weld, I couldn't afford you. From three dozen, I needed to get the head count down to one tight crew that could get us to the racetrack every week. How many people was that? I wasn't sure.

I started with Richie Barsz. Then, Mike, Brad, Tony, and Scott, my immediate team. I moved out from there. A couple of guys to build engines and a couple of guys to do other things. I couldn't afford twenty. I needed the best and the most diversely skilled. That was a heavy weight for someone so young.

At the same time all that was unfolding, Southland signed a broad marketing deal with Ford and their Special Vehicle Operations Division. They put together a multifaceted race team. Billy Meyer and Bob Glidden drove drag cars. Emerson Fittipaldi drove an IndyCar. Bruce Jenner drove a sports car. I drove the Cup car. It was a cool program with a bunch of really successful drivers and teams. I was lucky to be part of this crowd with their depth of knowledge and experience, especially in a year as high-pressured as this one.

As if all that weren't enough to juggle, I also had a houseguest. Michael Waltrip. I knew Michael first as Darrell Waltrip's much younger brother, who dreamed of being a race car driver himself. But I liked Michael on his own as soon as he moved to North Carolina from Kentucky, where he and Darrell grew up. He'd been working in the garage with me. He needed the money, and he was just a good guy. We became friends. He also needed a place to live, and even though my house was filled up with two little kids now and one more coming, I told Michael we'd make space for him. We even gave him his own room.

Things were going fine for a while. Heck, we even had a built-in babysitter. Michael has a way with kids because he treats them like equals. More than once we'd see him balancing young Adam on his knee while my son pretended he was driving a race car "like Daddy and Grandpa." But as sometimes happens with houseguests who've stayed a little too long, this setup started to stink. Literally. I have never in my life smelled stinkier sneakers than Michael Waltrip's. One day, I came home to find those smelly shoes of his right in my living room. I did what anyone would've done under the circumstances: I held my nose, picked them up, and threw them into the lake behind our house.

I felt a little bad. Not because of the shoes. They were beyond salvation. But because I knew Michael would wonder what to make of their sudden disappearance. Would he think he was the next one destined for the lake? I didn't want my friend to be homeless—but, really, something had to change!

I called my mom, and she was sympathetic. She promised to do something. She didn't say exactly what, but she must have done it. All I know was by the next afternoon, Michael Waltrip was living at my parents' house.

I was driving a race car. I was managing a beloved but challenging houseguest. I was trying to steer a business through a difficult time. I was certainly ill prepared for the last one. But there I was, my family's race team balanced on my narrow shoulders, and I had to get through the year. Clearly, I needed help.

You can't win a race if you can't get the car to the racetrack! And sometimes, it can be a challenge just getting all four tires on! The other Ford teams—especially Wood Brothers Racing, Bud Moore, and Junie Donlavey—really stepped forward to help. I don't believe I would have ever gotten a car built, much less put it on a track, without Junie, whose no. 90 Fords had spanned NASCAR's rise from a regional series to national phenomenon. Junie was also one of the nicest people in racing. We had no idea how to build a Ford. No idea what we were doing. At his garage in Richmond, he loaded up one of his Fords, the only Speedway car he had, and delivered it to Level Cross. He let us look at it from top to bottom. He let us measure everything. He let us copy whatever we wanted to. He truly got us to Daytona and allowed us to compete.

"Whatever they do, we do," I told my guys. "If they built it wrong, we're showing up with it wrong."

There were parts and pieces that were just not available to new teams. But Junie had them. Bud Moore had them. The Wood Brothers had them. And because we were part of the Ford family, they loaned us stuff. The only reason I got through the '84 season was because of the other Ford teams. We didn't have a great year. But without their help, it could have been much worse.

As the season came to an end, I knew I couldn't keep doing what I was doing at Petty Enterprises. I could see this wasn't going to work. I had started talking with the Wood Brothers. They had a ride coming open in time for the next season, and they were looking for a driver. I was already a Ford driver. I had 7-Eleven. Both companies liked me. The Woods and me: The more we talked about it, the more it seemed like a natural fit.

There was one problem that kept me up at night. I knew I'd have to shut down Petty Enterprises, at least for now. My dad was already thinking about returning, but he wasn't back yet.

That was a tough one, but I had no real choice. So we put together a deal. The only hitch was the predictable one: Southland and 7-Eleven wanted to run the no. 7. But the Wood Brothers weren't about to agree as quickly as I had. They always—*always,* since almost the beginning of time—had run the no. 21. The only other number I think they had ever run was the no. 16, which was Glen Wood's number. But at Wood Brothers Racing ever since, it had always been the no. 21. And what a rivalry that produced! Richard Petty's no. 43 Plymouth Chrysler against the Wood Brothers' no. 21 Ford Mercury. That was NASCAR's Hatfields and McCoys, as far as many race fans were concerned. Pearson and Petty brought that to a head all through the 1970s. Man, that was fun to watch and be a part of. Yet here we were, less than a decade later, and a Petty was on the verge of driving for the Woods.

I talked to Glen's sons, Eddie and Len Wood. "To put this deal together," I said, "we're probably going to have to change to the no. 7."

Eddie and Len were the future. They knew that to move ahead, they had to make this deal. But Glen owned the team, and I knew what a powerful force family tradition was. Glen's brother Leonard was still the crew chief and had been from almost the beginning. He had worked with some of NASCAR's greatest drivers ever. I'll write it in the sky if you want me to: The smartest man I ever met to work on a race car, bumper to bumper, is Leonard Wood. Knows more about engines, more about transmissions, more about gears, more about aero, more about making a car handle, more about everything. There have been other crew chiefs who might have known a little bit more about this or that. But Leonard is Einstein. He is the man.

I understood the struggle. It would have hurt my dad to give up no. 43. It all came down to Glen to make the final call.

People in racing often referred to Glen Wood as the Virginia gentleman. He showed why again this time. He took it all in stride.

"It's OK," he said. "We're not the number. We are the Wood Brothers. That's who we are."

For me, that no. 7 turned out to be lucky, after all. The Wood Brothers took real good care of me. Glen owned the team. Leonard was my crew chief. Eddie and Len ran the business side and looked after the cars. Their sister,

Kim, ran the office. When I looked around their race shop in Stuart, Virginia, it seemed like 80 percent of the people were related somehow—first cousins, second cousins, or something-or-other by marriage. They were a family operation every bit as much as Petty Enterprises was. I just felt like I had left one family and joined another one. That's how well we got along.

A couple of mornings each week, I'd try to drive up to Virginia. We'd work at the race shop until noon. Then, we'd all head over to Glen and his wife Bernece's house for lunch. Eddie would come. And Len. And their brother-in-law, Terry Hall. Whoever else was around. Bernece and Kim would fry up some Spam, and we'd have Spam sandwiches with mustard on white bread. I've always loved fried Spam. After lunch, we'd all go back to work. From the Petty family to the Wood family: It was the perfect transition for a guy like me in my midtwenties. It was like going away to college, and your aunt lives right off campus. You hang out with her and your uncle, and she'll also do your laundry. The Woods were all that, plus some of the best racing people in the world. It was a bond I'd never had before with anyone who didn't share my last name.

The second race of 1986, we went to Richmond and showed everyone what we were capable of. The Richmond International Raceway had a lot of history for my family. Grandfather Petty had won the first NASCAR race ever held there, in 1953. When I arrived with the Wood Brothers thirty-three years later, Geoff Bodine had the pole. My 1986 Ford Thunderbird with the big no. 7 qualified twelfth. Little did we know this would be our lucky day. After tangling with Bodine for the early lead, Dale Earnhardt led for 128 laps. Late in the race, he found himself in a classic throw-down with Darrell Waltrip. It started with a fender-banging duel and ended with Dale pushing into Darrell and Darrell's car turning into the guardrail in turn 3. I was running fifth at that point. Somehow, I made my way through the debris and managed to be the first car across the start-finish line, my first-ever Cup victory and my first win since the ARCA race in Daytona in 1979.

Man, did that feel good!

After the race, Dale had to pay a $3,000 fine and a $10,000 security bond for behavior judged overly aggressive. Darrell complained of a sore neck and blurred vision. And I wasn't paying attention to either one of them. I was high-fiving in Victory Lane with the Wood Brothers.

In racing, we all remember the first time we do a lot of things. The first time you crash a car. The first time you sit on the pole. The first time you win. Well, there is nothing like winning with the Wood Brothers, unless maybe it's winning with the Pettys.

One note for the history buffs: Richmond was the first race in eighteen years in which a Wood Brothers car rolled into Victory Lane without a big no. 21 on the side.

After the race, we tried to figure out what the special sauce was, exactly what we'd done to make the win possible and how we could do it again. We'd all gone out for pizza the night before. So maybe it was the pizza. Then, it hit me: *No, it was my underwear.* I'd had on my favorite pair. That must have done it. I was sure. I kept that pair and wore it for every race that followed.

But six or seven weeks later, something terrible happened. After the race, I left my driver's suit and my lucky underwear in the truck. My uniform was sent to the cleaners, and my underwear got thrown in the dumpster. Only after I got home to North Carolina did I realize what I had done. At that point, I had only one choice. I hopped back in the car and drove from Level Cross to Stuart, a three-hour haul. I climbed into that dumpster and rooted around in a huge pile of garbage until I found my lucky underwear. They were stained with dirt and grease and grime. But I put them in a plastic bag and drove back home.

I'm no expert at laundry. I'll admit that right up front. And before I turned on the washing machine, I may have let my good-luck underwear soak in Clorox for a little too long. OK, for *a lot* too long. All I know is that by the time they came out of the washer, the cotton part had totally disintegrated, and all that was left was a bright-white elastic waistband.

But I didn't want to risk anything more. For the rest of the 1986 season, I raced with that waistband beneath my uniform. No lucky underwear—just, I hoped, a lucky waistband.

The next year, Southland switched their sponsorship from 7-Eleven to Citgo, the Venezuelan oil company that had a lot of gas pumps outside

7-Eleven stores. Now, Citgo also wanted a piece of NASCAR. In switching the sponsorship, the Wood Brothers reaped one other benefit: They could finally give up the no. 7 and switch my car back to no. 21. They were happy, very happy, about that. I was happy for them and happy for me: Though I never minded the no. 7, I finally got to drive the iconic no. 21 that Cale Yarborough drove, that David Pearson drove, that Buddy Baker drove, that Neil Bonnett drove, and that Curtis Turner drove. All those legends drove the no. 21 for the Wood Brothers, and now so did I.

The victory in Richmond wasn't my only checkered flag with the team. We also won the 1987 Coca-Cola 600 at Charlotte, a race the Woods had dominated many times over the years. With so many race teams located in the Charlotte area, a lot of people considered Charlotte Motor Speedway to be NASCAR's home track. To win there was a big day for me, and not only because Level Cross was just an hour and twenty minutes up I-85. It also proved that Richmond wasn't a total fluke for me. Who needed demolition derbies? I could also win against exhaustion.

I was as much a survivor as a victor that Sunday at Charlotte. The grueling action claimed all but seventeen of the forty-two starters, including Bill Elliott, who'd started on the pole. But we just kept grinding till the end, running our race. And it wasn't even close. I finished more than a lap ahead of Morgan Shepherd and Lake Speed.

Wasn't that what we came there for?

Before I went to the Wood Brothers, I had never envisioned myself driving for anybody but Petty Enterprises. My dad drove for his dad. What else was I gonna do if not drive for my dad? But no one was more family focused than the Woods.

We were talking one day, Len and Eddie and I, along with several others, and we were joking about family businesses, something we all very well understood. "Listen," I said, "I know you've had a lot of drivers."

"Yeah," Eddie said as the others nodded.

"And when I look around here, I know that someday this train is going to pull into a station. And the person who's going to get off is going to have to be me. Because my last name is Petty, and everybody else is a Wood."

Everyone kind of laughed. But all of us recognized, I think, that I wasn't entirely joking. I had two eyes and a brain, and so did they. And I had a larger point I wanted to make.

"When that day comes," I said, "just let me know, OK? I want to leave here with all of us being friends."

I think they were a little taken aback by my frankness, but I also think they appreciated it. It kind of cleared the air. I understood how competitive racing could be and how complicated families are. But I had the distinct impression that the Woods felt the same way that I did. They wanted to be friends, no matter what the future might hold for any of us. And sure enough, that day eventually arrived.

It was during the 1988 season that Eddie and Len called and said they needed to speak with me.

"Sure," I said.

By then, we had kind of plateaued in our performance, running ninth, tenth, seventh the previous three years and doing about the same this season. Solid performances, to be sure. But we hadn't gotten any further than where we were. And I hadn't won a race since Charlotte.

"I think we're gonna make a change," Eddie said.

"Okay," I answered. "I appreciate that, man."

That was pretty much the end of the conversation, but my appreciation was completely genuine. Neil Bonnett would go back to drive for the Wood Brothers. They had a special relationship with Neil. Just like they'd had with David Pearson. Neil and David were more than drivers for the Woods.

When I'd tell that story later, a lot of people would have trouble believing me. They would shake their heads when I tried to explain.

"They told you, 'We don't need you anymore,' and you told them, 'OK, but let's stay friends'? Really?"

"Yeah," I'd answer. "That's about it." And it really was.

That's just life sometimes. People move on. To me, it's so much better if we don't have to take it all so personally. It's business, family business. I grew up in it. Really, I think I know what that means.

13

NASHVILLE BOUND

"Has anybody seen the Meat Man?"

Way back in the mid-1970s—1975 I want to say—a man showed up at the track one day with a wild idea. His name was Jim Donoho, and he was the publicity director for Nashville Fairgrounds Speedway. He knew people in the music business, and he wanted to make a record that featured NASCAR drivers.

Singing.

Yes, singing.

"Ninety percent of race fans like country music," Donoho explained. "So let's give 'em country music by some of the country's top race car drivers."

Well, as it turned out, a lot of those drivers were country-music fans too.

Thinking "we're gonna do this and make some money," six drivers signed on. Donoho dragged them all to Bradley's Barn, a legendary studio outside Nashville. He had some first-class musicians in the studio, and somebody pressed Record. Cale Yarborough belted out the honky-tonk classic "Six Days on the Road." David Pearson raced through Chuck Berry's "Maybellene." Darrell Waltrip took a stab at Billy Swan's "I Can Help." And my dad weighed in with his unique version of "King of the Road."

Before you laugh too loud, let me just throw this out there: I'd like to see Roger Miller running the Daytona 500! How do you think he'd do?

Oh, I almost forgot: They all joined in for a rousing rendition of "Ninety-Nine Bottles of Beer (On the Wall)," a song I suspect some of the drivers had actually sung before. By the time they got to six or seven beers, they were arguing over whether it was six or seven, and there was also the sound of breaking glass.

How can I say this nicely? The record wasn't great, musically, but you could tell they were having a good time.

Not even the silver-voiced Jordanaires, who lent some much-needed vocal support, could smooth out this ride. But in June 1975, MCA Records released *NASCAR Goes Country* as an album and an 8-track tape. If you're too young to know what an 8-track is, I'm not gonna bother explaining it to you. But you know what? Fans loved it. It sold twenty-five thousand copies. And there was just something goofy and fun about hearing Cale and Buddy and Darrell and the rest of them trying to sing.

Fast-forward (which you could do on a cassette but not on an 8-track) a decade, and another guy came around. His name was Mike Hopkins, but everyone just called him the Meat Man. I never did learn why, but that's even what he called himself. If you were looking for him in the garage area, you'd just say, "Has anybody seen the Meat Man?" Someone could usually point you in the right direction.

The Meat Man figured that enough time had passed since *NASCAR Goes Country* and that the race world might be ready for another musical go-round. This time, the Meat Man signed up an even larger team of singing drivers: Bill Elliott, Dale Jarrett, Rusty Wallace, Ricky Rudd, Terry Labonte, Buddy Baker, Cale Yarborough, and a few others, including me. Geoff Bodine was one of the instigators, as I recall.

Why not? I figured. *I'll give anything a try. I've been playing guitar and writing songs since I met Brother Bill, and Marty Robbins inspired me when I was twelve years old.*

The Meat Man had his own spin on the singer-driver idea. Instead of the old-gold country classics, he wanted to make a record of original songs, reflecting the lives of the drivers themselves. So he brought in some professional songwriters. Each of us sat down at the track or in a hotel room with one of the songwriters and answered a bunch of questions about our lives. Just talking. From those conversations, the writers went and made up original songs for everyone.

And just like the first group did, we all went to Nashville and recorded our songs.

Bill Elliott had "Crazy Racin' Man." Buddy Baker sang "I'm Puttin' You in My Rear-View." Dale Earnhardt's song was "Hard Charger," which made a certain amount of sense. Richard Childress recounted a famous wreck in "T-Bone." There was Ronnie Bouchard's "Super Speedway Man," Terry Labonte's "The Iceman's Hot," and Rusty Wallace's "It's What's Up Front That Counts." When the double album came out in February 1985, it had a real mouthful of a title: *World Series of Country Music Proudly Presents Stock Car Racing's Entertainers of the Year.* My song, "The People Who Love Me (Worry a Lot)," came right after Ned Jarrett's spoken-word intro.

The song concepts were great. As for the general quality of the singing, well . . .

As a collection, was this better or worse than the one a decade earlier? I'd have to put it in about the same category. *Fun but highly unlikely to take country radio by storm.* Still, that record, whatever the critics might have thought, actually did me a life-changing favor, even though it took a minute for me to realize it.

Part of the deal was that we were all going to help with promotion. Each of us was supposed to make one or two appearances or do one or two interviews. I was fine with that. I'd always liked talking to people about the crazy stuff I'd done.

I was getting ready for the race in Riverside when I got a call from the Meat Man. "I need you to come to Nashville and help me promote this album," he said.

"No problem," I told him. "I'm heading out to California for the race. I'll just stop in Tennessee on the way." I figured I might as well get my appearance done.

The Meat Man picked me up at the Nashville airport and drove me to Opryland. "We're gonna do this show," he said. "They'll ask you some questions about the album." He gave me a couple talking points to remind me how it all came about.

(Left) Grandfather and Grandmother Petty:
NASCAR pioneer Lee with wife Elizabeth.
(Photo courtesy of the author)

(Below) Granddaddy and Grandma Owens:
Leonard and Helen, my Mom's folks.
(Photo courtesy of the author)

Going steady: Lynda Owens and Richard Petty.
(Photo courtesy of the author)

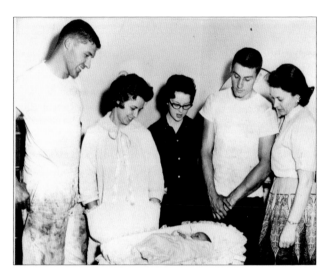

(Above) Couldn't take their eyes off me: Proud parents Richard and Lynda, Patsy, Uncle Maurice, and Grandmother Petty, June 1960. (*Photo courtesy of the author*)

Beach boy: With mom at Daytona's Royal Beach Motel, 1961. (*Photo courtesy of the author*)

Sick with the measles: Mom had to keep little sister Sharon and me at the hotel, but Dad surprised us all with a trophy, winning his first Daytona 500, 1964. (*Photo courtesy of the author*)

Growing family: Sister Sharon, Uncle Randy holding little Lisa, with sock-footed me, 1965. *(Photo courtesy of the author)*

Sunday best: With Dad and the family station wagon, 1967. *(Photo courtesy of the author)*

What's on TV tonight? At home with Dad, Sharon, and Lisa, 1967. *(Photo courtesy of the author)*

Easy riders: With Dad in 1969, first taste of speed.
(Petty Museum Archives)

Party on: My tenth birthday, my first broken leg, 1970. Grandmother Petty made those pants for me.
(Photo courtesy of the author)

Sharing secrets: With my favorite race car driver, 1970.
(Petty Museum Archives)

Another one: By 1971, my dad had a pretty big collection of these. (*Petty Museum Archives*)

(Center) Family fun: That's Uncle Randy between me and Sharon, Daytona 500, 1971. (*Petty Museum Archives*)

(Bottom) Full house: Introducing baby Rebecca, 1973. (*Photo courtesy of the author*)

Tiger pride: In the Randleman High
Marching Band with my sis Sharon, 1977.
(Photo courtesy of the author)

(Center) What a crew: With Dad, Wade
Thornburg, and Dale Inman, 1977.
(Petty Museum Archives)

(Bottom) Victory Lane: At Daytona
between Grandfather Petty and ARCA
cofounder John Marcum, 1979.
(Photo courtesy of the author)

(Top) Dirt devil: Back to basics in Myrtle Beach, 1979.
(Photo courtesy of the author)

My boys: At Charlotte Motor Speedway with Austin and Adam, 1985.
(Charlotte Motor Speedway Archives)

(Below) Daddy's girl: With Montgomery Lee at Charlotte, 1987.
(Charlotte Motor Speedway Archives)

Family ties: Victory Lane, 1987 Coca Cola 600 with the Wood Brothers.
(*Wood Brothers Collection*)

Grand gesture: When we won at Rockingham in 1990, Felix Sabates said to me: "Just take it. Just take the Rolls." (Rolls Royce not pictured.)
(*NASCAR Hall of Fame, gift of R.J. Reynolds Tobacco Co.*)

Mello Yello: With Felix and crew chief Robin Pemberton at Charlotte, 1992.
(*Charlotte Motor Speedway Archives*)

Another win: Rich rewards at Rockingham, 1992.
(*NASCAR Hall of Fame, gift of R.J. Reynolds Tobacco Co.*)

Eternal bond: I'll always be my mother's son, early 1990s. (*Photo courtesy of the author*)

Hang time: On the Kyle Petty Charity Ride with NASCAR's Mike Helton, 1995. (*Jim Fluharty for* NASCAR Illustrated)

Race ready: Checking in with Adam before the green flag falls. (*Kevin Kane Photography*)

(Above) Petty times three: In Victory Lane after Adam's ARCA win at Charlotte, 1998. (*Harold Hinson*)

Debut: Adam's only Cup start, Texas Motor Speedway, 2000. (*Kevin Kane Photography*)

(Below) Charity Ride heroes: With Click Baldwin and Don Tilley. (*Kevin Kane Photography*)

(Top) Adam's dream come true: Opening Victory Junction with Rick Hendrick, Paul Newman, Tony Stewart, North Carolina Governor Mike Easley, Dad, and Darren Singer, 2004.
(*Kevin Kane Photography*)

Horse power: With Montgomery Lee, 2004.
(*Photo courtesy of the author*)

(Bottom) So blessed: With Austin at Camp Boggy Creek, 2003.

Different kind of ride: From the wild bull to the hard dirt at Texas Motor Speedway, 2012.
(Texas Motor Speedway/Getty Images)

(Below) Beautiful bride: Morgan and I, December 12, 2015.
(Boonetown Story)

(Bottom) All Petty: With my dad and my sisters on the Kyle Petty Charity Ride, 2016.
(Kevin Kane Photography)

(Top) Texas welcome: Cheering on the Riders in Presidio County, 2016.
(*Kevin Kane Photography*)

(Above) NASCARnival: One of my favorite nights during summer camp at Victory Junction, 2019.
(*Victory Junction*)

In the Circle: At the Grand Ole Opry in Nashville, 2021.
(*Grand Ole Opry*)

Young riders: In Durango, Colorado, with Morgan, Overton, and Cotton.
(Photo courtesy of the author)

History lesson: At Darlington with Overton and Cotton.
(Photo courtesy of the author)

The Ride never ends: At the Charity Ride Revival with the Petty and Castano families, 2021.
(Kevin Kane Photography)

Keep on mowing: At 91, nothing slows down Morgan's grandad, PaPete, 2021.
(Photo courtesy of the author)

(Below) My muses: Trying out a new song on three of my biggest fans, 2021.
(Boonetown Story)

"I'm good," I told him.

Once we got to the studio, one of the people said to me, "Hey, do you want to sing your song?"

I looked around. There was a studio audience. "Sure," I said. "I'll sing it. I don't care."

"Do you remember the words?" the Meat Man asked. That was a good question.

"Actually, no, not really," I had to admit.

"Don't worry," the studio guy piped up. "We'll put it on cue cards for you."

"OK, let's do it."

I thought it went pretty well. I read off the cue cards. I sang the song. The audience seemed to like it. By the final verse, I was even starting to remember the words.

The people who love me worry a lot,
But they understand the dream that I've got.
So I'll keep on runnin' till I reach the top.

And as I sang, I was also thinking: *This is pretty darn good right here. I'm in Nashville. I'm standing with a microphone. I'm singing. And I'm gonna be on local Nashville TV. Sweet!*

When I got finished, the Meat Man seemed happy. He drove me back to the airport, and I flew on to California for the race.

Well, a couple days later, I was in the garage area at Riverside when a guy working on someone else's car came over to me. "I saw you on TV singing," he said. "You did a pretty good job."

"You saw that?" I was surprised. "Wow! Thank you very much."

"I didn't know you could sing," he said.

"I *can't* sing," I assured him. "But I appreciate it."

A little later, a race fan came over and said he'd seen me too. Then, a third person said the same thing. It made me wonder: *Did all these people live in Nashville? Maybe they'd all gone on Music City vacations that year.*

Come to find out that the program I had sung on was not some local production. It was *Nashville Now,* the number-one, prime-time program on the Nashville Network, which was carried all across the country on cable TV. We didn't have cable yet in Level Cross, so I didn't know about any of that. It wasn't quite *Hee Haw*, which was syndicated on regular television. But Ralph Emery, who hosted *Nashville Now*, was called the Johnny Carson of country music. A lot of people watched that show.

It was just about the last thing I expected, but my song on the record and my appearance on the TV show actually started getting some buzz. I didn't make the cover of *Rolling Stone*. But William Barnhardt, writing in *Sports Illustrated*, did call my song "the best of the 21 cuts on the album." He said young Petty "can trade in his crash helmet for headphones anytime."

The next thing I knew, a man named Don Light was calling me up. I had known Don on and off, but he was really a friend of Childress's, and he drove a race car out at the old Nashville Fairgrounds. Don had been in the music business a long time. He had come to Nashville as a session drummer and then got into artist management. At one time, he'd been Jimmy Buffett's manager. He'd also managed Steve Wariner, Marty Stuart, and Mark Collie and was working with Keith Whitley at the time. Don was a well respected guy in Nashville. He was close friends with Chet Atkins, the brilliant guitarist and record producer who helped create the Nashville sound.

Don didn't waste any time. He got a record deal for me with RCA Records, Chet's longtime label. Joe Galante, the young head of RCA's Nashville division, was the one who signed me. I was in excellent hands with these guys. Joe had worked with Waylon Jennings, Dolly Parton, Vince Gill, and a bunch of other top-tier country stars. This was all a little intimidating. Other than Ralph Emery's studio audience, I had hardly played in front of anyone. And now I had a deal with a major record label. I told myself, *If I'm gonna do this, I'm gonna do it right,* which to me meant paying my dues in front of live audiences.

So before I jumped into the studio to record my first album, I began flying from Greensboro to Atlanta every week.

Don got me a regular gig in a bar called Stonewall's so I'd get some experience playing in public. I had the house band, Gordon Dee, behind me. I was there every Wednesday night. I'd play the first set. I'd play the second set. Then, I'd hightail it to the Atlanta airport and catch the eleven-thirty flight home. I'd be in bed by two, then get up the next morning and go to work.

It was hard, but how else was I going to learn my new trade?

Don was a terrific manager. During this period, he got me hired as the opening act for some major country stars. Randy Travis. The Oak Ridge Boys. Janie Fricke. The Forester Sisters. Don even got me on *Hee Haw*. The other guests that night were Reba McEntire and Tanya Tucker—*I was the new talent!*—and I sang a song called "The Other Guy."

You found out your heart's with another guy.
I found out so you don't have to tell a lie.

The first big act I opened for was Janie Fricke, who was huge in the 1980s. The show was at the Hampton Coliseum, just up I-64 from Virginia Beach. That's a ten-thousand-seat arena. Kyle Petty and the Petty Larceny Band, we called ourselves. I did ten songs, and the people seemed to be loving 'em, especially when I dedicated the song "Oh, King Richard," written by Rodney Crowell, to my dad for his birthday.

Oh, King Richard, you rum runner's dream
The swiftest of outlaw that I've ever seen.

As I bounded off the stage, feeling triumphant and gripping my guitar, the audience was still clapping and cheering. The thought did occur to me: I think they'd like an encore.

Then a second thought dragged me down to earth.

Nope. Can't do it. I know ten songs, and I just sang all ten of 'em.

As I headed backstage still high from my performance, the next thing I heard was the boom of a local country DJ: "Ladies and gentlemen, Miss Janie Fricke!"

I flew back that night to Charlotte. If anyone was worried that my singing career would distract me from racing, I thought I'd put that to rest right away. That was the Sunday I stood in Victory Lane after winning the Coca-Cola 600 in the Wood Brothers' famed no. 21.

The Hampton Coliseum *and* the Charlotte Motor Speedway: Now, that was my idea of a weekend!

That wasn't the only time I'd be singing right before a race. Even after Charlotte, there were plenty of critics out there who said my music would distract me from whatever race was coming up. That never made any sense to me. I'd tell those folks that if I wasn't out doing a show, I could have been out with the other drivers going to bars and concerts anyway. My way, instead of being on the dance floor, I'd be up onstage with people throwing things at me.

When I opened for others, it was usually at large outdoor festivals and in giant arenas. Ten, fifteen, twenty thousand people. I'd leave the race-track on a Friday or a Saturday afternoon. I had a little twin-engine Beech-craft Baron that I bought just so I could get in and out of those shows. I might fly from Darlington to Forsyth County, Georgia, and open for Randy Travis at Lanierland, then jump on the plane and fly back to Darlington and practice or qualify or even race the next day.

On September 11, 1987, Don got me a gig with Hank Williams, Jr., at Reynolds Coliseum in Raleigh. Hank's crowd in those days was a little wild. When he sang "All My Rowdy Friends Are Coming Over Tonight," that's pretty much who turned out to see him play. Marie Osmond had been part of the tour, but she'd been replaced with Tanya Tucker, and I was going to open the show.

We were racing in Richmond that weekend. Richard Childress, Chocolate Myers, Will Lind, and Danny Lawrence—Dale Earnhardt's car owner and crew—all wanted to go see Hank Jr. They said they'd fly me down there if I could get them in.

Before the show, one of Hank's guys came looking for me. "Hank wants to see you," he said and walked me to the singer's tour bus. When I knocked, Hank answered the door.

He was a big man. We shook hands and chatted a little. Then, he looked at me, and he said, "What's it like having Richard Petty for a father?"

I said, "I don't know, man. It's like having Hank Williams Senior for a father. It's the only guy you know. That's your dad."

"Yeah," he said. "But it's a big shadow, isn't it?"

I wasn't sure if he was talking about his father or mine. Both of them, probably.

"It can be," I said. "It can be a big shadow."

"I know, man," he said.

Then, he just kinda sat there. He changed the subject. We talked about some other stuff, and then I had the feeling that it was about time for me to leave.

"Hey, it was good to meet you," I said. "Thank you."

"OK," he said. "Here's what I want you to do. This crowd, these people—and I don't mean this in a bad way. But they came to see me. And they're waiting on me to come out."

I just nodded.

"What I want you to do is go out there and do your thirty-five- or forty-minute set. You turn everything up as loud as it will go. You don't talk. You don't make eye contact. You just sing your songs. And I want you to end with Eric Clapton's 'Cocaine.' You know that song?"

I did.

"And then wave to the crowd and walk off the stage. Tanya will go on, and she'll do the same thing. Then, I go out."

"I hear ya," I said.

And that's exactly what we did. We did our forty minutes. We played a little country. We played a little rock. We turned our stuff wide open, and we ended with the Eric Clapton song. And I walked offstage, my ears still ringing from that wall of sound.

"Hey, man," Hank said as I passed him backstage. "You did a great job. I really appreciate you being a part of this."

"Thank you for letting me be part of it," I said.

Then, I went out and watched the rest of the show with Childress and Earnhardt's guys. We got in the plane and flew back to Richmond and ran the race the next day.

It's funny, but it's also true: The best part about being onstage, other than singing to the people and making them happy, is that if you mess up, you don't get hauled off in an ambulance, even at a Hank Williams, Jr., show. If you miss a chord or miss a lyric, you just missed it. It's not like at Daytona or Martinsville, where if you miss a corner, you get a quick ride to the Infield Care Center. That's your consolation prize.

I enjoyed playing my music. I loved being around people who played, people who were creative, people who could find words and make a song out of them, people who could take a guitar or a mandolin or a fiddle and make it talk.

Between playing at Stonewall's and opening for different acts, I kept at it for three or four years. The pace was grueling. But when you're in your midtwenties like I was, you think you can do just about everything.

But by 1988, my last year with the Wood Brothers, some of that was starting to fade.

It just got to the point where my deal with RCA was kind of fizzling out. Playing every week in Atlanta and opening other people's shows, I didn't make time to get into the studio like I should have, and that was probably a mistake. A lot of time had passed, and I didn't have an album. Really, I think my window had opened and shut. I was pushing myself so hard, racing, singing, flying all over the place, the music was starting to feel like a job. I didn't want to lose the fun of it. That's what attracted me in the first place. I enjoyed it. I was on a treadmill. I was scared I might be losing that. Being so naive, I'd thought at the beginning I could be a professional musician just by standing up and singing a few songs and that would be the end of it.

I didn't know the half of it.

Let me tell you: That whole experience gave me huge respect for anyone who pursues a career in music or the arts.

Don was still going strong. He was out trying to find another record deal. But one day, it just hit me: You can do a lot of things. But you can't be the best at any of them if you're trying to do sixteen things at once. It was time for a change. I still enjoyed the music. I loved it. I wanted to keep playing. But it was time to make a choice:

I'm going to do music or I'm going to drive a race car.

I'd been playing guitar since I was twelve years old. But I had wanted to drive a race car since I was even younger than that. I decided: *That's really what I'm here for.*

By the late 1980s, the job of race car driver was transitioning, as well. A lot more was being expected of the drivers than what had been. It used to be, if you could drive a race car, no one cared if you had three arms and two heads as long as you got to the track on time and did your job out there. But as the sport was evolving and sponsors were paying bigger and bigger dollars to put their names on the side of the car, they still wanted drivers to run well. But now they were also saying, "I need a driver who can win on Sunday. But I also need a driver who can walk and talk and sell my product the other six days of the week."

That was making side gigs harder to maintain.

I told Don how much I appreciated everything he had done for me, but it was probably time to focus on what I had grown up with. I knew I'd always keep playing music. But from then on, I figured, it just might be for myself.

14

TEAM FELIX

"There will be a man waiting for you when you get off the plane."

Though I knew I'd be saying goodbye to the Wood Brothers at the end of the 1988 racing season, it wasn't like I had anywhere else to go. I didn't. I had no job prospects at all. Twenty-eight years old, a family to support, I knew nothing else but racing, and there I was: making cold calls on the phone. Knocking on doors. Going to see people. This is how an out-of-work NASCAR driver finds his next ride. If they put "driver wanted" ads in the classified section of the *Charlotte Observer* or the *Winston-Salem Journal,* I'd have been poring over those, as well. Whatever field you're in, there's nothing glamorous about looking for a job when you don't have one.

People were friendly, which I appreciated. But no one had anything for me, not right away.

One of the people I called was Rick Hendrick, who my dad was going to drive for three years earlier but then changed his mind. As part of Hendrick Motorsports, Rick also had a test team at the time that did tire testing for Goodyear. There'd been rumors that at some point, he might want to turn that test team into a Cup team. I had done some tire testing for Goodyear, so I knew the team and the guys.

"Hey, man," I said to Rick when I got him on the phone. "I know you don't have an opening now, but is anything gonna happen with that Goodyear test team?"

"Probably not," he said. "But let me think about it. If something comes up, I'll keep you in mind."

"I appreciate that," I said, and I meant it. Rick was a good guy and always true to his word.

I talked to a couple of other teams that were just teams. They got to the racetrack on Sunday, but they were not the caliber of the Wood Brothers or Hendrick Motorsports. Not anything near. It would have been a step backward going to work with any of them. At the same time, I was in no position to be picky.

I did manage to put together a small, personal service deal with Ford and Peak Antifreeze. They had a V6 program. I ran a few races for them and did some appearances. I was in Chicago with those guys for a trade show at McCormick Place when I got a message to call Rick.

"Something's kinda going on," Rick said vaguely. "I'm going to sell that test team to a friend of mine. And he might be looking for a driver. Would you be interested in talking to him?"

That might have been the easiest question I'd ever been asked.

"Yes."

"Can you meet him tonight?"

"Well," I said, "I'm in Chicago. But the answer to that is yes. Tell me where to meet him. I'm on my way."

I went back to the trade show booth. As nicely as I could, I explained to the Peak people that I had to get back to North Carolina right away. "I have an emergency that pertains to racing." They were more than gracious. I got a taxi to O'Hare airport and jumped on the first flight to Charlotte. I checked in with Rick along the way. This was all pre–cell phone. Everything was over pay phones—remember them?

"There will be a man waiting for you when you get off the plane," Rick told me.

This was getting more mysterious by the minute.

In fact, there was a man. He was standing outside the gate with a little sign that said MR. PETTY. At this point, the Peak people knew I'd gone back to Charlotte. Rick knew where I was supposed to be. And so did the man with the sign, who said his name was O'Brien. But nobody else I knew had a clue about any of it. I didn't tell anyone because even I didn't know who I had flown back to meet.

O'Brien walked me to a Chevy Suburban, and we drove around the airport property to the area where the private planes were. He put in a code and we drove up to the door of a giant aircraft hangar. We got out of the Suburban, and he unlocked the hangar door. It was dark in there. When O'Brien flipped on the lights, the first thing I saw was a small jet. I didn't know a lot about private planes, but I knew enough to know this was a nice one.

O'Brien led me to an office and told me to have a seat and make myself comfortable.

All of a sudden, it occurred to me:

I was at a private hangar at the Charlotte airport, way in the back where no one could hear me screaming, if it ever came to that. Nobody knew I was here. I had no idea who I was meeting or when they might arrive.

Was this a mob hit or a business meeting? I wasn't entirely sure.

"I'm leaving now," O'Brien said. "They just told me to drop you off here."

Still no word on who *they* might be.

I sat in that office and watched the minutes tick by, half of me hopeful about a new driving opportunity, half of me wondering if I'd ever walk out of that hangar alive. I'd certainly never had a job interview like this one. If it even was a job interview.

That's how far race car drivers will go just to get an opportunity to drive a car. Just an opportunity. Nobody promised me anything. Nobody said, "Fly down to Charlotte immediately, and you can drive my race car." Nothing like that. It was only that I knew a guy who knew a guy who might want to meet me.

Just say when. I'm coming. I didn't think twice about it. I was there.

Then, *bam!*

Without any warning, the office door suddenly swung open, and in walked two guys.

I have to admit I was relieved to see that neither of them appeared to be armed.

They introduced themselves as Felix Sabates and Ted Conder, and they thanked me for flying back from Chicago to meet with them.

I was happy to meet, I said, skipping right over the wild adventure that had just unfolded in my head. The two of them seemed to be business partners, but I got the distinct impression that Felix was in charge.

He spoke with a Cuban accent. I'm not a great judge of men's fashion, but I could tell he was wearing an expensive suit. His black hair was combed straight back. He was talkative and enthusiastic. Instantly, I felt like I'd known him my whole life.

Felix told me a little about his background.

The oldest of seven children, he left Cuba at age fifteen seeking opportunity and freedom in America. Slowly his family members followed him, except for his father, a doctor, who wasn't permitted to leave.

Felix scrubbed pots and pans in local hospitals. He was a sander in a furniture factory. He washed cars at the Charlotte airport, where he'd later keep his private jet. He met Rick Hendrick at the grand opening of City Chevrolet in Charlotte. Soon, Felix and Rick were the best of friends and calling each other "Brother." Felix had a knack for selling. He could sell anything. He went to work for a local company called Top Sales, helping manufacturers get their products into retail stores. Felix bought the company in 1971 and steered sales up into the billions.

Teddy, I learned, sold Rubbermaid and other household goods to stores like Family Dollar. But it was Felix who had a real knack for business. He sold consumer electronics. He wholesaled millions of TVs and hair dryers to retailers all over the Southeast. He was in the right place at the right time for Atari and for a talking teddy bear named Teddy Ruxpin. That bear was big! And what a numbers whiz Felix turned out to be. If you told Felix you'd sell him a phone for $22.22, don't come back two years later and tell him it's $22.53! He remembered every penny.

In the years since, Felix had acquired an interest in several other businesses, and he was looking to expand his holdings in the sports world. He, Rick Hendrick, and a former North Carolina state senator named Cy Bahakel were minority partners in the newly formed Charlotte Hornets, the city's NBA franchise. Kelly Tripucka, the expansion team's star shooting guard, would be staying at Felix's house. Why pay rent? Felix had plenty of room. Felix and Teddy had also invested in NASCAR. They were the owners of a Busch Series race team. Their driver, Bobby Hillin, was a nice kid a few years younger than me. Now, Felix and Teddy were wanting a Cup team. "And this deal kinda came along," he said.

We just talked. He didn't quiz me about my driving or say, "Do you want to be a champion?" or anything corny like that. We just spoke about racing and where NASCAR was heading next. Teddy was straight up with him.

"Cup racing's really expensive," Teddy warned. "A lot of people have come into the sport with a lot of money and left with a whole lot less."

"I understand," Felix said.

"There's opportunity," Teddy emphasized, "but it costs."

Felix didn't blink, but he did ask me one question I wasn't expecting. "Why didn't you sign that trading card deal?"

How did he even know about that? This was just about the time that trading cards were first coming into NASCAR. Baseball, football, and now racing! I had been asked to license my likeness. I knew a lot of the other drivers had signed up with them. But I passed. It wasn't about the money. I just figured that, everywhere I went, those cards would be something else I had to sign.

I explained that to Felix. He just nodded.

Nothing happened quickly. Since I was job hunting, every day that passed felt like weeks. But Felix and Teddy and I kept talking over the next couple of months, and I came to see how serious they were about the racing business.

The third week of September, we were all at Dover. I was there with the Wood Brothers for the Delaware 500. Felix and Teddy were there for the Busch race. After their race, we all went back to the hotel to talk.

We discussed the importance of having a talented engine builder, good mechanics, and a great crew chief on a Cup team. Felix wanted to know if I had any potential sponsors. I told them we could certainly talk to Peak Antifreeze. "They might be interested, and also STP. I think we can talk to them."

Felix said he had no intention of running the full 1989 season. Gary Nelson, his crew chief, and John Wilson, his engine builder, wanted time to get up and running. He asked if I had an issue with that. "No," I answered truthfully, "I just want something to drive."

After we'd talked for a couple of hours, Felix finally said to me, "OK. I think we have a deal."

"I'm gonna drive y'all's car?" I asked.

"Yes," they answered. "On one condition."

"What is that?"

"You're gonna sign that damn card deal!" Felix said. "We own that card company, and you're gonna sign the deal." From what he said, I guess I was the only driver at any level of NASCAR who hadn't signed on.

That was an easy one for me: "No problem. I'll sign."

If you go back and look, the first year they had those cards, I wasn't on any of them. The rarest card is the card that doesn't exist, right? Good luck finding it! The following years, I was in every series they had.

And with that, I was back in the game. I'd be driving the no. 42 Pontiac for owner Felix Sabates and his new Cup Series team, SABCO. And yes, tell everyone in Level Cross: I was getting my old number back again.

My first year with Felix, 1989, we went to Daytona. We didn't qualify. We ended up renting a car from Eddie Bierschwale. He had already qualified for the 500. We put our Peak Antifreeze decals on the car to make it look as much like ours as possible. Eddie started the race in the car, and I got in at the first caution. We ran tenth, and Eddie was credited with the finish. It was a good day. Next up, we went to Atlanta, where we finished fourth. We had a pretty solid first year together with some flashes of "this could be really good." In 1990, we won at Rockingham right off the bat. Not a bad way to start our first full year of racing together.

Days of Thunder, starring Tom Cruise, Robert Duvall, Randy Quaid, and Nicole Kidman, reached theaters on June 27, 1990, and was a major box office hit. Cruise plays Cole Trickle, a young, open-wheel racer whose sights were set on the Indianapolis 500 before he decided he'd have a better shot in NASCAR. "To win at Indy, I'd need a great car," he said, "but stock cars are all the same." Oh, did young Cole have a lot to learn! His no. 51 Chevrolet Lumina is sponsored by Mello Yello, Coca-Cola's southeastern-regional answer to Pepsi's Mountain Dew.

In 80 percent of America, people thought Mello Yello was a made-up movie name. Who'd call a soda that? Well, Coke did. When the movie hit big, the people at headquarters in Atlanta decided, *Let's capitalize on all the national attention Mello Yello is getting.* The obvious answer: sponsor a real Cup car in NASCAR.

Right place, right time.

There was a flurry of pomp and circumstance when we signed that Mello Yello deal for 1991. We had the exact same color scheme that Cole's car had in the movie, black with neon green around the bottom. He ran no. 51. We ran no. 42. But other than that, it was the Mello Yello car from *Days of Thunder.* We started off the season strong. We won Rockingham again in 1991.

I had long hair. Felix hated long hair. He'd been on me to get a haircut. Bringing it up often. "When are you gonna get your hair cut?" he must have asked me every day. Finally, just before the race at Talladega in early May, I went to a barbershop.

"Cut it off," I said to the man.

Maybe that wasn't such a great idea.

On the backstretch at Talladega on lap 71, Mark Martin's Ford was clipped by Ernie Irvan's Chevy, sending Mark's car briefly airborne and setting off a chain reaction that ultimately included twenty of the forty-one cars. I got the worst of it when Ernie careened into my driver's side door. My car spun around. There were cars everywhere. At that point, I was just along for the ride.

I was stabbing and steering. Turning left and turning right. Tires were squealing. It's always loud inside a car in a crash—until it's not. The only thing quieter is a racetrack packed with one hundred thousand fans, once all the cars have finally stopped after the big one.

I knew instantly I was hurt.

I looked down. My left foot was turned at a very strange angle. I couldn't feel anything. Not yet. Is that what it means to be in shock? It was scary looking. *It's gotta be broke,* I thought.

I'd mostly been wearing black uniforms like Tom Cruise did in the Mello Yello car. But on this day, I happened to be wearing white. I looked down at my white pants legs, noticing a red stain and something poking through. That didn't look normal. It was a bone sticking out of my left thigh.

A big bone. A very big bone.

I couldn't move at all.

Dale Jarrett was the first person at my window. He pulled the net off and called and waved to the rescue squad. They got there in a hurry and got me out of the car and to the Infield Care Center. At the Care Center, they didn't want to push the bone back in the way it was poking through my pants leg. The wound was dirty. All they could do was put a sheet over me and load me into the helicopter for the quick flight to the University of Alabama Hospital in Birmingham.

In Birmingham, the doctor walked in and started poking. "Does that hurt? . . . Does that hurt?" None of it hurt. Though I was immediately grateful for that, it didn't seem like a great sign. How come I wasn't feeling anything? The diagnosis was a compound fracture of the left femur.

All I remember telling the doctor was, "It's my left leg and remember to get it the right length."

It's funny what pops into your mind in times of crisis. But as the doctors prepared to insert pins and rods in my leg, I knew that leg length could be an issue. I didn't want to limp for the rest of my life.

The race had been rain delayed for a full day. We'd finally run on a Monday. Surgery was that night. I'm not good with meds. So I don't remember Tuesday at all. But by Wednesday morning, I was feeling awful. My leg felt weird. I was nauseous from the meds. And suddenly, there were two nurses in my room.

"Please," I said, "y'all gotta take this medicine out. It's making me sick, even if it helps with the pain." They unhooked one of the IV lines. It took awhile, but the nausea eased. After lunch, the same two nurses were standing at my bedside again. "Good afternoon," one of them said, all cheery. "How ya doing?"

"I feel a lot better," I said.

"Good, 'cause you're going to therapy."

"Excuse me?"

"You're going to therapy."

"I am not going to therapy."

"Yes, you are."

"No, I'm not," I said, correcting her. "I'm going to lay right here on my butt and feel sorry for myself for at least a week because I can't get back in a race car. That's what I'm gonna do."

I had just enough willpower and hard-headedness that no one could possibly reason with me. The nurses recognized that and didn't even bother. They just declared:

"You know what *we're* gonna do, Mr. Petty?"

"What?"

"We're gonna snap you up out of that bed, and we're going to therapy."

And that's exactly what they did.

They snatched my butt out of that hospital bed. Put me in a wheelchair. By now, my leg was really hurting. A few minutes later, I was down in therapy. I know they were trying to be gentle. But *man*! It hurt. All that pain my shock had suppressed came rushing forward, and I didn't have the meds in me anymore to stop it. But I started with physical therapy. The therapists were ruthless, as I knew they'd be. Isn't that their job?

"You can put two percent of your weight on it." That was excruciating. I doubted I'd ever get to 3.

I was at the hospital in Birmingham for a week and went home to Carolinas Medical Center in Charlotte, where I spent another week. I was out in time to watch Kenny Wallace drive the no. 42 Mello Yello in the Charlotte race at the end of May. Because of the surgery, I had a rod in my leg and a couple of plates in my hip and a fistful of screws holding it all together.

I went to therapy every day for four or five months, a slow and painful journey. Bending my leg at all was a huge accomplishment. I stood next to a wall and put a towel behind my back. Saw how low I could go into a squat. At first, I slid down only a few inches and couldn't get back up. And every few seconds, pain shot through my leg as the scar tissue began to break apart. I did thousands and thousands of wall slides.

Sometimes I said, "This is never gonna happen," and I almost believed it. But slowly, my leg could hold more and more of my weight. Ten percent. Twenty percent. And it was up from there. And I got better at everything. I could squat so well, I didn't even need the wall anymore.

My leg could hold me. It could bend. It was the right length again. I was ready to drive a race car. Again.

I returned to racing at Darlington in September.

The Coca-Cola people always seemed happy when I came around.

While I was off recuperating, even though I couldn't drive a race car, I made tons of appearances for Mello Yello. I went to bottlers all over the Southeast and promoted the growing national brand. I spent countless days with Gary Azar of Coca-Cola as we made the trips together. To this day, we're still close friends, and the Mello Yello program really took off. I'm not saying it was all because of me. But the combination of *Days of Thunder,* the real race car, and all those visits with the bottlers, it was a perfect marketing opportunity for them. It didn't turn Mello Yello into the next Coca-Cola. But it gained a lot of popularity and attention.

And I couldn't help teasing Felix about one thing, the fact that just before the Talladega race, he had made me cut my hair. Felix could be a little superstitious. So I told him, "It's the hair, man. You made me cut it. And right off the bat, I got in a wreck. I never should have cut my hair."

I'm not sure if Felix believed a word of it or ever thought I was serious. But I will say this much: He never got on me about my hair again.

We could laugh together because we cared about each other so much. We'd talk about ways to make the team stronger and bring more sponsors in. I would even tease him about the cars he drove that I wanted.

One of them was a gold-colored 1978 Rolls-Royce Silver Shadow II. I'd always wanted a Rolls. I didn't care what color, what year, or what model it was or anything else about it. I just wanted that flying lady on the front of the hood. Once Felix let me drive his Rolls, and that made me want it even more.

Back in February, at the start of the 1991 season, Felix had said to me as we were heading down to Florida, "If you win Daytona, I will give you the car."

That's the way Felix was. Even a Rolls-Royce was just "the car."

Felix's offer quickly became a big deal in the media. It certainly gave the reporters and the fans something to talk about. Personally, I needed no extra incentive to win the Daytona 500. I'd grown up my whole life wanting to win that race. But part of being a car owner is generating interest for the team. In that way, Felix was the best!

I started sixth that day and ran a good race, leading for fifty-one laps, the most that day. But unfortunately, we did not win. I got in a crash with three laps to go and was credited with a sixteenth-place finish.

And I still wanted the Rolls.

I told Felix after the race, "Tell you what. Why don't I just buy it from you?"

He was OK with that. He'd had the car for a while by then. We came up with a way I could pay him out of my earnings.

Then, we went to Rockingham two weeks later, and I won the Goodwrench 500. After the win, Felix said, "Just take it. Just take the Rolls."

"Really?" I said.

He meant it! "The original deal was I'm going to give you a Rolls-Royce for winning Daytona," he said. "So now I'll give you a Rolls-Royce for winning Rockingham." I was dumbfounded. I couldn't believe he was giving me his car.

I didn't know what to say. Really, all I could say was, "Thank you." But I smiled about that all year long.

Those years with Felix and Mello Yello would be some of my very best as a race car driver. Felix took care of the business side and let me drive the car. As his driver, I was the public face of the team—working the sponsors, meeting the fans. But Felix was always there, always involved. And did we ever have fun! We went to Europe together. We went to the Bahamas together. He and I never had a written contract. One day, we'd be sitting in a restaurant and he'd write a number on a napkin, my driver's salary for the next year.

"Is that OK?" he'd ask.

"Good with me, man," I'd answer. "Let's just keep going." And that would be our entire negotiating process.

One day, he called me up and said, "I need to cut your salary back." In exchange, I got a small percentage ownership in the new Charlotte Checkers of the East Coast Hockey League. The team did well, well enough that I even got my own 1996 ECHL championship ring. Felix always did what he said he would do, and I did the same.

He had his own unique way of doing things. On the way to a meeting in Las Vegas with a potential sponsor, Felix pulled a friend away from a casino craps table and brought him along. "You'll be my lawyer," Felix told his friend. "Whatever I say in the meeting, you just nod and agree." When the negotiating got heavy, the man dutifully supported every position Felix took.

"We can't do that, can we?"

"Nope. We can't do that."

"We need these guys to cover the insurance, right?"

"Oh, yeah. They have to cover the insurance."

Who needs a real lawyer? I'm pretty sure Felix's casino friend didn't charge $300 a quarter hour. He got the job done!

We came *this close* to letting Peak pay our sponsorship fee in antifreeze—five hundred thousand gallons, if I remember right—instead of the usual cash. It was like a farmer paying in chickens for a tractor repair. Only Felix could do that. If you gave me half a million gallons of antifreeze, I wouldn't have a clue what to do with it. But Felix knew he could sell anything. Why should antifreeze be any different from video-game consoles or flat-screen TVs? In the end, Peak decided to pay us the normal way, but I know Felix could have made it work either way. Those years were when I really felt like I came into my own as a race car driver. And it would never have happened without Felix's friendship, support, and love.

15

CHARITY RIDE

"Do you know a guy named Don Tilley?"

It's only fitting, I suppose. But the earliest inspiration for the Kyle Petty Charity Ride Across America came at a rest stop off I-95 as a much younger me glanced at a very large, black Harley-Davidson motorcycle. We're talking 1973 or 1974, which would make me thirteen or fourteen years old.

I was coming home from Daytona, riding with my dad's crew, still in my sweaty STP uniform. It was getting close to midnight when we stopped at a rest area just across the Georgia–South Carolina line. I stretched my bony legs and walked over to get a Coke out of the drink machine. It was dark, but not so dark that I didn't notice the Harley-Davidson parked nearby.

"Hey, boy," I heard a gruff, male voice say just as I was bending down to pull my Coke out of the machine.

I looked up. It was the man on the motorcycle. He wasn't a big guy, maybe five-five. He was wearing jeans and a leather jacket.

"Yes, sir," I said.

"What's your name?"

"Kyle." I didn't know what he wanted.

"You're Richard's son, aren't you?" he said.

"Yes, sir."

"You tell him Don Tilley said hello."

"Yes, sir."

And as I walked back to the van with my can of Coke, I thought, *That's the coolest guy I've ever seen in my life.* I mean, it's eleven thirty at night. He's out riding his bike. That's all I ever wanted to do, ride motorcycles. He was a grown man, and there he was.

The next day at the race shop, I said to my dad, "Hey, do you know a guy named Don Tilley?"

"About yay tall?" my dad asked. He was holding his hand right at chest level.

"That's him," I said.

"Was he on a motorcycle?"

"Yes, sir."

"He worked here when you were born," my dad said. "He was a damn good welder and a good race car driver too. He ran some races for your grandfather and for me too. Then, in 1972, he started a Harley dealership in Statesville. Been a Harley-Davidson dealer ever since."

I could tell Don Tilley was cool. And my dad knew him.

It wasn't until I got older that I traded my little Yamaha dirt bike for my own black Harley. Everybody in the race shop who had motorcycles had Harleys. Harry Gant had a saying: "If you're gonna have a pickup, it's gotta be a Ford, and it's gotta be black. If you're gonna have a luxury car, it's gotta be a Cadillac, and it's gotta be white. If you're gonna have a sports car, it's gotta be a Corvette, and it's gotta be red. And if you're gonna have a motorcycle, it's gotta be a Harley, and it's gotta be black."

Harry had strong views about such things. Those were his rules to live by. And people in the race shop pretty much did just that.

Every year after the Rockingham race in November, Don and some of his friends would ride to Phoenix. They were always leaning on me: "Come on, ride with us. Come on, ride with us."

I was like, "Man, that's a long way."

I'd ridden to Dover, Delaware. That's four or five hundred miles. But Phoenix? That was close to 2,100 miles if you went straight there. "That's a little too far for me," I said.

Don kept pushing. "No, man. Three days. It takes three days." Eventually, he wore me down. In November 1991, I agreed to ride with Don and his buddies.

Besides Don, it was Click Baldwin, who owned the Harley shop in

Gastonia and showed up looking like he just stepped out of a Harley catalog. It was Robin Pemberton, a legendary mechanic, fabricator, and crew chief—and, later, NASCAR executive. It was Harry Gant, still at the wheel of his no. 33 Skoal Bandit car. It was Darren Jolly, crew member for Robert Yates. A couple of others. And me. We had this group, and we all headed west. We rode and we rode, and the farther west we rode, the colder it got. Phoenix was a long way from North Carolina. We stopped in Oklahoma City and picked up some guys and continued on. It was that night, right around midnight, that it suddenly dawned on me. *What a cool idea this is!* A motorcycle ride where we pick up people all across the country and just keep riding. Like a bike-a-thon, only much farther and much faster than anyone could pedal on that kind of bike. I knew I could get a few drivers and other NASCAR people to come along. We'd really take Don's ride to the next level if we could pull off something like that!

We rode a little farther. And when we got to Arizona, we stopped south of Phoenix near the Salt River Canyon and picked up another group there. It just kept getting better, the farther we went.

I didn't do anything right away about expanding the ride. We did Don's ride, the usual way, for a few more years. But I started talking to Harry and Don about it, and I mentioned, "You know, going from Statesville or Charlotte to Phoenix is really not coast-to-coast. You're getting close but it's not all the way across." Now, I was the one who wanted to go more miles. So, I said, "Let's haul our bikes to California and ride back after the California race." That's June, right in the heart of the racing season. "Much better than November. And it's coast-to-coast."

We kept talking, and people seemed to get into it. "Let's do it!" I said.

I told my owner, Felix. Harry told his guys. We told our sponsors and our crews. And the answer came back, "No way! You've got appearances you have to make on Wednesdays and Thursdays. You've got other things you need to do. You can't be out there riding motorcycles in the middle of the country in the middle of the season. That's just crazy."

These were our teams and sponsors. This wasn't family. We didn't even mention it to them.

We wouldn't let it die, though. We wanted to do this. We talked about it a little bit more. And then it dawned on me: "We'll do it for charity."

Harry and I both floated that idea with our teams, and we both got the same reaction.

"You'll do it for charity?"

"We'll raise some money. We'll give it away. Everywhere we go."

And everybody—especially our sponsors—said, "Great idea. Why don't you all do that?"

So, in the summer of 1995, the Kyle Petty Charity Ride Across America was born. We left the San Francisco 49ers NFL training camp. We went down to Huntington Beach. Then east to Las Vegas. Down to Phoenix. East to Odessa, Texas. To Fort Worth. To Little Rock. To Nashville. And back to North Carolina.

There were about thirty-five of us that first year. We took up donations, raising money as we went along. We confirmed our suspicion that summer is a much better time for motorcycle riding than November is. Sometimes at night, we'd do an event at a bar along the way because Coors was my sponsor at the time. We gave the money to a firefighter in Huntington Beach who'd been burned really badly and to a hospital in Phoenix and other deserving groups in the places where we stopped. And when we got back to North Carolina, we couldn't believe how much fun we'd had.

"Holy crap, man! That was the greatest ride ever! We've never done anything any better than that before!"

We weren't as organized as we could have been. We missed a couple of turns and ate fried chicken on the side of I-10 (Interstate 10). Sometimes, we ran five hours late or someone ran out of gas. But everybody loved the Ride. We got a bunch of media publicity for the charities we supported and for our sponsors. And we gave away, I believe, $35,000. So, of course, we decided to do it again.

We couldn't possibly have known what a long-running tradition we had just begun and how many worthy causes we would support in the many years to come, including a very special charity project that wasn't even a glimmer yet in any of our eyes!

Part III

DAD

16

BOY WONDER

"Let's go to Caraway . . . Let's go to Myrtle Beach."

Adam was just a kid. That's what I remember most. He was just a kid. I have in my mind a chunky little boy of eight or nine years old wanting to drive a go-kart. And I had to think for a minute how I was going to answer him.

I had seen other kids whose fathers I knew. Other racing people. At some point, the kid said, "I wanna go go-kart racing." The dad would get a pickup, get a big trailer, buy two or three go-karts and some spare motors, and pay a guy to go with his son to the go-kart track. Within six months or a year, most of those kids didn't want to race go-karts anymore. They were done with it. They would get bored and go off in some other direction.

I thought Adam would be better off if it wasn't all handed to him.

When he asked about go-kart racing, I said, "OK, you can go-kart race. I never go-kart raced. You can, but it's supposed to be fun. Always remember that."

We had a friend who eventually ended up driving my dad's bus, Archie Kennedy. And Archie would take Adam to the go-kart track. He didn't go all the time. I went with him a couple of times. I couldn't always go with him because he would run while I was at the track. Archie would always take him, whether I was there or not.

Adam would drive the go-kart, and as soon as the race was over, he would just go play with the other kids. That's what Archie told me, and that's what I saw when I was there. That's what kids do when they're eight or nine and they're driving a go-kart.

Adam came back after he'd run five or six races, and he said to me, "They're faster than me. I need a better motor."

I thought, *Here we go!*

"You don't know how to drive yet," I told him. "How do you know you need a better motor? You learn to drive and do the best with what you've got, and then we'll start working on it."

He went back and won a go-kart race with the equipment he had.

He called me, all excited. "I won," he said.

"That's great, man," I told him. He had a right to be excited. He'd done it with his driving ability. His excitement made me excited. It wasn't the motor. It was him.

"I got fifteen dollars for winning," he said.

"Fifteen dollars? You're kidding!"

"No."

"That's good," I said.

He'd thought it all out. "I'm gonna help pay for the go-kart," he said, "and I'm gonna help pay for the tires, and I'm gonna pay for the gas."

"That sounds good," I said. "What about the trophy? They give you a trophy?"

"I didn't get a trophy," he told me. "You could get a trophy or you could get fifteen dollars. I took the fifteen dollars."

Was he his great-grandfather's great-grandson, racing for the money and nothing else? I had to think about that for a second. No, it wasn't that. Winning just made him feel good and he wanted to share his good fortune in a kid's idea of a grown-up way by helping to pay for things.

Nothing wrong with that. What a great instinct! But to me as a father, it seemed like a teachable moment. When I got home, I said, "We need to have a class. Let me show you something."

We sat down together at the dining room table. On a piece of paper, I wrote down some numbers. "This is how much the go-kart cost," I said. "And this is how much tires cost. This is how much fuel is. This much is going to the racetrack. This is for food. It all adds up to this much. These numbers are going to keep changing because you're going to keep going, but this is how much it adds up to. Now, let's take that number and divide it by fifteen."

So, we divided it. "According to this, you're going to have to win about two hundred and fifty races for us to get back even. That's a lot of races. I appreciate your wanting to help pay for stuff. Believe me, I do. But we don't need the fifteen dollars right now. It'll be gone fast. But that trophy will mean something many years from now, the first race you ever won. So, take the fifteen dollars back and get the trophy."

He took the $15 back, and he got the trophy. The guy at the go-kart track said, "Sure." I'll bet that trophy cost him less than $15. It was a cool deal all around. Adam kept that trophy in his bedroom. He showed it to people. It meant a lot to him. We still have that trophy. Now it's priceless.

Felix had a Legends car, and he let Adam drive it.

Legends cars are 5/8-scale replicas of American automobiles from the 1930s and 1940s, powered by air-cooled Yamaha engines. Even though there are a few different body types, all the Legends cars are mechanically identical. So they're a low-cost way to get into racing where the skill of the driver is what wins races, not who has the most money to spend on a car. Though experienced drivers participate, there's a Young Lions Division for twelve- to sixteen-year-olds. Adam wouldn't be one of the first future NASCAR drivers to hone his skills at the wheel of a Legends car. So did Brennan Poole, Ryan Blaney, Reed Sorenson, David Ragan, Joey Logano, Kyle Busch, and Kurt Busch. For Adam and the others, it was a step or three up from go-karts.

Archie brought Adam to the Legends races at Charlotte Motor Speedway, just like he'd taken him to the go-kart races, giving Adam his first taste of a real racetrack. Adam ran a few races, and he really enjoyed it.

When he was fourteen, we decided we'd get a late-model car, which is a real car. We put it in a shop close to where we were living. It was just a chassis. We didn't have a body on it yet. It didn't have an engine. But he'd go over a couple of times a week and work on the car, and I'd go with him.

It was nice. He enjoyed it. I enjoyed it. We'd make a little progress every time. One day, he had some reason he couldn't go over there. He was playing football or doing something else. I can't remember exactly what, but he was busy. The next time, he had another reason. And then another reason. And all those reasons started sounding more like excuses. Next thing I knew, he wasn't going over there anymore.

I never said anything about it, and neither did he.

Five or six months went by. Maybe a little longer. Then, out of the blue one day, he said to me, "Have you been over there working on that race car?"

"Not my race car," I said. "It's your race car. I'm not working on your race car."

"What?"

I think he was surprised to hear that.

"Listen," I said to my son. "We got a race car because you said you wanted to drive one. If you don't want to drive one, that's fine. That's not an issue. But I'm not going to put a race car together that I'm not going to drive, and I'm not going to put one together for you to drive. We're going to do this together or we're not."

"Okay," he said. "Let's go back over there."

So we did. We started working on the car again. And from that day forward, I don't ever remember Adam looking back. He just kept saying, "Let's get it ready . . . Let's go to Caraway . . . Let's go to Nashville . . . Let's go to Myrtle Beach . . . Let's race."

Ah, the short tracks. Where racing begins.

Our local short tracks, and hundreds of others like them, are the grassroots of American racing. Always have been. Caraway Speedway, just down the road from Petty Enterprises in Level Cross, is typical. Four turns. A couple of straightaways. Not quite half a mile (0.455 miles) from the start-finish line back to the start-finish line. Built as a dirt track in 1966, it was paved with asphalt in 1972 and has been a regular part of the NASCAR Weekly Series ever since. Think of tracks like Caraway as racing's semipro division. The fans get to mix with the drivers after the Saturday night races. Friday nights are added to the schedule outside of high-school football season. No sane operator would want to compete with that.

Not in North Carolina.

Short tracks are dotted all over the South—and not only the South. You can hardly toss a football in North Carolina without hitting a short track. There's one in Concord. There's Ace Speedway in Burlington. There's Asheville-Weaverville in Asheville, of course. There's Carteret County by the coast. There's Orange County in Rougemont up near the Virginia border. There's Franklin County across the state line. You've got dirt tracks like Madison 311 and Lancaster. I've never added up how many there are altogether, but there are a lot more short tracks in our part of the country than there are minor-league baseball parks or college stadiums—for sure.

A guy might work at a gas station, but he loves racing. So he puts together a street stock or late-model car or a limited late-model, depending on the engine size. You may have eight to twelve guys in that area who like to race and eight to twelve others in the next area and ten or fifteen others a little farther down the road. They'll race at their local tracks, then try their luck at a track in the next county or the one after that. Before you know it, you have some regional rivalries heating up.

This is where the racing starts to get thrilling. It's all about the racing.

The racers do get paid. It could be $1,500 or $2,500 for a win. Lesser amounts for those who finish just behind the winner. Racing on that level is not a profitable venture. However much the prize money is, it all goes back into the car. It really is like playing semipro ball, like the ex-high-school pitcher who says, "Yeah, I work down the street here at the grocery store, but I've still got some stuff on the mound."

You win a bunch of races, and all of a sudden you're a local celebrity.

You'll see a similar mix of characters at most of these short tracks. Some older drivers, in their forties and fifties or older, who've been doing it their whole lives. This is as far as they ever made it, and that's OK with them. They just love racing. Then, there are some drivers a few years younger, in their thirties, give or take, who still have that burning desire to move up. Their dream hasn't faded yet. They haven't turned into that older group, but a lot of them will eventually. Then, there are the hungry young drivers, the eighteen- to thirty-year-olds. Sometimes, you'll see them out there way younger—I mean *really* young, thirteen, fourteen, and fifteen years old. Somewhere in that group—*somewhere!*—is the next Richard Petty or the next Jimmie Johnson or the next Tony Stewart. Can you spot him? One of the thrills of going out to your local short-track races is being constantly on the lookout for the next superstar.

You might see an eighteen-year-old who's incredibly hot. There's another kid, and he's nineteen. He's just as hot in another part of the state. When those two come together—and you can bet they will—it's gonna be a show! People in the know in those communities will be paying close attention. You know what local race fans love saying more than anything else in the world? "I paid eight bucks to watch Jeff Gordon race just down the road here, and now he's on my TV."

That, right there, is the grassroots connection between racing and the people who love to watch it. Those hundreds of little tracks around the country—or is it thousands?—that's where the sport and the learning really get started. Without them, there is no big-time racing.

After working his way up through the go-karts and Legends cars, Adam was certainly ready to give his late-model car a run on the short tracks. So that's what we did. He ran at Caraway and Myrtle Beach and Nashville and a handful of others. He was fifteen years old.

It really wasn't about winning, though of course that's all any driver wants to do. It was more about learning and keeping your head about you and getting used to being in the mix. Caraway was close to us. On a shorter track like that one, a young driver could learn to be aggressive. Everyone was packed so tight together, you just had to knock people out of the way. Myrtle Beach and Nashville were small but long enough and wide enough to help prepare Adam for what was coming next. On tracks like those, you learned to pass people. You could develop some finesse. With a little more room to maneuver, you could get another driver to watch you in the mirror and set him up. You might fake to the outside and pass him on the inside because he took the bait. It's on tracks like those where you really learned to race. There's a difference between people who can go fast and people who can race. Real racers will tell you that speed has nothing to do with racing. Some of the greatest races you'll ever see will be on short tracks at 55 miles an hour.

I know that sounds crazy, but it's not 100 percent wrong.

This much is undeniable: Mashing the gas isn't all it takes to be a great racer. There are other people with you on the track doing what you are doing. You have to be able to outrun them.

As Adam's talent improved, so did his enthusiasm for racing. Witnessing his wide-eyed wonder, that was so much fun for me. What dad wouldn't get a kick out of watching his son discover such a passion inside himself, a passion that in Adam's case I shared too?

But witnessing my son fall more and more in love with racing also gave me a lot to think about, some serious questions that I really had to wrestle with as a dad. I wanted to be encouraging. I wanted to be helpful when and where I could. But I also wanted to be sure—double-sure, triple-sure—that these were Adam's choices, Adam's desires, Adam's interests, not a path he was pursuing because his father, grandfather, and great-grandfather had pursued it before him. As far as I was concerned, nothing in our family needed to be preordained.

"*You* have to want to do this," I told Adam on more than one occasion, always emphasizing the word *you*.

"Don't become a racer because I did it or because anyone else did it before you. Those were *our* choices. You have to make *yours*."

I didn't only say that. I also meant it. And I believe that Adam got the message loud and clear. I certainly pray he did.

"You sure you wanna do this?" I asked him many times.

If there was any hesitation in his voice, I certainly didn't hear it. He was as gung-ho as any young racer I had ever been around.

I delivered the exact same message to my son Austin, Adam's younger brother, with precisely the opposite result. Austin never showed that same level of interest in racing. He loved a little bit of everything, and that was totally fine with me. I've always been proud of Austin, just like I've been proud of their younger sister, Montgomery Lee, who chose her own path without a second's hesitation or regret.

I always knew this was slippery territory for a parent, not just letting your kids be kids.

In my short time on earth, I had witnessed too many fathers living vicariously through their sons, pushing their sons to do things the fathers wished they had done themselves, things the sons didn't really have a passion for. The sons just went along with it because they didn't want to disappoint the dad.

Mothers do that with their daughters too, I suppose. But I'd seen it more with fathers and sons. I vowed I would never do that with any of my children.

Maybe that's just me talking, drawing from my own experience as a father and, especially, as a son. But too many of us spend too much time in our youths either being forced or pressured to act like adults. And then when we get to be adults, it's too late to act like children. Certainly until you're out of school and on your own and you have to pull that trigger on some kind of grown-up life—just enjoy yourself. Try to learn. Figure out what you're good at and what you love. Discover what you really can't stand. Try things, even if they turn out to be the wrong things. Keep an open mind. You're never going to be twelve or fifteen or eighteen or twenty-one again. Before you take on all the responsibilities of adulthood, take the time to figure out what you care about and who you are.

Believe me, you'll never be as young as yesterday again.

Despite all that, Adam was getting deeper and deeper into racing. By that point, he certainly never had to be told, "Get on over to the shop." It was scary sometimes, seeing how focused and exacting he was.

Sometime around then, I went out to Michigan to test my Cup car. There's no record of this, thank God, so I can't look up the exact date, and no one else can. But it was right around then sometime. It was a hot day. I remember that much, and Adam tagged along with me. And I'll never forget what happened once we got there. We weren't the only ones testing at Michigan International Speedway that week. Eight to ten other race teams were also at the track, running their own tests. The second or third morning, I went around to the other teams and asked for a favor.

"When the track opens up after lunch," I said, "can you all give me about fifteen minutes and let us be the only ones that go out on the racetrack?"

Everybody said, *Yeah, sure, no problem.*

One p.m. is the steamiest part of the day. The track was sure to be sweltering and slick. No one minded missing a few minutes of that.

Without asking anyone's permission, I put Adam in the driver's seat and let him go out in a Cup car.

He was fifteen. Actually, he might have still been fourteen. Whichever, he was crazy young to be doing something like that. But I gotta say, he looked pretty good out there. Fast down the straightaways. Smooth through the turns. Keeping control the whole way. And he was going fast. He ran ten or fifteen miles an hour slower than what we were running. But it's still ungodly fast for a fourteen- or fifteen-year-old. Stupid fast. No one at the track said anything about it. I'm not sure that anybody was paying attention enough to notice. If they did, no one mentioned anything to me.

All I know is that Adam got out of that car with a giant smile on his face.

17

FAMILY PLAN

"You know what, Felix? I think I'm leaving too."

I was always a lazy driver.

If I had to describe my style behind the wheel of a race car, that's the word I would use. *Lazy.* Not lazy in the sense that most people use the term. I'm lazy in that I always wanted the car to do most of the work.

If I could make the car do 95 percent of the work, I was in good shape. If I could make the car do 75 percent and I had to make up 25 percent, it was harder for me to make up that difference and win. I could make up some, but I couldn't carry a car.

That's why we worked so hard in the shop to have the best possible car—and at the track to get the best possible performance out of the car we had.

Over time, these are the kinds of things you learn about yourself.

I always respected the equipment I had, partly because I'd had to work so hard to build and maintain it at some point in my career. I was never that overly aggressive guy who would put a car in a bad situation I didn't think I could get out of. For me, this went all the way back to working on my dad's car as a kid. Understanding what it was to take care of your car. Understanding what it was to have to put that car back together on Monday morning after you were the one who drove it on Sunday afternoon into some place you never should have gone.

With the teams today having so many cars and so much more money than we had, that's the way a lot of guys race now. The car isn't something they have to take care of. The car is more of a commodity. You throw it away after the weekend. It doesn't mean anything. The race is over with. That one's wiped out? That's OK. Get another one. That's just the way the sport is now.

It's like watching NBA players who wear new shoes every night. Compare that to Julius Erving, who probably wore the same pair for a solid year. There's a huge difference in how a player is going to treat those shoes.

I'd like to think I thought about things before I did them. That wasn't always the best attribute for a race car driver. Sometimes you have to seize the moment, consequences be damned. Sometimes I did, and sometimes I didn't. And that probably hurt me as a driver. I can be honest with myself about that now. But at the same time, I was that guy that if things were right, I could win you a race. If things weren't right, I could get you a decent finish. And if we were way off, I couldn't save you. I probably fell into the same category as a lot of other guys, most guys except for those at the very, very top of the game.

Some of those guys will tell you, "Just get it close, and I'll drive it."

That wasn't me. That's a different style. That's one of the things that makes racing so interesting. Drivers have such different styles. Before we ever left the race shop, I wanted the car to be the best that we as a team could take to the track.

There are people who are fast. There are people who are fearless. There are people who are also a little reckless. At some time in my driving career, I fell into each of those categories. Most drivers do.

My dad liked to explain how the handful of truly great race car drivers were fundamentally different from the much larger number of good ones. "There's guys who can go fast," he'd say, "and guys who can race. But not all guys who can go fast can race. If you find someone who can do both—can go fast and race—that's your guy."

I wasn't that caliber of driver. My father was. And he had two hundred victories to prove it.

I couldn't go as fast as he or Dale Earnhardt or Jimmie Johnson. They soared in both categories. They could race *and* go fast. Up against double-threats like those guys, most days I would come up a little short, but I wasn't the only one.

I did have confidence, and that helped. I always believed that if you and I were in equal cars, I could beat you. It didn't always work out that way, but I was always convinced of it. I had that confidence in myself. If you beat me, I would make myself believe that you had a better car than I did that day. Was I kidding myself? Was I letting myself off the hook too easily? I don't know. But believing in myself was useful either way. It made me want to work that much harder to make the cars better than they were. And I had the chance to try. With Felix, at Petty Enterprises, and with the Wood Brothers, who already had a great team of their own, I was in that position. I always felt like I had input. I had helped to build a car, and that gave me confidence. I wasn't some guy hired off the street who could just drive the car. That's why I'm comfortable saying I was a good race car driver.

At that time, if you drove a race car long enough, eventually certain things would happen to you. They just would.

You're going to be on pit road in the heat of battle and somebody's going to scream into the radio, "Go!" You'll blast out of your pits, and the next thing you know, the tires are rolling off the car.

You leave before the lugs are tight.

That's going to happen. And you're going to have to get out of the car and walk all the way back alone. The fans will be watching. It's embarrassing. And it won't even be your fault—well, *maybe*. But who else will they all be looking at but you?

There's something else that will happen eventually. And this one is before the actual race begins. You'll leave the garage area and go out to practice and somebody will have forgotten to put hood pins in. The hood will fly open, and you won't be able to see a thing. You know how bad this looks, driving blind with the hood up, and then it will also occur to you: The TV cameras are already set up for the race. Highlight reel!

Because everybody likes a good laugh, right?

But at least those two racetrack mishaps won't usually get you hurt.

What happened to me at the 1996 Brickyard 400 in Indianapolis easily could have.

When NASCAR first came to Indianapolis Motor Speedway, we would cut the corners and drop our left fronts in the grass. That might seem a little strange, driving 170 miles an hour. The cars would rotate as we skimmed across the edge of the grass. The corners at Indy were tighter than what we were used to, and that was the best way we could get in the turns.

Well, Tony George and the other fine people at what is quite possibly the most famous racetrack in the world, they loved their grass. They didn't like a bunch of stock car drivers trampling all over it. So the morning of the Indy race, they put down little rumble strips to keep us off the grass! And they put what looked like croquet wickets over the rumble strips to secure them in the ground. Just a bent piece of wire, but that's what it was there for.

Unfortunately, the rumble strips and the croquet wickets didn't deter anyone. We still ran out in the grass, just on the other side of the rumble strips, even farther out. But that also had the effect of popping those metal pieces out of the grass and scattering them up and down the racetrack.

Predictable result: Soon enough, drivers were running over them and cutting their tires.

It happened to Jeff Gordon and five or six other guys. Then, it happened to me.

Turn 4. I was running second behind Johnny Benson. I dropped off in the corner—and *pop!* It was loud. I heard it, and I immediately felt the car stop turning and head straight toward the outside wall.

I hit it almost head-on.

The car ricocheted back to the left, right into the path of Sterling Marlin. He was trying to avoid my spinning car, but slammed into my left front near the driver's side door. That jammed the left front tire up onto the engine, and the throttle hung open. It also knocked me out cold.

Sterling's impact turned me back toward the outside wall, which I hit almost head-on again, turning the car back across the track and slapping the driver's side door against the inside wall before the car finally came to a stop. I wasn't awake for the last couple of hits, but I know it's true because I've seen it on YouTube!

If you've ever been under anesthesia or been knocked unconscious, then you know how you can sometimes hear people talking in a distant kind of way. You know they're there, but you're not quite sure what's happening or what is going on.

I knew I was in the car at the racetrack. I knew people were talking nearby. I didn't really understand what had happened. All I could think to do was to pray.

I prayed that I was alive. I wasn't sure about that because I couldn't move.

I was thinking in my head, *Move your hands*. But I couldn't feel anything moving. *Move your legs*. But I couldn't move them either. I couldn't feel anything down there. My body wasn't responding to what I wanted and what I thought it should be doing.

I thought I heard voices. Maybe I didn't. That's when it hit me: *I'm not alive. I must be dead*.

I prayed harder then.

"Please, God, when my eyes open, let me see the Pearly Gates."

I don't believe I had ever prayed so hard in my life.

Then, all of a sudden, out of nowhere, I recognized a voice.

I wasn't positive at first, but then, yes! It was Sterling Marlin.

"Crap!" I said to myself. "If I'm dead and Sterling's here, we're not in Heaven."

I always loved Sterling. But probably neither of us was on a fast track to Heaven at that point in our lives.

I went back to praying that I was alive.

"Please, Lord. Let me be alive."

They had to cut the top off the car to pull me out of there. They slid a backboard down in the seat and put that neck brace on me that looks like it's made from Styrofoam cups to keep my head from moving.

They lifted me up out of the car and onto the ground. Where the wreck was, they couldn't get me directly to the ambulance. They needed to pull the car out of the way.

I was lying on the asphalt on the backboard with that thing around my neck, with my hands strapped to my chest, still mostly unconscious, still unable to move.

I was in. I was out. I was in. I was out. With a lot of twilight in between.

I could hear people's voices, then I heard nothing.

What happened next I learned from Sterling when we talked the next week. Thankfully, I didn't experience it firsthand.

"There was a wrecker driver and two EMTs," he said. "Every time they tried to pick you up, you screamed like a girl."

"Like a girl?" I asked him.

"Yeah, a girl," he said. "They bent over. They picked you up. You screamed like a girl. They put you back down. They bent over. They picked you up again. You screamed like a girl. They put you back down. And then the wrecker driver said to one of the EMTs, 'If you get off of his ponytail, he'll quit screamin'.'"

And sure enough, that EMT was standing on my hair.

Each time they picked me up, my head would yank back, and I'd scream again. God as my witness, that's a true story. That sort of thing doesn't happen to everybody, but it happened to me.

Nothing's forever, right?

By the summer of 1996, I'd been driving for Felix and Teddy's SABCO Racing for seven years, and I loved Felix like my own dad. That's saying something in a business as up and down as ours can be, where millions of dollars are on the line every week of the year. I felt like Felix and I had done pretty well, but what we had was more than owner and driver. We cared for each other deeply. He was my friend. Still, as the season wore on, I have to admit I was feeling down about where we were as a team. There were no two ways about it. We weren't having a good year, and 1995 hadn't exactly been great either.

Sunday, June 23, we were on our flight home from the race in Michigan, where I'd finished thirty-eight, almost last, and our race winnings were a not-so-impressive $17,080. That would barely cover the fuel for the plane ride home. I could tell that Felix was feeling just as down as I was. And so was Ty Norris, our team manager.

We were all sitting together on the plane, and no one was really talking.

Ty finally broke the silence. "I've got something I need to talk to you about, Felix."

Felix glanced up from his seat. The look on his face said, *Now what?*

"I think it's time for me to take another job," Ty said. "I need to try something different."

It caught Felix completely by surprise. He wasn't out-of-control angry. That doesn't capture it exactly. He was just very upset.

He didn't say anything to Ty. He just turned to me and said, "I guess you'll be the next one."

"You know what, Felix?" I answered. "I think I'm leaving too."

"What?!" Felix said.

"Yeah," I said, "I think it's time for me to go do something else too."

I hadn't planned on saying that. I can't say I hadn't thought about it. I had thought about it. But I didn't know in advance about Ty's announcement, and I hadn't made any decisions to make one of my own. It just came out.

Looking back, I should have talked to Felix about it one-on-one. I shouldn't have just dropped it on him like that. He had always been kind and fair with me, and he deserved better from me than that. I've always been ashamed of how I handled myself that day.

Though my resignation may have seemed sudden, coming to that moment was a long and winding road. When you grow up in the rural South like I did, working in a family business, watching the business be successful and then watching it struggle, then watching it have limited success again—well, you're awfully slow to walk away from anything, even when things aren't going great. You kinda learn to keep your head down. *Just keep grinding. Tomorrow's another day. Don't give up. We're counting on you here.* You try to live up to all that because that's what family does.

In my time with Felix, I'd gotten to the point where I felt like I was part of his family, and that's a big part of why I loved driving for him. But over our years together, a lot of changes had occurred inside the race team. Just natural changes. The crew I started with in 1989, many of them had moved on. The guys I worked with earlier, they were some of the greatest people I'd ever been around. The new guys were great too, but we didn't have quite the same connection as you do with a group you build something with. The sport was changing in the mid-1990s, and SABCO Racing was just a different place than when we started.

I really like music, and I never understood how a band could break up. If you write the music and you love to play it and the audience loves to hear it, how could you ever let the band break up? But eventually, I came to understand. A lot of bands break up just because they've run out of that creative drive. After a lot of time together, they lose that spark. Where did it go? Hard to say. They just reach a point when it's time for something new.

That's kind of how it was, I think, for me and Felix. But a lot of it was me.

Somewhere along the way, I lost that drive to try to be the creative spark for the team. We'd fallen into a rut somehow. We weren't running that well. It was sad, but I didn't feel the same drive I once had. And consequently, I felt like I was letting the team down. I needed something new. I needed a fresh challenge. So despite my Southern-family-business upbringing, I was getting the sense that it might be time.

And then there was my son Adam. Adam had a lot to do with it. I had an old family tradition staring at me.

At the beginning of NASCAR, Grandfather Petty had started a race team, and when my dad came along, he drove for my grandfather's team. The fact that my grandfather came before him meant that my father had a place to start. My dad didn't have to go find a job. He didn't have to go anywhere else. He just walked down to the shop and started racing, once he'd passed the magic age of twenty-one.

Same thing when I came along. I had the exact same opportunity. It wasn't the first time I'd ever walked into the Petty race shop. I'd been hanging out there almost since I first learned what a race car was and how to count to ten. No one in the family had made any promises to me.

But that race shop was always there, a place to begin my driving career. I always understood that.

Now, Adam was coming along.

He was itching to be a race car driver. To show everybody how serious he was, he was taking all the steps he should be taking as a young driver working his way up the ladder.

I could see it coming and coming fast. There was really no doubt about his interest or commitment.

But where was he supposed to go?

Working with Felix, I didn't have a race team. And that had been nagging at me. As much as I loved Felix, at that time I couldn't offer Adam the same opportunity that my grandfather had given my father and my father had given me. That came from being a Petty, and it came from the family business being a race team. Unless I made a change of some kind, I knew, that family tradition would not be handed down again.

The family business hadn't been a forever thing for my father and it hadn't been for me. We'd both left home. My dad had left Petty Enterprises for Curb Racing in 1984, won his two hundredth race, and then come back to Petty Enterprises in 1986. I'd left for the Wood Brothers and then for Felix. I stayed away longer than he did. And those were the right decisions at the time for both of us. I had no doubt about that. Right for me. Right for my dad. Right for our family. And right for Petty Enterprises. I wasn't second-guessing any of that. But I was suddenly hearing the loud call of home.

In Adam, I had a son who was clearly focused on being a race car driver, and it didn't seem like a passing phase. As he'd come up through go-karts, late-model cars, and ASA (American Speed Association), he was reaching a crossroads of his own. "What's he gonna do next? Where will he go now?" For me, that question hung heavy in the air.

And now I had an answer.

"I think I'm gonna go and start my own race team," I told Felix on the plane that day as we headed home from Michigan. "I think the time is right now."

18

HOTTEST WHEELS

"It had always been her dream to qualify for a race."

Did I really want to be a car owner?

Truth is I'd never given the idea much thought, never even dreamed of it. I hadn't seriously considered putting myself in that position since my short-lived experience at Petty Enterprises the year my dad left. I still remembered the weight of that time, the pressure I felt and the lessons I learned. But I could see the bigger picture now, what Grandfather Petty had built and my dad had carried on and what I had benefited from. For me, continuing that tradition meant making a big change.

Yes, it was impulsive, the way I handled things with Felix. I realized that from the minute the words tumbled out of my mouth. I still ask myself, "What the heck were you thinking? How could you just leave like that?" It was about the only thing I had ever quit in my life. I had never been someone to walk away from stuff. I'm the kind of person who sticks it out no matter how bad things are. That's who I am. But maybe we were just at a place, Felix and I, where we'd been together too long. Something else was calling me.

Given how unplanned all this was, I hadn't laid any groundwork for what might be coming next. I hadn't coordinated anything with my dad. I was thirty-six years old, old enough to know better. Felix and I had the fourth-longest continuous association among all active drivers at that time. When word got out about what I had done, somebody looked that up. But in that moment, in that airplane at eighteen thousand feet, I gave my official notice—and there it was. Felix's statement to the press was all class.

"The last two years haven't been good, and we haven't seemed to be going anywhere," he told reporters when they started calling. "We've had a crew change, engine-builder change, and basically, we haven't gotten any better. Sometimes you get in a rut . . . Sometimes a change is good, and I think it's going to be for both of us."

Sometime later, Felix spoke to a reporter. "My relationship with Kyle Petty was probably the most fun and satisfying of my life as far as the racing career is concerned because Kyle is a wonderful human being. I was his adopted father. Richard Petty, the King, tells me when I hired Kyle, 'Well, I am going to give him to you to raise him up and when you get him raised up, I'm going to take him back.'" Yeah, that's about what happened.

Because we never even had a written contract, the unwinding of our partnership wasn't complicated at all. It was more like two friends just saying, "Goodbye for now." Leaving Felix was emotionally wrenching. I'm not gonna lie. He was a brother to me and more, one of the best people I have ever known. Felix was very important to who I am today. I loved the guy and always will.

I knew how hard it would be to start my own race team. I had no illusions about that. My brief time running Petty Enterprises in the mid-1980s hadn't exactly been a bed of roses for me, when my dad went off to race for Mike Curb and left me holding the keys. But that was more than a decade earlier. I figured I should have learned some things since then.

I called the new team PE2 Motorsports, for Petty Enterprises Squared. And as Grandfather Petty had first taught me all those years ago, I needed a sponsor before I could go racing. I was thrilled to connect with Hot Wheels.

Jack Baldwin put us together. Jack was a sports-car racer I'd ridden motorcycles with. Jack said to me at the exact perfect time, "I think Hot Wheels might be interested. Let me hook you up with Mattel."

Yes, it's good to have friends.

I met with the Hot Wheels people. We clicked, and they were interested. And from their perspective, I think the deal made a lot of sense. They had an instantly recognizable brand that featured mini replicas of cool-looking cars. I'd played with Hot Wheels when I was a kid. Almost all my friends did. Why wouldn't Mattel want to associate their popular action toys and die-cast collectibles with a real race car and go into business with the people who built, marketed, and raced them?

That was my pitch, and it must have been a good one because we made a deal. I think they really saw me as their ambassador to the NASCAR community, someone who could open doors and introduce them to other drivers and owners who might be willing to license their own cars to Hot Wheels.

The company wanted to make a Dale Earnhardt car and a Dale Jr. car. They wanted to make a Jeff Gordon car and a Hendrick car. I knew all those guys. They were my friends. I was happy to make the introductions. Basically, I said, "Would you talk to the Hot Wheels people about the possibility of working with them?" And the Hot Wheels people took it from there.

Almost all the drivers expressed interest. Some of them would say, "We're exclusive in the 1:24 scale die-cast with another company, but I'd love to do a 1:64 scale with Hot Wheels." That was an explosive time for die-cast cars. To collectors, these were more than toys. There were limited editions, signed and numbered. For some models, prices started in the hundreds of dollars.

Hot Wheels put together a great program with a lot of different teams and a lot of different drivers. It worked out for everyone. Hot Wheels got cars they never would have gotten. The drivers made some unexpected money. And I got a sponsor who was willing to pay for me to go racing.

I was running my own team again—without some of the pressure I'd had the last time I'd tried. I was also a dozen years older, and I had learned a few things since that last, tough season at Petty Enterprises. We even built some of our own motors for the no. 44 Hot Wheels Pontiac Grand Prix, though we did buy some from Petty Enterprises. And we had a good year for a brand-new race team. Two top 5 finishes. Nine top 10s.

Overall, we finished fifteenth in points, the highest of all the new teams to run during the 1997 season.

There were some only-in-NASCAR opportunities that came along with driving the Hot Wheels car for Mattel, and I still shake my head and smile about some of them. Like Barbie. I don't have to tell you how beloved Barbie is or that the bestselling fashion doll of all time is also a Mattel product. And Barbie, like the rest of life, is always changing with the times. In those years, the mid- to late-1990s, Barbie was feeling empowered. She was taking on all kinds of jobs that women didn't traditionally do.

When the Barbie race car driver was introduced in 1998, she was wearing a figure-hugging blue fire suit with "50th Anniversary NASCAR" emblazoned on the front. She had a true-to-life blue-and-orange helmet under her arm. And look, there I am on the box in my own uniform, gazing at racing Barbie with pride.

The box copy certainly brings Barbie lovers into the action. "NASCAR racing is the fastest-growing spectator sport in America today . . . and almost half of the fans are women!" Barbie lovers learn. "Barbie doll is no exception. A fan of stock car racing, and a big fan of champion Kyle Petty, it had always been her dream to qualify for a race."

Why not, right?

"Making sure her racing helmet is in place over her long, honey blonde hair, she lowers her working visor and straps herself into the car for the race of a lifetime. Suddenly the checkered flag falls . . . Barbie has come in first! A true NASCAR winner!"

I still think Barbie was ahead of her time, reminding little girls that their dreams could take them anywhere, up to and including the driver's seat of a race car. A quarter century later, that's a message still worth repeating.

Even before we connected with Hot Wheels, I'd already been part of some memorable sponsor promotions. For a Coors Light contest, I was along for the ride on a record-setting round-the-world Concorde flight. With our partner Caterpillar, I was part of breaking another speed record, this one around the tip of Florida with the American Power Boat Association. But I have to say some of the hardest-to-forget promotions came through Hot Wheels and Mattel.

Who else would make me an honorary Blues Brother?

In February 1998, Universal Pictures was releasing a long-awaited sequel to *The Blues Brothers* movie, which had been a mammoth hit in 1980 for John Belushi, Dan Aykroyd, James Brown, Aretha Franklin, Ray Charles, director John Landis, and everyone else associated with it. Sadly, Belushi was gone. But in *Blues Brothers 2000,* the Dan Aykroyd character, Elwood Blues, is being released from prison after an eighteen-year sentence for the crimes he committed in the first film. And Hot Wheels was definitely along for the ride.

They created a special Blues Brothers paint scheme for my race car, which of course was duplicated on a Hot Wheels car, and it was one of the coolest-looking cars when I showed up to drive at the 1998 Daytona 500, just as the new movie was coming out. But it was my uniform that got just as much attention as the car did. The suit had all the required safety features. But it also had a perfect, retro Blues Brothers look, boxy suit jacket, white dress shirt, skinny black tie and all. If my sponsors' logos weren't there, you probably couldn't even tell the difference.

That *Blues Brothers* promotion also signaled the explosion of what would become a major social trend, Hollywood's increasing reliance on cross-promotion and product marketing. When I was a child, we loved *Dumbo* and *Snow White and the Seven Dwarfs* and lots of other kid films, especially the ones that Disney put out. But movie merchandising wasn't anything like the monster it would become. Over the years, the studios learned that they weren't just making movies. They were also creating massive marketing platforms for film-branded T-shirts, pajamas, hoodies, backpacks, toilet paper, and yes, miniature-size cars, which all together could sometimes generate even more revenue than the tickets sold in theater box offices around the world.

The Blues Brothers car was like a trial run for that trend.

NASCAR has deep ties to Hollywood. Fans will debate forever which NASCAR movie they love best, and there are some strong contenders in the race. You hear those arguments whenever race fans get together: What's the best NASCAR film ever made?

Some people are partial to Tom Cruise in *Days of Thunder*. Hey, it got me the Mello Yello car! Others like the Kenny Rogers vehicle *Six Pack*. *The Last American Hero*, the Junior Johnson biopic with Jeff Bridges, has its fans. So does *Greased Lightning*, where Richard Pryor takes a serious turn as early Black driver Wendell Scott. (I think it's fair to say that one was before its time, like Wendell's career was.) Few films wrung more humor out of the sport than Will Ferrell's *Talladega Nights: The Ballad of Ricky Bobby*, proving that, yes, we really can make fun of ourselves. There were also some laughs in Burt Reynolds's *Stroker Ace*. Did you catch me in that one? If you blinked you coulda missed me. It was my film debut. That was me in the purple shirt table-racing through the hotel lobby.

One that's often overlooked is the Elvis musical *Speedway*, which was shot at Charlotte Motor Speedway and includes cameos by Cale Yarborough and my dad, which many have cited as the only time the King and the King shared a bill.

But I would argue that all of those movies, along with our *Blues Brothers*–NASCAR tie-in, merely set the stage for the 2006 release of *Cars*, which, even though it's animated, is still one of the most NASCAR of NASCAR films. The familiar voices. The knowing characters. The car-centric plot line. The producers' intricate knowledge of NASCAR. The glamorous red-carpet premiere. *Cars* goes much deeper into NASCAR history, culture, and gear than anyone could possibly have expected. This was so much more than another kids' cartoon!

All these years later, I still get a laugh from the cast list: Richard Petty as "Strip 'Mr. The King' Weathers." My mom, Lynda Petty, making a rare step into the spotlight as the ex–demolition derby queen "Lynda Weathers." Dale Earnhardt, Jr., as "Junior." Darrell Waltrip as "Darrell Cartrip." Humpy Wheeler as "Tex Dinoco." And Mario Andretti as "Mario Andretti."

Wait, how did Mario get to keep his own name? Nobody knows.

My dad was really excited when the producers showed him the car he was going to be, a 1970 Plymouth Superbird. "That was a good race car," he said. "But they only let us race one year. The deal was, it looked like a race car, whether it had a number on it or not, with the big wing and sloped nose."

When they asked my mom what kind of car she should be, she suggested a 1969 Ford Ranch Wagon station wagon because that's what she drove us kids to the races in. As for the right color, she didn't hesitate.

"Petty blue, of course!"

Produced by Pixar Animation Studios and released by Walt Disney Pictures, the film learned the *Blues Brothers* lesson well, launching a multimedia franchise, producing two sequels and two spin-offs and grossing $462 million worldwide.

You think all that was an accident? I don't. I loved that they asked me to voice Mr. The King's nephew, "Cal Weathers," in *Cars 3*.

To this day, kids still come up to me because of that movie, including kids who've never watched a NASCAR race in their lives.

I'm used to being stared at. I've been stared at my whole life. It happened all the time when I was little, and it still happens to me. I'll be out to dinner with friends and one of them will say, "That table over there is staring at you." Truth is a lot of the time I don't even notice. Growing up with my dad, whether we were in Daytona or Michigan or California or wherever it was, fans were staring at him. And so they were also staring at us. We all just kinda got used to it. The people were almost always very kind. They'd wait until my dad had finished eating. Then, they'd come to the table and ask for a picture or an autograph. NASCAR fans are some of the friendliest people in the world, and I know they always will be.

I learned at a young age from my dad that fans are what make the cars go round. Without fans, sponsors don't sell products, and there is no money to sponsor a car. Without money to sponsor a car, there is no race. Everything starts with the fans. My dad always signed his autograph so you could read it. He always felt that if someone took the time to ask for it, he should take the time to do it right.

I love running into race fans, whether it's at the track or at a gas station or a supermarket or a motel. Sometimes people are surprised when they look up and see my lanky frame standing there. They'll say things like, "There's no way Kyle Petty would be in this place!" Or "You're Kyle Petty! What are you doing in the Piggly Wiggly?"

And I'm like, "Whadaya mean? I need paper towels too!"

I know I'm a fairly distinct-looking person. I don't necessarily blend in everywhere I go. I mean, really, how many race car drivers or ex-race car drivers look like *me*? I'm fairly tall. And the long hair in a ponytail—I get it. Those things can make me stand out. But some of the times I've laughed the hardest are when I've encountered race fans who *don't* recognize me—or they aren't quite sure whether they do or not. Like the woman I met in the gas-station convenience store after a long day at the track in Darlington. I filled my car and went inside to grab a snack and a cup of coffee. She was in the checkout line right in front of me. She had a case of beer in either hand. Two cases of beer. And I couldn't help but notice she was swaying. Rocking forward and rocking back and rocking forward again. At first, I thought she was just rocking. But then it occurred to me: "Those may not be her first two cases of beer today."

She had on a race T-shirt, and she seemed friendly enough. But as she was rocking along there waiting for her turn to pay, I noticed she kept looking back at me. She looked to her left. She looked to her right. And she kept looking over her shoulder back at me. Then, she started nodding her head up and down.

"I know who you are," she said.

"You do?"

"Sure do."

I just nodded. We moved up a space in line.

"Yep," she said. She'd rolled around and was staring straight at me now. "You're Michael Waltrip."

"Nope," I answered. She held her gaze right on me like she didn't want to let me get away. "I'm his brother, Darrell."

She lit right up. "I knew I knew you!"

She kept smiling the whole time she paid for her beer. The last I saw her, she was standing outside her car, pointing me out to her friends. "I just met Darrell Waltrip," I heard her say. I gave a little wave before I got back in my car.

All I can say is I hope I didn't do anything to embarrass Darrell. Michael, I'm not so worried about. He's done worse things than that!

Over the years, there's almost nowhere I haven't ridden on my motorcycle. One June night, I was cruising through West Virginia on my way up to Michigan. It was rainy. It was late. I'd ridden longer than I wanted to ride that night. It had to be ten thirty or eleven o'clock. Even at that time of the year, the mountains in West Virginia can get chilly after dark. I had a bandana around my neck, and my leather jacket was zipped up tight when I eased into the motel parking lot.

"Do you have a room?" I asked the young woman behind the desk.

"We got one room left," she said.

"Well, I'll take it."

"License and credit card."

I pulled both of them out of my wallet and slid them across the counter. She picked up my license and gave it a good look. Then, she looked up at me. Then, she looked at my license, and she looked at me again.

"So," she said. "You think you're Kyle Petty?"

"I used to be," I said.

Honestly, I didn't know what to say. She did not appear convinced.

"Kyle Petty's got a ponytail," she said.

Perfect, I thought. I turned my head around. Yep, there it was. "I got a ponytail," I said.

"Listen," she said, the tone in her voice sharpening. "I'm a Kyle Petty fan. And that's not a ponytail, OK? Kyle Petty's got a *pony*-tail." The way she said it, a ponytail sounded like a very substantial thing.

"OK," I said with a shrug, "that's fine."

"You watch racing?" she asked me.

I nodded. "I watch it every now and then."

She was definitely a race fan. "It's great," she said. "It's a great sport. I've watched it my whole life." She went on at some length about how much she loved racing, how her dad had been a race fan and her brothers were race fans, but none of them loved NASCAR the way that she did.

The whole time she and I were talking, she was getting me checked in. She slid the registration card to me. I filled in my name and address and signed "Kyle Petty." I did everything I was supposed to do to check into a motel. She ran my credit card. It went through. She handed me the plastic key card for my room. She couldn't have been any nicer. She slid back my license and my credit card. Then she said to me, "Let me give you a little advice. If you're gonna go around pretending to be Kyle Petty, you need to try to look a little bit more like him."

"Thank you very much," I told her. "I'll take that into account."

I put my license and credit card back in my wallet. And under the name Kyle Petty, I headed off to my room, relieved to be inside but still trying to wrap my head around what had just happened at the front desk. This nice young lady had checked me into a motel under the name Kyle Petty, with a license that said Kyle Petty, with a credit card that said Kyle Petty—and went through—and she still didn't believe I was Kyle Petty. But she was willing to check me in anyway. Well, the credit card did go through.

Me? I was just happy to be in for the night.

At the end of the 1998 season, I decided it didn't make sense for me anymore to run a single-car team. The sport was changing, and each year there were more multicar organizations. So I took all my stuff home to Level Cross, bringing the no. 44 Hot Wheels car with me to Petty Enterprises. I turned PE2 into a Busch Series team for Adam.

My dad had finally retired as a driver in 1992 at age fifty-five. After thirty-five years and more wins than anyone else, he was not behind the wheel of a car but he would never really leave the sport. And Petty Enterprises was still roaring on. Rick Wilson, Bobby Hamilton, John Andretti, and Jeff Green all drove the famed no. 43. Petty Enterprises very much remained an operating race team, now with two cars again, the no. 43 STP car and the no. 44 Hot Wheels car both running out of there. After all those years, there were still some familiar faces around the shop.

There I was, back where everything had started, at Petty Enterprises.

Apparently, you *can* come home again. Once I settled in, I also took on the title of company CEO.

In 1999, we had nine top 10 finishes, though we finished a disappointing twenty-sixth in points. That year, I also stuck my toe into broadcasting, making some guest appearances on ESPN to provide commentary during Busch Series races. As long as I was driving, I couldn't very well comment on the races I was competing in. But I slipped into the broadcast booth for the Busch races, and I really had a blast doing it.

I didn't know how much longer I'd keep driving. But sitting around talking with a bunch of my friends about the races and getting paid to do it—that wouldn't be the worst way to ease out of the car.

And with Adam coming along, I was starting to think the time was getting near for me to pass the Petty racing torch to him.

19

FOURTH GEN

"You're always going to be compared to us."

I rented a building in Thomasville and moved Adam's race team in. That way, he and his guys could work all day and night if they wanted to on their Chevrolet no. 45 car.

As 1999 came around, they were ready for another step up the racing ladder. The steps were coming quickly. Right, wrong, stupid, or indifferent, that was our plan. When we'd first gotten started, I had asked Adam, "Where do you want to end up?"

His answer was, "I want to be a Cup driver."

"Well, if that's the goal," I told him, "you don't need to spend a lot of time dinking around at all these different levels. You can experience them. That'll help you. But let's get you to Cup as soon as we can."

So that was the route we followed. Late-models on short tracks for a couple years. *Boom!* ASA for a year. *Boom!* Quick toe-dip into ARCA. *Boom!* And now came the Busch Grand National Series, the final step for drivers who had their eyes on NASCAR's top level, Cup Series racing. These Busch Series races, which started in 1982 under the sponsorship of the Anheuser-Busch beer company, are typically held the day prior to Cup Series races at the same tracks. So the competition is stiff, and the visibility is high. The series has had various sponsors and various name changes over the years—Budweiser Late Model Sportsman Series, Busch Grand National Series, Busch Series, Nationwide Series, and Xfinity Series. But don't let that confuse you. It's all the same thing. Our plan was to run a few Busch Series races in 1998, then in 1999 and 2000 run the full Busch Series schedule, and finally move to Cup full-time in 2001. This was perfect timing for the future of Petty Enterprises as 2001 also marked Dodge's reentry into the Cup Series.

In NASCAR, there's always someone ready to second-guess whatever decisions you make. But it seemed to me like things were going pretty good so far for Adam.

He finished sixth in his Busch race at Daytona. He finished fourth at Fontana. Both were impressive drives. But he failed to qualify for three Busch races and finished the 1999 season twentieth overall in points. There was no denying he was a talented young racer. And some people were talking about him like the second coming of Jeff Gordon, Dale Earnhardt, and Richard Petty, all rolled into one. Of course, they were all Petty fans through and through. That seemed wildly premature to me. But more and more, people in the NASCAR media—and people at the track too—kept talking about Adam. He also had the distinction of being the first fourth-generation professional athlete in the history of American sports.

I wasn't much for hype like that. Labels like those, I figured, only come back to bite you. I used to see that in the media and laugh about it. Frankly, I didn't understand what the big deal was, anyway. I knew a bunch of fifth- and sixth-generation farmers. No one thought that was anything to write a bunch of feature stories about. So it just didn't seem like that big a deal to me. The truth of the matter is that some other professional sports haven't been around long enough to have so many generations, and in others the entry process is totally different from racing. In baseball, we have Ken Griffey and Ken Griffey, Jr., but it was harder for Ken Griffey, Jr., to get to the majors. His dad couldn't just put him on his baseball team.

Once Adam started running Busch Series, the "fourth-generation professional athlete" thing was kinda hard to deny. There was no getting around his family legacy, that's for sure. And by then, he was a professional racer by any definition.

Ninety-nine percent of the people who run those races make their livings as race car drivers. So that's a professional. Truck Series, not so much. ASA, I don't know. That's a different game. If you looked at Adam's tax returns, you'd certainly have to say "yes." Racing cars is the only job he ever had and the only way he ever made a nickel in his life. Never worked on anything but race cars. Never did anything but drive them, and that's what he got paid for. When he started driving the Busch car, he had a driver contract. He didn't get paid to work on the cars, though he showed up and did a lot of work on them like he was supposed to.

So, guilty as charged, I guess: My son was America's first fourth-generation professional athlete.

So what does any of this mean about Adam's future as a racer? Hard to say. And the truth is no one held the answer to that except for Adam.

It isn't always easy predicting something like that. You can watch thirty guys drive a race car, and they all look pretty good. They are all technically strong. They all say the right things when you interview them: "I'd wreck my mom to win this race." That same ol' BS you hear all the time. But what you can't see sometimes from those spins around the track or those testosterone-fueled comments to the media is the desire. The passion. The heart. The *something more*. Those things often reveal themselves over time.

A long time.

For me, growing up with Richard Petty, I think I have some ability to spot that *something more*. Being around Adam, there were moments of that, flashes of that, glimpses of that. Can I sit here and honestly say that that's what it would be always? Nah.

It's the same in any sport. You'll see it in great college players who never make it in the pros. You can judge the skills, and they're important. But you can't judge heart. You can't judge that desire. Those things reveal themselves over time.

As a father, I'd like to say, "Yeah! Absolutely. One hundred percent. Adam was on his way to greatness. No doubt about it." But at the same time, only he could answer that question. That's one of the millions of unanswered questions the universe holds.

Though I never pushed Adam to race, at the same time, I had to recognize that it wasn't totally an accident that he developed a passion for the sport his father, grandfather, and great-grandfather had built their lives around. He'd been exposed to it. It was always right there for him. He'd been around racing and race cars since before he could say "dada" and "mama," just like I'd been. It was always there, silently calling to him no matter what any of the rest of us said or didn't say. He chose to seize it just like I had.

Did he and I ever talk about the pull of our legacy? The answer is yes and no. We never just sat down and talked about it. I got the distinct impression—and I've always carried this impression—that he looked at it the same way I looked at it. Maybe it's just the way both of us were raised. It was a one-generation influence, not two or three. I raced because that's what my dad did, not because that's what my grandfather did. I did what my father did. I watched him go to the racetrack. I went with him. I watched what he did there. I wanted to do what he did. And oh yeah, my grandfather also raced. For Adam, I think it was something similar. Even though I never pushed him, he raced because that's what I did. I took him to the racetrack. When he was interviewed, he talked about things we did as an immediate family, not things his great-grandfather did. And you know what? Where we were raised, there was nothing unusual about any of that.

Growing up in a mill town and a farm community like I did, it wasn't uncommon to have a great-grandfather, grandfather, father, and son all in the same business. That wasn't uncommon at all. Even today, it's not uncommon for four generations to be working on the farm at the same time. It's perfectly normal in the rural South or in rural North Carolina to have a fifth- or sixth-generation farm still up and running. The dairy farms and tobacco farms, they didn't just pop up last week. They've been in the same families forever.

The outside world looked at us—third- and fourth-generation race car drivers—as oddities of sports nature. *To have four people doing the same thing, are you kiddin' me?* Anytime someone talked like that, I knew I could drive them to three or four different sixth-generation farms right down the road. *You see that piece of property there? That's been the Hocketts' dairy farm since the 1850s. So what's your point? We're just getting started over here!*

Being a Petty could be a burden as well as a blessing, especially in the expectations department. A blessing and a burden in lots of other ways too, plenty of both. No one knew that any better than I did. I wanted to help Adam avoid one of the bigger traps, which was feeling like he had to be something he wasn't. All his life Adam was surrounded by larger-than-life characters, people—to put it mildly—with some distinct personality traits, his father and grandfather at the top of the list. My message to Adam was loud and clear: "You can't be Kyle Petty. And you can't be that man with the cowboy hat and sunglasses. All you can be is who you are. You be you."

It was important, I thought, for him to hear that directly from me. I didn't want my silence to raise any unintentional expectations. We all lived with enough of those already.

It is possible, I told Adam, to be proud of where you come from and *who* you come from and still not be defined by that. That was a topic that came up naturally from time to time. "Richard Petty's grandson didn't win that race," I told him. "Kyle Petty's son didn't lose that other race. Adam Petty did both of those things. That's you. That's not us. We didn't drive that car at I-70 Speedway when you won the race in Missouri. That's not us. You're connected to us, but that's not us. That's you. And you have to take ownership of that and just be who you are."

We had the flip side of that conversation when he missed a race at Rockingham on account of rain. When you start a new team, you don't have any points. So if qualifying gets rained out, you don't get to start. He was devastated that he wasn't going to get to race. Not because of anything he had done. That's what I tried to tell him. "You didn't cause this. You didn't miss the race because Adam Petty didn't run fast enough. You didn't miss the race because we gave you bad equipment. You didn't miss the race because of something we did as a team or we did as an organization. You missed this race because of circumstances that we can't control."

Did Adam understand? I think he did. Intellectually. Did it make him any less upset or hurt? Not that I could tell. Not right then anyway.

"There are things you can and things you can't control," I reminded him. "Don't let not making a race define what this moment is. You just come back the next week and run again. It's part of life. It happens."

I think that particular time at Rockingham was especially hard for him because, the week before, he had run sixth at Daytona. So he was already up in points and now he knew he was going to lose some. He took it all so personally. It was hard on him when people criticized him.

He was too young to have thick skin yet. If somebody wrote something negative, it upset him. Especially if he was being measured against his father or his grandfather. I told him one day, "You're always going to be compared to us because you're part of us. You have to embrace that. But you don't have to be defined by us. You're you. Don't let what people write about you rattle you too much."

Then I added, "You're going to be here a long time. There's gonna be a lot of bad stuff, but there's gonna be some good stuff too. It balances itself out eventually."

All that was right except for the "long time" part.

It can be a tricky line to walk, our own identities and the ones we get from our families. I understood that. I told him I wasn't pretending it was easy. I tried another analogy. "Listen," I said, "the Beatles were a great band, but Ringo wasn't their first drummer."

I thought the analogy was perfect, but he looked at me like I was speaking Martian or something. Maybe I should have picked a band that hadn't already broken up by the time he was born.

"Ringo played the drums," I explained.

20

GROWING FAST

"Richard Petty's finally got the son he never had."

That trip to Michigan, where I let fifteen-year-old Adam take a test run in a Cup car, wasn't the only time the two of us bent a well-established track rule, like the one that says that children may not drive 200-mile-an-hour race cars. The second time was even crazier. Later that same year or maybe it was the next, he came with me to Indianapolis Motor Speedway, home of the Indianapolis 500, the Brickyard 400, and for quite a few years the United States Grand Prix. With a permanent seating capacity of over 250,000, it also happens to be the highest-capacity sports venue in the world. That place is big and intimidating for every driver that enters the gates, I don't care how old you are. We were there for another test.

In the garage area at Indy, they have walls that separate the different race teams, sliding walls like you might see in a hotel ballroom. They give each team a bit of privacy.

We were in our area with the car we were testing when I said to Adam, "You want to go drive this car?"

"Here?" he asked. I'm not sure if he thought I was serious.

"You wanna?"

He nodded. Then, he thought for a second and nodded some more.

This was Indianapolis, the nation's first track to be called a speedway, about as far as you could get from a local short track.

"Let's do it," I said. "Let's see if we can."

Adam was totally game.

"Go get a uniform," I said.

We kept the door shut and hid out in our room. Nobody else was in there. He dressed and went and got in the car. I snuck out and went into one of the suites to watch him run.

He ran five or six laps. I have to say he looked pretty good.

We weren't on the radio. So when he came back in, I took down the window net and said, "Hurry. Get to the room next door and don't make a sound."

He scrambled out of the car and ran into the stall next door. Meanwhile, I was standing there next to the car like I had just gotten out.

Not two minutes later, two or three speedway officials showed up. They looked as stern and serious as FBI agents, though I don't believe they had the power to arrest anyone.

"Who was driving that car?" one of them asked in a tone I would have to call accusatory.

"What do you mean?"

"Who was driving the car?" he said.

"I was. It's my car."

"That wasn't you," one of the others said to me.

"Yeah, it was. It's my car. We were just trying some stuff that didn't work."

They looked at each other, and then they looked at me.

"Listen," the first guy said, "don't let your kid in that car again."

"He wasn't driving," I said. "I swear."

"Where is he?"

"I think he went across the street to Steak 'n Shake. I don't know where he's at."

Finally, the second man sighed. I took that as a good sign that the interrogation was ending. "I know that's your story and that's OK," he said. "But don't let him go back out there. Don't do it again."

They were pretty upset and sure of themselves. But they didn't quite have whatever evidence they needed to take it to the next step, thank God.

With Adam, every little thing had to be just so. He was like my dad in that way. I remember one time when I was sixteen or so, being at my dad's shop, installing a back panel on the car. The panel went behind the bumper. No one would ever see it once the bumper went on. While I was working, my dad wandered by. He took a close look at what I was doing. He ran his hand over the panel like he was patting a prized pony. He began to frown. "We don't do that kind of work here," he said. "We use a bead roller. The bead makes the metal stronger. We don't cross-break."

He looked again at what I was doing. "We don't do that," he repeated.

"Okay," I answered, "but nobody's going to see it."

That was not the best thing for me to say. I know that now. As far as my dad was concerned, it was barely worth responding to. "I'll know it's there, and it's not right. So, take it off."

I removed the panel and got a new piece of metal. I rolled some beads in it. And I put it back. Then, I went and got him and asked, "How's this?"

Only then did my dad's frown fade at all. "That's the way we do things here," he said.

Adam had a couple of friends who would come by at night and help him in his shop. He and I would work on the car in the afternoon, and then his friends would go over and hang out with him at night. They thought it was cool that Adam had a race car and they could help him work on it.

He called me at ten o'clock one night. "You gotta come over here," he said. I didn't know what the problem was, but it sounded urgent.

I drove right over to the shop. Adam's friends had left by then. He was pacing next to the car, and he wasn't happy.

"It's terrible," he said. "Look at this."

It was a brake line that one of his friends had installed. Brake lines come rolled up. Adam's friend hadn't fully straightened this one. It looked a little wavy in there. It wasn't pinched. Nothing that would affect the fluid flow. It would work perfectly fine, I could tell.

"It'll be OK," I said.

"It's *not* OK," Adam shot back. "It needs to be straight."

"Well," I said, giving my son the space he seemed to need under the circumstances, "what are you going to do about it?"

He didn't hesitate a second. "I guess I'm gonna have to take it off and straighten it."

"Nobody's gonna see it," I reminded him. As I spoke those words, I could almost hear the echoes of my much younger self, standing behind my dad's car more than a quarter century earlier.

"I'll know it's there," Adam said. Then, he repeated himself: "I'll know it's there."

Damned if it wasn't Richard Petty talking to me!

I didn't argue with Adam that night. In a way, he was right. It was a level of focus and intensity I was fully familiar with.

"Let's take it off and straighten it," I said.

And that's what we did. We pulled the brake line out. We got it straight just like Adam wanted it, and we put it back in the car. We worked on that brake line for an hour.

Even as a teenager, Adam had a way he wanted things done. He could be just as exacting with anyone, himself at the top of the list. He was always toughest on himself.

As Adam pursued his racing passion, I wanted to be sure his education didn't suffer. He went to Trinity, one of the public high schools in Randolph County. We also had a tutor for him, Miss Martin, who'd been my seventh-grade teacher about a million years before. There were a couple of offices in the front of Adam's race shop that Miss Martin used for her lessons.

Miss Martin actually started out tutoring my son Austin. Miss Martin was great with Austin, and she was just as good with Adam, making sure those boys stayed on top of their schoolwork. Pretty soon, her efforts expanded to the point where Austin and Adam were doing most of their schoolwork with Miss Martin in the front offices of the race shop. You couldn't really call it homeschooling. Shop schooling, I guess.

Then, Terry Labonte's daughter, Kristy, began studying with Miss Martin too. So did Terry's son, Justin. And fellow young racer Brian Vickers, whose father Clyde had also been a race car driver and owned a car-parts company, was studying with Miss Martin too. And so were three or four other kids in the neighborhood. The front offices in the race shop were almost becoming their own little school district. The kids would go to regular school for band or football or PE, but they were taking English and history and most of their other courses with Miss Martin. It was a crazy situation, being almost an extension of Trinity High School. But that's how it was, and it seemed to work for everyone.

Sometimes, when I had time in the middle of the day, I'd stop over there so Adam and I could work on the car. There'd always be kids studying at the front of the race shop and others coming and going while I was there. There were a couple of other kids in the neighborhood who had medical issues, and Miss Martin seemed to know how to deal with that. It was a cool place, and she was an excellent teacher. The kids all really liked her.

The level Adam went to next, ASA racing, wasn't quite what I would call big-time professional stock car racing, but getting a little closer. It was a step up from the late-models and short tracks. It was a touring series with a national schedule. You might go from Toledo, Ohio, to Anderson, Indiana, to Nashville, Tennessee. Mark Martin, Rusty Wallace, Alan Kulwicki, Dick Trickle—real legends of motorsports came out of that incredible series.

When Adam showed up at the Peach State Speedway in Jefferson, Georgia, on April 11, 1998, for his first ASA race, he was three months shy of his eighteenth birthday. But by that point, I could really see he was becoming a race car driver. He just needed to do a lot more of it. He ran nineteen of the twenty ASA National Tour races that year. His one win on that circuit was the tenth of the season, and it was a big one: the Kansas City Excitement 300 at the I-70 Speedway in Missouri, where he beat future seven-time NASCAR champion Jimmie Johnson by 1.412 seconds, becoming the youngest winner to date in the series.

That *was* exciting!

Everywhere we went, the tracks posed new learning opportunities for him, and the competition was real. This was all part of Adam's development, and no one expected it to happen overnight. But watching him out on those tracks—gaining his confidence, working his way through the pack, trying to avoid the mistakes that will get a driver in trouble—I was beginning to get signs of real promise out there. Raw promise, but promise nonetheless. The diversity of tracks was especially important. Golfers will understand that.

If you're a good golfer and you play at the same golf course every day, eventually you'll know everything about that course. Even a great golfer will have trouble going in there and beating you on your own home course. It's the same in racing. There's a lot of big fish in small ponds. The true measure of a race car driver is whether he can race anywhere. Back in the 1960s and 1970s, some smaller tracks used to bring in a Cale Yarborough or a Bobby Allison for a match race or an exhibition. People loved seeing the legends of racing up close like that. They especially loved it when one of the local boys still won.

Out on the ASA circuit, it was easy to forget that Adam was still just a kid. But here's the funny part: He was still too young to book a hotel room or, ironically, rent a car. So we hired a young guy named Stephen Patseavouras to travel with him. I wouldn't call Stephen old. But at twenty-three or twenty-four, he was old enough to keep an eye on Adam and also walk up to the desk in a hotel lobby, put down a credit card, and sign for the room. To me, it still felt like we were sending two kids out on the road. I went when I could. But often it was just Adam and Stephen out there with the rest of their crew, barnstorming America like ASA's Thelma and Louise.

Then, tragedy came crashing down on them. For Adam and his team, it happened on Monday, September 7, 1998, Labor Day, and it happened to someone very important to them, their crew chief and friend, Chris Bradley. Chris had been working on race cars since he was a teenager in Grand Rapids, Michigan. At forty, he was the grown-up on Adam's team. The ASA series had brought them to the Minnesota State Fair for the Miller Lite 300. During a caution late in the race, as Adam pitted in the 215th lap, his guys sprang into action just like they always did. They jacked up the Pontiac. They threw on fresh tires. They gassed the car. And as all that was happening at the usual breakneck pit-stop speed, Chris slipped beneath the car to make a quick adjustment to the sway bar. No one else on the crew knew he was down there, and neither did Adam.

As the car came off the jack, Chris was still on the ground underneath the car. Adam hit the accelerator. He said later that he felt a bump as he pulled out. Did he run over an air wrench? A tire? He didn't give it a second thought until track officials stopped the race, and Adam learned what had happened to his crew chief and friend.

Chris was rushed to Regions Hospital in St. Paul. He was wheeled into surgery immediately. The doctors got right to work on him. But Chris's injuries were just too severe. The doctors couldn't save him. Two hours later, he was pronounced dead.

Adam headed home on Tuesday after spending some time with Chris's family. Adam was completely devastated. All of us were. When Adam got home, I wanted to make sure he understood that tragedy was part of racing and that, heartbreaking as this one was, he certainly wasn't alone.

I reminded him about my uncle Randy, how he'd been killed in the pits at Talladega at age twenty when a pressurized water tank exploded and I was standing there. Adam had heard that story before. But when I told it again, I saw the look on Adam's face. I think it took on a whole new meaning to him now.

But it was my dad, I'd say, who really reached Adam with the story he shared.

In 1965, when my dad was part of a Chrysler boycott of NASCAR in a dispute over engine specs, he'd competed briefly in drag racing, driving a car he called "Outlawed." At a drag strip in Dallas, Georgia, his dragster went out of control on his run. Something mechanical broke in the front of the car. He had no control over where the car went. It veered into a dirt embankment crowded with fans. The left front tire and wheel broke away from the car and made its way over the fence and into the crowd, killing an eight-year-old boy.

"I didn't know how I would come back from that," my dad told Adam. It was a horrible experience for him, something he still won't talk about to this day. But to my dad's credit, he understood immediately where Adam's head was and shared the story with him.

It was my dad's way of saying, "I've been where you are. I'm with you. I understand."

The unspoken message? We may never forget these tragedies, but life does go on. It has to go on.

There was one other lesson in Chris's death that I thought was important for all of us to remember. People in racing talk a lot about driver safety, and it's a vital topic. But it's also true that the crew members are at equal—sometimes even greater—risk. The conditions are tight. The work is frantic. The equipment can be dangerous. Cars are whizzing by. They work in pit stalls not much larger than parking spots. And everything happens fast. These guys are aiming to change four tires and complete the refueling in less than twelve seconds, and they almost always have other adjustments to make. The crew members do have helmets, gloves, fire suits, and other protective gear. But they aren't surrounded by a car the way a driver is. However much gear they have on, they're working under frantic time pressure around dangerous equipment and moving race cars. Though cars no longer zoom into pit road in excess of 100 miles an hour like they once did, the crew members are constantly working in a danger zone.

As a family, we put out a statement to the media, which felt totally inadequate, but we didn't know what else to do: "The Petty family and everyone associated with the race team are deeply saddened by the death of Chris Bradley. Our prayers are with the Bradley family and friends in their time of grief. Chris was not only a part of our racing family, but also a part of our extended family. Adam and everyone associated with the Petty family are praying today for Chris and his family."

Three weeks after Chris was killed, six weeks after Adam turned eighteen, he was still down. The shock had barely begun to wear off for any of us. But I had an idea. I had PE2 by then, my own race team. I was working out of Charlotte, and an ARCA race was scheduled for September 30 at Lowe's

Motor Speedway, which is now Charlotte Motor Speedway. Adam and I sat down and I said to him, "I've got eight or ten cars. We could just paint one up like your ASA car. We'll take you over there, and you can race it."

He'd never run an ARCA race before, and in terms of the competition, it was a great transition into what might be coming next. They ran a few speedways while ASA was a short-track series. I also thought it could help give him something to focus on after all he'd been through.

He didn't hesitate a second. "I'm in," he said. "Let's go."

So we went over there, and damned if he didn't win the race.

His first ARCA race, and he won it. And what a nice family tradition it was, a lot of race fans noted. I didn't have to remind anyone that I'd also won my first ARCA race.

We were all so proud of Adam, no one more so than his grandfather. "I was overwhelmed with pride when Kyle got into racing," my dad said in one of the postrace interviews, "but to see another generation begin is just incredible. Now Kyle can feel what it's like to see the family tradition go on."

After the race, we were all over at my parents' house, celebrating Adam's victory. It was a great feeling all around. I looked out the kitchen window at one point and saw Adam and my dad walking together in the backyard. I could see they were deep in conversation. But from inside the house, I couldn't hear what either one of them was saying.

As I looked out the window at them, I turned to my mom and I joked, "Richard Petty's finally got the son he never had."

My mom kinda chuckled at that, but it was the kind of laugh that said she knew exactly what I was saying.

As my dad later told a friend of his: "Adam had one, singular focus—driving a race car. When Kyle came along, he wanted to drive a race car, but he also wanted to ride his motorcycles, play his guitars, all sorts of stuff. Adam is on one thing alone."

You want to know how laser focused Adam was? He was focused about everything. And he had no filter that stopped him from bringing that focus home.

Adam loved his brother and sister, but they could get on his very last nerve. When we finally started paying him some money for driving a race car, he went to the local Chevrolet dealership and bought a rust-colored Corvette. He'd never had a car of his own before. He loved that car, and he babied it. He parked it in the driveway at home and almost never took it out. He kept driving the old pickup at the race shop. He wouldn't drive the Corvette because he didn't want the guys that worked with him in the shop to think that he thought was better than they were or that he had more than they did. I think he was a little embarrassed to own a Corvette. So he'd drive it only at night or sometimes if he was going someplace where he didn't think he'd run into anybody he knew.

Nobody knew it, but every time Adam drove that car, he would write down his mileage in a little notepad. One day, when he got back home from a race, there were eighteen extra miles on the car.

He asked me: "Did you drive my car?"

"Nope."

He asked his brother, Austin: "Did you drive my car?"

"Nope."

"Well," Adam said, before stomping off to their bedroom, "somebody drove my car." When Adam came out again, he had that notepad in his hand.

He looked at his younger brother again, and he said: "You drove my car."

"I didn't drive your car," Austin insisted.

But when Adam opened the notepad and began reading the mileage figures out loud, Austin's defenses began to crack.

"All right," he admitted. "I did drive it. I drove it to the end of the driveway."

"*Four hundred times!?*" Adam hollered. "It's got eighteen extra miles on it."

It was like watching a bad episode of *Cops*. Austin admitted to a little bit, then a little bit more, and a little bit more until he finally said, "Busted." He explained that he'd had some friends over while Adam was off racing and he'd taken them for a ride in his big brother's car. Austin pointed out that he'd brought the Corvette straight back home, that he'd cleaned the car inside and out, and that he'd carefully put the cover back on. But if he had known about it before, he'd sure forgotten all about Adam's notepad.

I really thought Adam was going to kill him. That's how mad he was. But then the two of them went back to their room, and a few minutes later I could hear them talking and laughing.

LEARNING IT

"Racing seems so unimportant right now."

To this day, I still feel connected to Mike Helton.

That call he made to me in London, breaking the news about Adam's accident, I can't even imagine how hard that must have been for him. It's a sad connection Mike and I share but a deep one. I have so much respect for him. All these years later, that call still comes back to me in my quiet moments, the fact that Mike drew that terrible duty and how well he handled it. It's strange. But as I was hearing his voice on the phone that day, I almost felt worse for him than I did for me. I have told him a couple of times how sorry I am that he had to do that. And when I think about it, I get teary all over again. I have tried to help Mike understand how much I appreciate what he did.

After I got Mike's second call, I went upstairs to the hotel room and talked to Montgomery Lee. But I didn't tell her everything. Not at first. I'm not sure if this was the right thing or not, but I thought it might be better to break the news to her gradually. Our father-daughter weekend at the horse show was being swamped by a horrible reality, coming at both of us from across the ocean. What was the best way for a young girl to absorb that? This was her big brother. They had always been close. I knew she would be devastated. What I told her at first was that there had been an accident at the racetrack in New Hampshire. That Adam had been hurt and they'd taken him to the hospital. And that we needed to get back home now. She was shaken, of course. I'm sure she could tell that I was shaken too. I told her I thought we would hear more in a little while.

That was hard, me knowing and not telling my daughter and trying to stay upbeat for her and give her some reason for hope. Someone called and booked us two tickets to New York on British Airways. We flew on the supersonic Concorde, the fastest plane in the sky. My dad's plane met us at Kennedy airport to take us the rest of the way home. Mark Malden, who had been the athletic trainer for the race team and worked with Adam really closely, was on my dad's plane and flew back with us to North Carolina.

It wasn't until we got on my dad's plane that I told Montgomery Lee what I knew from Mike's second phone call, that her brother hadn't made it after all. She was as devastated as I expected her to be. Her sadness made me even sadder. She just kept crying and crying and crying on the plane home. I didn't know what to say to her. She loved her brother so much. We all did. It was hard to imagine our family and our future without him. She knew this would change her life and all our lives forever. And there was nothing I could say to reverse any of it. But I did notice one thing: The more I got lost in feeling bad for Montgomery Lee, the less time I had to feel bad for myself. The importance of worrying about others in a time of tremendous tragedy: That would turn out to be a valuable lesson for me.

It was good to have Mark there, another person who cared about Adam and could share our feelings about the tragedy that had just been thrust into our lives. It wasn't so much what Mark said. It was him being there with us. We got back to North Carolina so quickly—the supersonic Concorde, the rushed transfer at Kennedy, my dad's private plane—that the people in New Hampshire hadn't even released Adam's body yet. They needed time to perform an autopsy. The medical examiner had to do whatever medical examiners do. There were all kinds of procedures the people up there had to go through. NASCAR had procedures of its own. As you might imagine, none of it was quick.

Personally, I didn't mind the delay. What happened had happened.

It wasn't changing. And the slow pace of things gave me some time to collect myself.

From what Mark told us, the accident threw a dark cloud over the whole race weekend in New Hampshire. Everyone up there was shaken, and they looked to each other for support. Steve Park, a driver from Long Island, was especially shook up. "Adam and I were joking around this morning right before practice," he said. "And then to have this happen is unreal. This hurts. I'm numb. Racing seems so unimportant right now."

At the track on Friday night, the other drivers and the crew members gathered for a small memorial service. During one of the pace laps, Tim Fedewa pulled out of his pole starting spot and left it empty, his own four-wheeled version of the missing-man formation the U.S. Air Force has flown since World War II as an aerial salute to fallen comrades. A group of fans constructed their own tribute on the backstretch hill, lining up an array of rocks to read: *Adam 45*. The drivers and crew members joined the fans in a moment of silence before the race on Saturday. Everyone was invited to take a moment and think of Adam and his family.

When Tim won the race, he walked into Victory Lane and declared, "This one's for Adam."

Class act.

"I wasn't Adam's best friend, but he made you feel like that," Tim said. He told the fans that he loved being part of Adam's "contagious smile and laugh. Every time I think of this weekend, I'll definitely think of that."

It wasn't just New Hampshire. From all across the racing world, the tributes poured in. "Adam and I came into this sport at roughly the same time," Dale Earnhardt, Jr., remembered. "I looked at him almost like a classmate. We shared a lot of interests, and we shared a lot of laughs."

Racing and family: Those were the two things everyone mentioned—and for good reason. They really were at the center of Adam's life.

Sterling Marlin said his mind flew right back to the day in February 1981 when Richard Petty won his last Daytona 500 and carried baby Adam on his shoulders into Victory Lane. "He looked like he was a natural there, and I've got the feeling he started making plans right then to get back to Victory Lane for the Daytona 500 as fast as he could."

I can't say Sterling was wrong.

The race media, normally a fairly cynical bunch, seemed genuinely moved by the tragedy and what it meant to racing. So many of them wrote beautiful pieces. I am still touched by the words of Shav Glick, the legendary motorsports writer at the *Los Angeles Times,* who recalled seeing me with my dad and my son, "a tall, slender teenager in the mold of his forefathers," the night before the 1997 Daytona 500. Shav beautifully captured my fatherly grief.

> "It was inevitable that Adam would follow us," said a beaming Kyle, whose grandfather Lee had won three NASCAR championships and father Richard a record seven.
>
> He was asked how he felt having a son racing. "What do I think about it? Probably just what Granddaddy and Daddy thought when I started out. You just hope they make it back."
>
> Adam didn't make it back Friday.

NASCAR didn't seem to have any answers, not yet, from their own investigation into how drivers could be kept safer in the future. They were looking. They would eventually, but not yet. NASCAR president Bill France, Jr., called Adam's death the biggest tragedy to strike a major racing family since 1993, when Davey Allison, son of Bobby Allison, was killed in a helicopter crash at Talladega. That Allison-family comparison was not one anyone was looking for. No one had to tell me that the last driver fatality in Busch competition was Clifford Allison, another of Bobby's sons, killed in 1992 during practice for a race in Brooklyn, Michigan.

"It is difficult to express our sadness over the passing of Adam Petty," the NASCAR president said. "The entire NASCAR community will miss him."

The media had been calling since Friday afternoon, looking for some kind of statement from our family. None of the reporters knew how to reach me in England, and there were no phone calls on commercial airplanes back then. It fell to my dad to put out an initial statement. What could possibly be said? Here's what he came up with: "This is a very difficult time for all of us, but we so appreciate the way our friends and fans from all over the world have expressed their love for Adam. We thank each and every one of you."

Be gracious. Turn the lens outward. He was showing all of us how to respond.

I don't even remember how I got home from the airport. I have a vague recollection of arriving at our house and seeing a large number of cars in our driveway and parked out front. I know there were people in the house, but I couldn't tell you who they were or what they were doing or what anyone said to me. I'm sure it was all the things you'd expect to hear when something tragic happens. But I'm sorry, my mind was so overwhelmed at that point, I really can't recall any of it.

I believe Austin had already left and gone up to New Hampshire to be with his brother and fly back to North Carolina with him. I can't imagine how hard that must have been. Pattie was as devastated as I was. I was so shaken by what had happened and from looking after Montgomery Lee, I was physically and emotionally drained.

I do know that Austin handled a lot of the details. He was stronger than I ever believed someone his age could be. Me? I was somewhere. I just don't remember where.

The sympathy notes and the prayer cards and the heartfelt letters were already pouring in. At our house. At the race shop. A lot of them were just addressed to the Petty Family, Level Cross, NC. I guess folks figured that the people working at the post office would know where to find us. They did. It wasn't just a few cards and letters. It was more like an avalanche of condolences and love. Even before all of those got to our mailbox, there were the thousands—I don't know how many thousands—of emails that were coming into the Petty Enterprises website.

I have to say I was stunned by the sheer volume of it and how deeply personal so many of the sentiments were, this instant outpouring of sadness and grief, much of it from people I had never even met before, or if I'd met them it was only in passing. These were race fans, and they felt connected to our family in a deep, personal, multigenerational way. They wrote with such emotion, it was almost like they had lost a child or another loved one of their own.

"I am so heartbroken. I want to hug all of you."
"I have been following Adam since he won his first ARCA race, just like I have been following you since you won your first ARCA race. There were so many more things I was waiting for Adam to do."
"God bless you and your whole family."

And we didn't just get letters and cards in the mail. Some really nice people sent me books. Books on how to mourn. How to deal with grief and loss. I'm sorry, but I can't say I was ever able to read any of them. What I already knew was everybody mourns differently when they lose a parent or a child or brother or sister or a good friend. There is no one set of rules on what you should feel at a time like that. And that made me feel a bit better because what I was finding out is I didn't fit any one mold. My feelings were my own and that was OK.

Grandma Owens, I remembered, had her own book she turned to after losing Randy. "The answer is in the Bible," she would say. "All you've got to do is open it up. It'll take you where you need to go. You don't even have to know where you're going. Just pop open that Bible. It'll take you there."

I had never experienced anything like all of this in my thirty-nine years on earth—Adam's death *and* the reaction to it. And I didn't quite know how to respond at first. I knew there were Richard Petty fans out there and maybe some Lee Petty fans still around. I knew I had some people who followed me. But this was more than just being a fan. This was more than following a driver someone happened to like. This was something deeper. Emotionally deeper. What was it exactly? As I read people's notes and thought about their kind messages, it soon became clear to me that they really did think about our family as part of their own families. Whether we'd ever actually met before, the Pettys really were people they knew. We'd already been through a lot together through racing. Victories. Defeats. Surprises. Disappointment. And now this! In Adam, they really had lost somebody they cared about and couldn't help but share in the pain of his blood family. They didn't have to imagine what the rest of the Pettys were feeling. They were feeling it too.

They hadn't only watched Adam grow up. A lot of these people, the ones of a certain age, had watched me grow up too, from being a kid lugging my dad's tires to being there every week on the Cup circuit for the previous two decades. What other sports provide such a long-running connection, all wrapped up in a single family? Some of the people, the older ones, had even seen my dad grow up as he went from being Lee Petty's little boy to a promising racer to the greatest of all time. They'd watched me have kids and watched, expectantly, as my oldest son came into racing too. They had wondered, like we'd all been wondering, *How far can he go?* He was right on the verge. He had a lot of promise. And now that question just hung in the air, the storyline abruptly interrupted, a young life over in an instant.

It wasn't only sadness they were feeling. Just like us, they felt loss.

They'd watched all of us with their dads on all those Sunday afternoons in Victory Lane. They couldn't help but feel connections to us and think: *Man, that could be my nephew. That could be my grandson. That could be my son.*

They invested their time and attention and emotions. They had earned the closeness. They had earned their pain. I came to understand exactly what these people were feeling. Soon, I was feeling sadness and empathy for *them.*

It was like they had lost somebody in *their* family. You know what I mean?

To this day, I still have people come up to me with their own Adam stories, where and how they met him, how his death affected them.

This may sound strange, but I really wasn't all that curious about the details of what had happened.

Maybe I was protecting myself, I don't know. The less detail I knew, the less I had to picture Adam in his car that day. Adam was in a wreck at practice, a single-car wreck. Everything happened so fast. Nobody else got hurt. Those were the key facts, weren't they? I'd seen enough single-car wrecks and been in enough wrecks in practice and in races. Things just happen, whether a wheel comes off or a throttle hangs or an air tank explodes or whatever it is. I'd learned that lesson young with Uncle Randy. A freak accident. What could anyone have done about that? Nothing was going to bring him back. Adam was gone. Truly, I wasn't looking for anybody to blame. That's just not where my mind ran to.

I'd known other people to die—from cancer, from heart disease, from whatever it was—where their loved ones blamed the treatment or they blamed the doctors for not diagnosing it earlier. Sometimes, they even blamed themselves. I didn't feel like doing any of that. As far as I was concerned, there was no blame. There was just no blame. Things happen. You can't beat up on other people or beat up on the world and beat up yourself while you're trying to find someone to blame.

No matter how unprepared I was for this, I vowed I would never let that happen to me.

I've seen other people look for someone to blame, and I know it doesn't work. The blame leads to bitterness and bitterness will eat you from the inside out. I've watched that happen too many times.

Bad things happen. Sometimes quickly like with Adam. Sometimes slowly like with a long illness. I had been around enough race cars and been around enough death in race cars and seen enough to know that it just happens. You just never think it's going to happen to you. As a race car driver, you almost have to feel that way. Otherwise, the fear starts eating at you and you can't drive the car. Drivers put that fear in a box, and they don't think about it anymore. It's part of the sport. It was especially part of the sport during that time and before, part of what we did and what we chose to do. But to do the job, I don't want to say you had to ignore it—the truth is you couldn't realistically ignore the danger. But you had to separate it from all the other things you were thinking about. Otherwise, you couldn't go out and drive the car.

And no, the timing is never right. It wasn't right this time. It never is. How could it ever be right for a nineteen-year-old?

Not quite six weeks earlier, Adam had made his thrilling Cup Series debut in Fort Worth. The race hadn't gone as we'd planned. He'd finished fortieth with engine issues. But a bright new future was laid out in front of him, and he was grabbing hold of it. There would be bumps in the road. There always are. Three days after Fort Worth, Grandfather Petty passed away at age eighty-six from complications of a stomach aneurysm. It was so sad for all of us but not unexpected. I chose to look on the bright side. Grandfather Petty, who'd started this whole four-generation adventure of ours, had lived to see his great-grandson make his Cup Series debut. No one else on earth could tell that story to St. Peter at the Pearly Gates! And Adam was off and running. In all, he'd made forty-three Busch Series starts, one Cup start, an ASA season with a win, an ARCA win, and countless late-model, Legends, and go-kart races. But that doesn't begin to tell Adam's story. What mattered more were all the lives he touched along the way, in and out of racing, over the previous nineteen years.

22

SINKING IN

"When all is said and done."

The original idea was to have a private family service. Something small and simple. Just relatives and a few close, longtime friends. Adam's death was such a shock to all of us. The pain was still so raw. Organizing any of this felt surreal. The last thing I thought we needed was a major production or some big extravaganza. He didn't like to make a big fuss. Adam wasn't that kind of person.

I don't remember exactly who did it, but they started drawing up a list of whom to include beyond the immediate family, Adam's aunts, uncles, cousins, and grandparents. His team, of course. His good friends from school. His fellow drivers. People who'd been especially nice to him along the way. Some friends who were totally devastated by his death. Could we really exclude *them*? Before you knew it, that list was getting longer and longer and longer. Honestly, it was hard to know where to stop. Adam had touched so many people, and there were all these others who were connected somehow to our family and shared deeply in our grief. It just seemed wrong and cruel and impossible to hold a service and not invite them. You add three people, then ten more, and before you know it you need an auditorium to hold everyone. It wasn't what we'd originally intended, but that's kinda what happened, and it was amazing in the end. Definitely the right thing to do.

We ended up having a service at High Point University, Monday, May 15, at 11 A.M., nine days after Adam's accident. The investigation was concluded and the body was released. We were free to do whatever we thought was right.

A lot of people came. A *lot* of people. I couldn't count them all. Someone later said 1,500. It seemed like just about everyone we'd ever met and two-thirds of the racing industry showed up. They came out of respect for our family and the love and admiration and support they felt for Adam. It was stunning, really, to look around that auditorium and see all those faces I recognized, people from every part of the racing world over the past thirty, forty years. There was Humpy Wheeler and Dale Jarrett and guys I had been raised with who'd watched Adam grow up and watched him race and knew him his whole life. They all felt a certain pride in him. These were the people who defined our sport. Bobby Allison, who had stood where I was standing. Ward Burton. Bill Elliott. Bobby and Terry Labonte. I couldn't help but notice Ernie Irvan, who'd survived a terrible practice crash at Michigan International Speedway and had just retired on the advice of doctors. Adam's crew members wore dark polo shirts with the number 45 on the sleeve.

There were some people who, right or wrong, hadn't crossed my mind in years, and there they were. They felt moved to be there. But looking around that packed auditorium, what was I supposed to feel? I had no idea. I hardly knew what I *was* feeling, the emotions were rushing so frantically. Mostly what I was feeling was numb.

The pastor, Douglas Carty, recalled some moments from Adam's short life. His baptism. His sixteenth birthday. His sense of humor and his determination to continue the family legacy, his intention to be the absolute best he could. "From the time he was a little kid, I can remember that all he wanted to do was race," Reverend Carty quoted Austin as saying. "He wanted to grow up and be a race car driver just like my daddy."

There were so many layers to that comment, I knew I'd spend the next ten years unpacking all of them.

Reverend Carty quoted from the apostle Paul and the Book of Revelation. He told the mourners they could find comfort in the fact that even though Adam was absent from them, he was with the Lord. "Adam is in the presence of God, think about that," the minister said.

A duet sang "I've Been on a Mountain with Jesus" and one of Adam's favorites, Christian singer Geoff Moore's "When All Is Said and Done."

That's when my mom lost it. She broke down and sobbed out loud for her grandson. That was very hard to hear. It made the pain seem so real to me. It really broke my heart. My always-strong mama overwhelmed with grief, and there was nothing I could do to fix her pain. I didn't stand up to say anything. But Montgomery Lee, Adam's baby sister, was stronger than all of us. She stood in front of all those people and put words to the grief that all of us felt. On behalf of our family, she was the one who captured the hearts of everyone. She remembered Adam as her big brother, not just a race car driver or a fan favorite, but as a wonderful young man whose life was tragically cut short. "We not only lost a fourth-generation driver," she said, stopping more than once to regain her composure and dab her tears. "We lost a great friend and my brother. It's not the same without Adam here. Things will never be the same."

No, they wouldn't be.

I was so proud of Montgomery Lee. Through her tears, she put into words the impact of what had occurred. More than once I wanted to go to her and hold her tight. I marveled at how brave my fourteen-year-old daughter was, just being up there. I'm not sure I could have done that.

"Everyone loved Adam," she said. "He will always be with us, no matter what."

As she finished and walked slowly away from the microphone, my dad got up and escorted her back to her seat. By that point, I'm pretty sure there wasn't a dry eye in that auditorium.

I don't know if you've ever had to be at a funeral for someone so close to you that, later on, a lot of it was a blur. I know what Montgomery Lee said that day made me well up in tears. Try as I might, I cannot remember every word she spoke. But sometime later, she said something that moves me every time I think of it.

"You always have this thought in the back of your mind that one day you're going to wake and not remember anything about him," my sweet daughter said sadly. "That scares me. I have that thought a lot. That one day, I'll forget his voice or one day I'll forget the way his eyes looked."

That's a fear, I'm sure, that's shared by every parent who's ever lost a child. But Montgomery Lee was still a child. She and the rest of us would just have to make sure Adam Petty was never forgotten.

Before the memorial service, the people in New Hampshire had sent Adam's body to a funeral home in High Point. He was cremated there at our request. They put his ashes in a beautiful urn. It was up to us to decide what to do with them.

I know some people choose to take the urn with a loved one's ashes and leave it on a mantel or a bookshelf or in another special place at home. Some people sprinkle the ashes in the woods or at the seashore or some other place in nature. I have heard about people hiring a small plane to do this. Still other families bury the ashes in a grave at a local cemetery.

Those are all perfect choices for those families, but none of them seemed quite right to us. We decided as a family that we should do something that felt more like Adam.

I had no idea what that might be. Neither did Pattie or Austin or Montgomery Lee. But we talked about it for a while. Together, we knew we would come up with something we could feel right about and be proud of. We were all at peace with how the memorial service had gone. It was very real and very Adam. It was really wonderful having so much of the racing community and so many of Adam's friends there to honor him and commemorate his life and his passing. It gave strength and comfort to all of us. But the question of what to do now—well, that was a quieter, more private decision for our immediate family to make.

The people in New Hampshire not only sent Adam's body home. They also returned his possessions to us.

All of them.

Everything they had.

His helmet.

His uniform.

His shoes.

His gloves.

His regular clothes along with his wallet and his keys and the other things he'd brought with him to the track that day had come home earlier on the race truck along with his race car. So we already had his personal items.

I wasn't really expecting all that. I have to be honest: Some of it was jarring to see. But these were Adam's things, and now they were ours.

We chose a spot. I'll never say where it is. But it's a special spot, somewhere that Adam knew well and cared about. Somewhere calm and restful and private and beautiful.

We didn't seek anybody's permission. We didn't file a permit with the county or ask for approval or get anything official like that. What we decided to do may have violated some rule or regulation or local ordinance. It probably did. But I don't think we disturbed anyone, and to us it was the right thing to do—for us and for Adam.

I had a backhoe Caterpillar had given me years before when they were an associate sponsor on my Mello Yello car. We went to the place and dug a hole big enough for a car.

I had brought the car over earlier. So it was already there.

We folded Adam's uniform and laid it neatly inside the car.

Then, we put his helmet on the driver's seat.

And right beside his helmet, we carefully placed his ashes.

We made sure that everything was laid just so. Then, as gently as we could, we slid the car to its final resting place.

It took a while to get the hole filled in. We wanted it all to be just right. We needed it to blend in so no one who didn't know what was there would ever have the slightest clue.

Then, we planted a tree in the fresh dirt so we would always know the exact spot where Adam was.

I have no doubt that Adam's soul and his spirit are in heaven now, exactly where they belong. But what remained of his body would forever be in the company of the physical things he treasured most of all.

His race car. His uniform. His helmet. And it was the people he loved who put him there.

Almost from the day Adam died, fans and people in the racing world were talking about what might have been.

It's a natural question. I get that. A talented young driver is killed in an accident. People wonder how far he might have gone. What had the future held for my race car–driving son? If he'd lived, what might he have achieved in life and in this sport of ours?

Honestly, those weren't the first questions that popped into my mind. I was far more shaken about losing a son than I was about the world losing a race car driver. At the same time, Adam loved racing. And in the fog of all my sadness and grief, I can't say those questions didn't find their way into my thoughts.

Let me just say this: Some of the talk was totally over the top.

I am always fascinated when people say, "The first time I saw this kid drive, I knew he was going to be a superstar." You can toss out that race program right now! That's like saying, "The first time I heard Bob Dylan sing, I knew he was going to be Bob Dylan." Highly unlikely. Chances are, you heard a nasal-voice folk singer from Minnesota who seemed to have something to say—but what exactly was he getting at? That took awhile to come out. Yes, it was in there somewhere between his guitar strumming and his harmonica riffs. But only over time did Dylan's true genius become clear to the world. You can see that progression of the greats in almost any field.

There is young promise, and there is true greatness. One becomes the other over time.

People were saying, "If this happened and that happened, Adam coulda been one of the great drivers of his generation, maybe any generation. . . ." Well, maybe. But there's just no way to if-and-but something like this. Life gets a vote too.

And still, there were moments—I can't deny it—when I looked at Adam driving and I could say, "Wow, I cannot believe someone so young did that" or "could do that." Having driven race cars for so long myself, having sat in the seat my son chose to sit in, these were things I could see and understand. I was like, "I can't believe you won this ARCA race and beat Mike Wallace. I can't believe you did that. You won at Charlotte."

I know my dad saw something in Adam. Or let me put that more precisely: He saw something of himself in Adam. And so did I.

Then again, there were moments where I was watching my son do something stupid or inexperienced. I was shaking my head and saying, "You're eighteen. You'll learn."

So, put me somewhere in the middle.

I saw examples on both sides. And I sometimes felt like an imposter, as if I were looking at the real deal when I stood back and looked at him. I could see traits in him that I saw in my father. A certain intensity. A certain single-mindedness. A brash ambition that wasn't going to let anything stand in the way, no matter what. But had he run enough to have reached that stage yet? No. He hadn't. Was he getting there? He seemed to be. He'd run ASA. He'd won there, which was impressive. He'd certainly learned a lot. But in ASA, he also did things where you had to say, "That's a rookie mistake . . . Shoulda never put yourself in that position." He was just establishing himself in the Busch Series. He'd only run one Cup race. So he was still very much on that learning curve. Given the evidence we have in front of us, it's just impossible to say where he might have ended up. He had talent. I think that much is clear. How far could he take it? It's how I imagine it might have been watching a young Picasso experiment. He had something . . . but *what*?

What I knew at the time was this: I could look at him and look at my dad and I could think, *Yeah, he's gonna be OK.* How far he goes will depend on two things: Whether he can keep up that intensity and whether we're able to furnish him with the equipment he needs to win.

Can we give him good stuff?

Can we give him competitive stuff?

Can we give him winning stuff?

Because if we can't, I don't care how great he is. He's not going to win anything.

If you could have put Adam in a Jimmie Johnson situation with Hendrick Motorsports, if you could have done for Adam what Joe Gibbs Racing did for Denny Hamlin, what Roger Penske did for Brad Keselowski, then the sky's the limit for Adam Petty.

If you put him in a lesser car, then he's just another driver.

But I don't believe at eighteen or nineteen that you can tell for sure. I couldn't answer that. I wished it for him. With all my heart. Because that's what he wanted for himself.

Maybe, just maybe, Adam could've done it all. We'll never know.

Part IV

THE ROAD AHEAD

23

FITTING TRIBUTE

"We should build a camp."

Here's the thing about a major tragedy that's easy to lose sight of: Your own life goes on.

I wasn't prepared for that at all.

I knew my world would always have a giant hole in it. But how could I channel this terrible grief I was feeling so it didn't keep gnawing away at me? And what was I supposed to do with the rest of *my* life? Those questions would take some struggle to get my head and my heart around. And truthfully, I didn't even know where to start.

I got to thinking about when Uncle Randy died. Randy was Granddaddy Owens's only son. Granddaddy Owens never recovered from what happened in the pits that day. He was never himself again, just a shell of the person he'd been before. I didn't want that to happen to me.

On the opposite side, Grandma Owens turned to her faith in God. She was the one who took the tragedy and could find a place for it in her heart, a place that wasn't exactly acceptance but did include understanding. It's not that her heart wasn't broken, and it's not that she wasn't crushed. But instead of feeling bitter, she decided to feel blessed. She decided she was blessed that she'd had Randy in her life at all. To me, these seemed almost like conscious decisions. All I knew was that you could be around my grandmother and never feel sorry for her because she didn't feel sorry for herself. You could not be around my granddad and *not* feel sorry for him. His life was over. It was like he was just waiting around to die.

After Adam's accident, I came to realize that I too had a choice: I could look at things in one of two ways. I could feel bitter. Or I could feel blessed. I wanted to be like Grandma Owens. I wanted to feel blessed. I didn't have the old-time devotion that my grandmother had. It wasn't easy. As much as I wanted to, I couldn't just flip a switch and turn off the grief. But at least I knew the direction I wanted to go. I should go out and help other people who were in the same position our family was in or might be in the future. In Adam's name, I should go out and do good.

I just had to find a way to bring that direction to life.

Over the years, I'd been fortunate to meet a lot of people through racing. One of the people I'd met was the actor Paul Newman. Besides acting and making his Newman's Own products, Paul loved racing sports cars. He was a regular at the historic Lime Rock Park track near his home in Connecticut, and I'd driven in some sports-car races with him. He was a talented racer. Not just a celebrity fooling around. He knew what he was doing out there. He caught the bug when he did a movie called *Winning*. After that, he tried to avoid filming between April and October when he was out racing for real. I think he loved racing, though maybe not as much as he loved acting. He liked it a lot, anyway. Paul didn't keep the money he made selling dressing, popcorn, pasta sauce, frozen pizza, lemonade, salsa, and other food products. Every nickel went to charity. And his main charity was starting a children's camp near his home in Connecticut—the Hole in the Wall Gang Camp, he called it, as a nod to his movie *Butch Cassidy and the Sundance Kid*. Then, he helped to launch a group of affiliated camps. All of them were for kids with chronic medical conditions and serious illnesses.

I happened to know a little something about Paul Newman's camps.

In the fall of 1999, seven months before Adam's accident, he and I were in Daytona Beach for Biketoberfest, a big gathering of people who love motorcycles. Bruce Rossmeyer, who owned Daytona's premiere Harley-Davidson dealership, was a million-dollar donor to Camp Boggy Creek outside Orlando, which Paul had helped to create three years earlier with General Norman Schwarzkopf and some local sponsors. That year at Bike-toberfest, Bruce arranged a charity ride to Boggy Creek. Adam rode. Some other celebrities did too. I was asked to be the ride's grand marshal. The camp was amazing. Adam and I were totally blown away. Here were these kids with chronic or life-threatening illnesses going horseback riding, catching their first fish, and basking in the glow of just having climbed the camp's rope tower, all while making new friends, learning new skills, and developing new self-confidence. They were playing sports. They were bunking in cabins with other kids. They were learning, "I am not alone."

These kids had been through surgeries, chemotherapy, radiation—things no child should ever have to go through. Adam, as young as he was, had the same reaction I did. He was clearly affected by what he saw. Some of these kids had been in and out of the hospital for months or years. You couldn't meet them and not think how truly special they were. And for the campers' families, the camp was totally free. The kids were asked to contribute something else entirely: a positive, playful attitude and a willingness to have fun.

After we said our goodbyes and rode back to Daytona with Bruce's Harley group, Adam and I were almost unable to speak.

"What a cool friggin' place that is," Adam finally said. And I had to agree. What we had just witnessed was potent, inspiring, and hopeful all at once.

"We should build a camp like that back home," Adam said to me sometime before we left Daytona. He still had a thoughtful smile on his face, and his eyes were still wide with amazement.

"That'd be great," I answered, the way fathers often respond to the dreams of their children, encouragingly but without making any firm commitments.

Adam wasn't done. "You're already doing the Charity Ride Across America," he said. "You're going and visiting kids and going to children's hospitals and all of that. Why don't we build a camp like this and let the Ride help pay for it?"

I said, "Sure." And the next day, I went back to racing.

That wasn't the first time Adam had shown an interest in children's charities. He loved talking to kids at the racetrack. And when he was out racing, he'd often visit a pediatric hospital with his sponsor, Sprint. But there was something about Paul's camp in Florida that pushed his natural compassion to the next level. And he didn't forget about it once we got back home.

He started looking into what it would take to open a similar camp in North Carolina. He even checked out a couple of pieces of property he thought might be suitable. Nothing formal or official. But in his mind at least, he was already moving forward.

After his accident, there were a multitude of people who wanted to do something in Adam's memory. Someone suggested naming the grandstand at a racetrack in his honor. A group of people in Charlotte wanted to name a YMCA for him. They were prepared to raise the money and do everything else to make it happen. These were caring people, ready to do something lasting in my late son's memory, and I was touched by their generosity. But none of the ideas that people suggested felt right to me. Adam never sat in the grandstands. He was always in the infield or garage area. Why name a grandstand after him? He hadn't been to the YMCA in years. He played soccer at a Y when he was four or five years old for about six games. Why have an Adam Petty YMCA? The dots didn't connect.

Then, it hit me. All of a sudden, Pattie, my dad, and my mom—all of us collectively—said, "Let's build a camp." The camp idea: Now, *that* was something Adam really cared about.

I called Paul Newman. I told him what we were thinking. He knew about Adam's accident. I told him we wanted to start a camp.

"That's a cool idea," Paul said.

I was thrilled to hear him say that and even more thrilled when he offered to help.

"Let me tell you what we'll do," Paul said. "I'll send down two or three of my guys for you all to talk to. You've got to understand what this involves. It's a lot. You can see if it's really something for you, and maybe we can see if it's something for us to be involved in." I knew we couldn't have anyone better guiding us.

A few days later, three of Paul's guys showed up at the race shop. My dad, Pattie, and I sat with them in the back office. We told them what our vision was. We wanted to build it over-the-top, everything first class. We wanted one building that looked like Adam's race car. Adam being a racer, we wanted the camp to have a whole racing theme.

They said, "You've got to build a hospital."

We said, "OK."

They said, "You've got to build cabins."

"Got it."

"You need a cafeteria."

"Yep, a cafeteria."

In our minds, we also wanted a theater, an indoor gymnasium, a swimming pool, and several other facilities over and above the things they said we needed for a basic camp. We were ready to start.

It was a good talk we had with Paul's guys. We learned a lot listening to them. We didn't know anything about building camps for children, sick or healthy, or running them. These people were the world's greatest experts. After we'd talked for a couple of hours, one of them asked, "Can we talk a minute . . . by ourselves?"

Sure, we said and stepped out of the office. About forty-five minutes later, they called us back in.

They were sitting across the table from us. The three of them on one side, the three of us on the other. Really, they couldn't have been any nicer. Then, one of them spoke. "OK," he said, "we've talked about it. And we think we have an idea of what you're trying to do, but we just don't believe it's feasible. And we can't afford to put our name on something that fails. We can't. So, we're going to pass."

I understood where they were coming from. I really did. I was disappointed. But I understood.

"We're sorry," Paul's main guy said. "So, what do you think you'll do now?"

"Oh, we're gonna build it," I said with absolute certainty.

I don't think he was expecting that.

"With all you are thinking, it'll be forty or fifty million dollars, just to build it," he said.

I looked straight across the table. I'll never forget what I said next or the look on his face when I said it. "We raise eight or ten million dollars a year just to ride around in circles. I'm pretty sure we can raise forty million to do something good."

He nodded, but I'm pretty sure he didn't believe me.

After the three of them left that evening, Paul called. "You meet with my guys?" he asked.

"Yeah," I said.

"What do you think?"

"We think they were really nice. We learned a lot from them."

"So, what did they say?" he asked.

"They said they were going to pass."

"What?" Now Paul was the one who sounded surprised.

"They said they'd pass."

"OK," he said. "What do you want to do?"

"We're gonna build a camp," I told him.

"OK," Paul said, sounding like he wanted to hear more.

"Raising money, that's the business we're in," I explained. "Raising money for racing. That's what we spend ninety-nine percent of our time on. We fundraise."

"They just don't understand," Paul said. Then, he added before he got off the phone, "Hey, you know what? I'll send you a check. I'm in."

A couple of days later, a check for $100,000 arrived in the mail. Paul Newman's personal check. Not a check from his company or his charity. Even before we started raising money, we already had our first major donor. At that point, our camp didn't even have a name.

At first, we thought about calling it Camp Adam, Adam's House, or something like that. A lot of charities are named after the people who inspired them, and that's good. It was Adam who'd brought us all together. It was Adam who sparked the idea to build the camp. It was Adam whose memory we were honoring. But we wanted the camp to stand for more than one individual, no matter how loved that person was.

A lot of ideas were floating around, not all of them fully thought out. This being North Carolina, someone suggested we might somehow incorporate Mayberry, Andy Griffith's famous TV town, or else Petticoat Junction, from another down-home show of that era.

Thankfully, we didn't go too far down either of those dirt roads. But we finally landed on Victory Junction. The Victory part was a nod to racing. The Junction part was left over from *Petticoat Junction,* the last time that TV show has ever been mentioned by any of us. And then we got into the real work ahead of us, turning a high-flying dream into a down-to-earth reality, raising a huge pile of money and building an amazing camp for some very deserving kids.

24

KEEP DRIVING

"It makes me feel closer to Adam."

While we all got busy honoring Adam's legacy, his sudden passing also created an urgent issue for Petty Enterprises. Adam was our future. What were we supposed to do now?

Even before Adam's Cup race, we had begun the process of switching manufacturers from GM to Dodge, and Adam was going to be a key part of that. That's what all of us were focused on. Our next big marks on the wall as a company were Adam and Dodge.

All through the glory days of the 1960s and the 1970s, when my dad won a million races, he was driving Chryslers, Plymouths, and Dodges. And now, after being out of the sport for sixteen years, the manufacturer was coming back to Cup Series racing and back to Petty Enterprises. The 2001 season, we believed, could be the beginning of a repeat of that earlier time. And we believed we could accomplish that with Adam.

In my mind, I thought I would probably drive through 2001 and maybe 2002 and then step aside and spend the rest of my time in the sport as an owner and going to the races with Adam. Being with him and John Andretti, who was driving the no. 43 car. That would be our group. We had put ourselves in a position to do that. We had a two-year plan, a five-year plan, and almost a ten-year plan, starting in 2000. We were thinking long-term. Since I'd returned to Petty Enterprises and taken on the job of CEO, I was steering the company into more of an engineering focus, an approach that was different from the way things had been in the 1990s. NASCAR was changing, and so were we. Multicar teams. An engineering philosophy. We felt like we had our bases covered. With Adam, we'd also be part of the youth movement in the sport. And the icing on the cake was the return of Dodge to Petty Enterprises.

Adam's death was hard enough for me to deal with as a father. But every day, I also had to go back to the race shop and run a company. I had to define our future all over again, while I spent a lot of that first year feeling lost.

I stepped out of Cup racing after the summer. Steve Grissom took over the no. 44 Hot Wheels Pontiac, and I finished the 2000 season driving my son's no. 45 Busch car. I had four top 10 finishes in the car over a span of fifteen races, but I couldn't say my head was really in it. I had an awful lot on my mind.

Fans were still coming out to see me, and I appreciated the support so much. But there was one thing I realized I was doing, and I wouldn't say it was a conscious decision—more like a heart decision. Ever since I'd started racing, I was always happy to sign autographs when race fans asked me to. "Kyle Petty no. 44," I would write, or "Kyle Petty . . . *whatever my car number was.*" But I never did sign anything "Kyle Petty no. 45." I guess you could say I felt like I was just a relief driver for the team. The no. 45 was Adam's number—never mine. And it never would be.

When we got back together with Dodge in 2001, it was supposed to be such a joyous season for all of us. But it was still a very tough time for me personally and a tough time for us as a company. We struggled. We really did. After bringing the no. 45 to Cup full-time and switching to Dodge, we failed to qualify for twelve races and failed to finish higher than sixteenth. I didn't think we were gonna struggle that much, but we did. At the same time, with Adam gone and a three-car race team to sustain, I couldn't really stop. Partway through the 2001 season, I realized I was going to have to keep driving longer than I had planned. And my heart wasn't 100 percent in it.

When you get in a race car, you have to be 100 percent committed every lap, 100 percent committed to driving. And you have to 100 percent believe that you can make that car do what you want and need it to do. And if any of that equation isn't in place, then you won't get the results.

I don't believe that when 2001 came along, I was 100 percent.

I can see that now. I didn't totally see it at the time. What I saw then was that I needed to drive the car. I needed to be at the racetrack. The sponsors wanted me to, and the company needed me to. We had to keep moving forward. We had to keep Petty Enterprises alive. And instead of Adam being the one driving the company into the future, that ended up falling back on me.

If you look at my driving numbers from before Adam's accident and after it, it's clear: My heart wasn't really in the driver's seat anymore. That's just a fact. My overall career numbers would have been a lot better if you had just counted what happened before. But after Adam was gone, it wasn't about me anymore. It was about the people around me. It was more about, "Let's make a better car for John Andretti . . . Let's make a better car for Buckshot Jones . . . Let's make a better car for Bobby Labonte . . . Let's make a better car so the guys who drive for us can do better." And that's what we tried to do.

Some weeks, we were barely successful. Some weeks, we weren't successful at all. But we had a plan, and we worked our plan, and we stuck to it. I was 100 percent trying to make the team better, trying to make the company better and trying to keep everything alive. All along, I felt like, eventually, we would hit on a combination that would work, and that was proving elusive.

Austin was seventeen years old and he, just like Montgomery Lee, was having a rough time with his own grief. Thankfully, my daughter had her love of horses and competition to keep her mind busy. These days you hear about how counselors use horse therapy to help with everything from anxiety to autism to rehab from abuse issues and depression. They call it Equine-Assisted Therapy. Montgomery Lee was before her time.

Austin took his grief in different and unexpected directions. One day he came to me and said, "I think I might like to race."

I can't say this came as a surprise to me, and I wouldn't say I was totally comfortable with it either. He'd shown some interest in driving before, but this was different. He went on talking, explaining a little more. "I've always stood back and looked and thought it was Grandpa and yours and Adam's thing. But I want to do this."

Austin loves so many things about life. One of his greatest characteristics has always been his natural enthusiasm. He wanted to fly jets in the Air Force. He wanted to play in an orchestra. He wanted to go to college. He loved girls, and they loved him back. Even as a young teenager, that boy was always dating someone. But this, I felt, might be a reaction to his brother's accident. They were incredibly close. They had always shared a bedroom. Austin came to the track with Adam, the two of them standing on top of a trailer or in the infield cheering for me and their grandpa. Austin would never be able to share these experiences with Adam again.

On Austin's sixteenth birthday, Adam had given him his old Legends car. Before Adam's accident, when he could, he'd gone along when Austin raced it. The car was painted up with the no. 46, and Austin wore a red fire suit that looked a lot like Adam's and had the Petty Enterprises logo across the chest. But now, Austin took it all more seriously, immersing himself in the Tuesday night races at Lowe's Motor Speedway, where local fans would come out to watch who they hoped would be the future stars of NASCAR.

I wasn't sure how I felt about this. But Austin had his reasons, and he'd clearly thought about them. He explained it to me like this: "It's not a Cup car, and I may never drive a Cup car. But I sit in a seat, and I'm buckled in, and I can look at everything the way Adam did."

That was not what I was expecting him to say.

He finished by saying, "It makes me feel closer to you, Dad. It makes me feel closer to Grandpa. It makes me feel closer to Adam."

All this was tough for our family, but we kept going because that's what we had always done.

It was almost a relief that we had something else we could all do together to honor Adam. We had Victory Junction to focus on.

25

CAMP KIDS

"Can I say a couple of things?"

Though we were struggling in the shop and on the racetrack, our plans for a camp in Adam's honor were moving full speed ahead. My dad and mom donated ninety acres of land behind their house in Level Cross. It was a perfect location for a kid's camp, and we didn't have to pay a nickel for it. And it didn't surprise me when all three of my sisters immediately said, "Just tell us what we can do." But I have to admit I was taken aback by how quickly and how enthusiastically our NASCAR family stepped up.

They'd all come to the memorial service. And that meant a lot to me. But helping to build a camp for chronically ill children in Adam's memory—that was a major project that would be hugely expensive and go on for years. Yet as soon as I said, "This is what we're gonna do," the sport's top drivers were all at the front of the line. I looked up, and there was Dale Jarrett, the NASCAR champion that year.

"Whatever you need, man," he said. "Just let me know."

And Bobby Labonte said, "I'm in." Bobby donated a car that we auctioned for camp, and he also wrote a check.

Kenny Schrader said, "We love your whole family. Tell me where to show up. Tell me what I can do."

These three guys appeared with me in uniform in the first Victory Junction print ad, "Join Our Gang." They made it happen. My dad, Bobby Labonte, Tony Stewart, Kenny Schrader, Jimmie Johnson, and Jeff Green joined me in the camp's first TV commercial. They were in, all in.

One by one by one, people just found ways to be helpful. Drivers, owners, crew chiefs, sponsors, everybody. They all said some version of "How can we help you?"

Some drivers, but not a lot, had foundations at that time. As a group, we were just learning how blessed we were and how we could use our platforms to help other people. But these were fast learners. They showed up when we asked them to. They hosted fundraising events. And pretty soon, it wasn't just the owners and the drivers and the crews and the other NASCAR people. The race fans jumped in too. Jeff Gordon's fans started sending $24 checks in honor of Jeff's car number. Dale Jarrett's fans started sending $88 checks. Too bad three-digit numbers didn't exist! It was crazy.

Kurt Busch went above and beyond and then some. He donated a whole building for the camp. Like me, Kurt had played Little League baseball when he was young. We knew that most of the kids coming to the camp would never have had the chance to participate in organized athletics because of their illnesses. We came up with a great idea. Why not build an indoor ball field where kids could play softball, baseball, and kickball?

We broke ground on the camp's construction within a short eighteen months, which is lightning speed for a project of this magnitude. We stuck with the racing theme and told Adam's story. Racing was Adam's passion. Racing was in the blood of most of the people who were helping bring this idea to life. We were racers and race fans, and that's what connected us, and we were proud of that. We wanted to turn that pride into action. So that is what we did.

Just like we imagined, one building was designed to look like a race car. We named the hospital area the Body Shop. The cafeteria became the Fuel Stop. We had all kinds of crazy ideas, and we turned a lot of them into reality. That indoor field Kurt donated became the Kurt Busch Superdome. Somewhere along the way, Paul Newman's guys decided we may have something here, after all. They sent people from Boggy Creek and other camps to advise us, and they provided other assistance, which we certainly appreciated. Paul came down and gave an inspiring speech, and we were thrilled to make Victory Junction an official affiliate of his Hole in the Wall Gang camps.

More than once I caught myself wishing that Adam could see how this dream of his was actually coming true. But then I remembered my son's laser focus, and I had to admit, he probably wouldn't have been surprised at all that we could really pull it off.

There was a moment early on, before the camp officially opened, when I had a moment of doubt.

I was standing at the construction site with a few other people as the buildings were coming out of the ground. We were all patting ourselves on the back for what we had achieved already and how quickly we were getting it done. That's when the thought occurred to me: *Oh, my God. Who's gonna give their child to us to look after? That's never gonna happen.* I could already hear people say, "No way am I dropping my kid off at that guy's house."

When we envisioned Victory Junction, we did give some thought to where all these kids might come from. It would be a total waste of time and money and everyone's hard work if we built a beautiful facility and nobody showed up.

We figured our best shot was with families from North Carolina and South Carolina—that was our core region—and maybe a few from eastern Tennessee. But just like in the movie *Field of Dreams,* it turned out that "If you build it, they will come." Because of NASCAR's fifty-state footprint and the wide reach of the drivers who were helping us, we started getting inquiries from kids and their families all across America and from other countries too. And when we finally opened in 2004, the best thing happened. The kids showed up. Hundreds of them, then thousands of them, some of the greatest kids and the greatest families you ever met, people who had been through things you couldn't imagine, coming to Victory Junction for a week at camp and the time of their lives. Clearly, there was a need out there. It turned out we had nothing to worry about when it came to boys and girls wanting to come.

My biggest worry that first year was that we would misplace a couple of them. Maybe they'd wander off. Maybe they'd be homesick and their parents would come and scoop them up in the middle of the night. We did a head count every day just to make certain. Actually, we had a much harder time getting them to leave.

We said everything we could think of. "The week's over. . . . We've loved having you. . . . Please, come back next year." Still, at the end of the week, some of the campers did not want to go home.

So many things at camp just happened. People had ideas. Connections were made. If something worked, we did it again. If something didn't, we changed. We took advice from the best medical specialists, and we listened to the campers and their families. They were often the real experts. We tried to be guided by them.

One thing we were committed to from the very beginning: All the children would attend for free. These families, even the ones who were well off, had been squeezed financially by the illnesses of their children. The last thing we wanted to do was add to that pressure. So, free. Totally free. For every family.

The days and nights were packed with activities. And soon enough, we were developing traditions and rituals of our own, like any great camp does. When the kids arrived on Sunday, they all checked in with the medical team at the camp hospital. That way, the doctors and nurses would get a clear idea of any physical limitations and what meds the campers needed. Then, the fun began. We had all the regular camp stuff and a full weekly calendar of events and activities. A cookout one night, our NAS-CARnival the next, where drivers and other NASCAR people come to hang out with the campers. The kids almost always put on a talent show. You should see some of their performances! They'll make you laugh and touch your heart. Friendships are made. Bonds are built. New possibilities are constantly opening. Friday afternoon, the kids go home. That may sound like just a regular week of summer camp, but that's exactly the point. This is not a camp for making kids feel different. It's a camp that treats kids like kids.

We've gotten to know so many amazing children and families over the years, it's hard to single out just a few of them. Everyone is special, and everyone sticks with us. Our second year, we had a boy who came from Richmond, Virginia. He was eleven or twelve years old, and he had burns over 85 percent of his body. He still could not move. He had only one unburned finger and a little bit of a thumb. To anyone who had known him before, I'm sure he was unrecognizable. I could hardly imagine a tougher place for a kid to be. He seemed so excited when he arrived. He hadn't ever been to camp before. He really hadn't been anywhere in the three years since he had been burned. And his mom, who had driven him down from Richmond, was just as excited as he was.

"This is gonna be fabulous," she confided to the counselor who showed the two of them around.

"I can't wait," the boy said.

But this boy from Richmond—when his mother left on Sunday night, he suddenly seemed to withdraw. He just stopped talking. As more kids arrived, he withdrew even more. When the counselors tried to talk to him, he wouldn't say anything. He didn't want to talk to anybody.

We have a rule at camp that no one has to do anything they don't want to do. But we encourage all the kids to have new experiences, to try things they've never done before. Often, those are some of the greatest moments of all, the look on the face of a kid who's just spent a month in a hospital and is now riding a zipline or getting on a horse for the first time. This boy, the next day, he didn't want to ride the horses. He didn't want to do arts and crafts. He didn't want to get in the swimming pool. Didn't want to do anything. All he wanted to do was sit in his cabin.

We sent several different counselors to talk to him. Often, if a kid doesn't click with one counselor, another counselor will find a way to connect. We have 120 kids at camp each week. Our ratio is one and a half adults for every child.

All day Monday, we got nowhere. By Tuesday, he'd been through a few different counselors. We were wondering what we were doing wrong. We're usually better than this. "I'll take him this afternoon," Pronto, our camp director, said. "Maybe he doesn't realize that there are other kids here with burns."

So Tuesday afternoon, Pronto tried. He wasn't having much success. "I just don't feel like it," the kid said to everything Pronto suggested, when the kid said anything at all. Finally, our twelve-year-old agreed to try archery, and that went OK. But he still wasn't saying much of anything. We were making a little progress, I suppose. But the week was ticking by, and we definitely hadn't achieved any kind of breakthrough.

On Wednesday at lunchtime, we did something we called the Circle of Thankfulness. We had a hula hoop with a long bit of ribbon that went around it. Everyone was invited to come and take the microphone and say what they were thankful for. Thankfulness. The point is to wrap the ribbon around and around until you can't see through the circle anymore. When you can't see through that circle, the circle is full of hope.

All of a sudden, as people were saying what they are thankful for, the boy from Richmond got up from his chair and got in line behind a lot of excited boys and girls.

"I'm thankful we're having pizza today," one kid said.

"I'm thankful for Chip the horse and how he let me ride him," another kid said.

"I'm thankful I'm in the cabin I'm in."

"I'm thankful I made a new best friend."

It's nice, some of the things the kids get up and say. As always, there are always touching moments.

All the counselors and volunteers were glancing over at the boy who hadn't said anything, wondering what he was going to say. He had hardly spoken to anyone, except for a few words to Pronto, and now he was going to speak to every camper, counselor, and volunteer in the building.

The adults got quiet as he reached the front of the line.

Finally, it was his turn.

"I just want to say . . . " he began. Then, he turned to Pronto. "Can I say a couple of things?"

"Sure can," Pronto told him.

The boy took the microphone. He held it in his hands. The room was silent. The other kids noticed that the counselors and the volunteers were listening carefully. So they listened too. Then, the boy continued.

"I'm thankful there's a camp like this."

Everybody was watching and waiting. "And I want to say one other thing," he continued. "I've watched everybody. I'm thankful that no matter how we were burned, we all survived."

It was a very emotional moment. Powerful words to come from a twelve-year-old boy who had been through so much. Pronto walked over to take the microphone. But the boy pulled back.

"No," he said with unexpected confidence. "I've got one other thing."

Pronto took a step back. And the boy continued.

"Because it's Wednesday," the boy said, "isn't tonight dance night?"

"It sure is," Pronto said.

"I've gotta warn everyone. I'm gonna dance tonight."

This kid was unstoppable, unstoppable the rest of the week, making up for everything he'd missed out on before he spoke.

His mom came on Friday, like all the other parents did to pick up their children. The boy jumped in the car and just like that, he was gone. But about thirty minutes later, he and his mom were back. His mom got out of the car. *Uh-oh, what'd we do?* In the end, the camp experience seemed to all go well. So why was his mom here again? She looked around a bit and asked where she could find Pronto. Once she found him and they sat down together, she immediately started to cry.

"I just want to thank you and everybody at this camp for giving me back my son, the son I had before his accident," she said. "That's the little boy he was. That's the way he acted. That's who he was—full of life, full of joy . . . and a total handful. Just being inquisitive. Just wanting to know things."

That week, for the first time in years, he saw himself without any of his scars. Camp opened that door for him.

It takes a lot of effort, love, and commitment—and a lot of money—to keep a dream like Victory Junction alive and thriving. Thankfully, we have been blessed with thousands and thousands of supporters who have continued to give generously. Dedicated individuals. Tireless volunteers.

Wonderful corporate sponsors, faith-based organizations, and charitable groups.

People give in so many different ways. Their big-heartedness never fails to amaze me. Sometimes, it's a kid no older than our campers, sharing a small allowance. Some folks make monthly gifts, sticking with us through the years, or sign up for commemorative bricks and custom benches on our Fan Walk. Others make tribute gifts to special people in their lives. Some even remember Victory Junction in their wills.

Looking back, it was inevitable, I suppose, that the Kyle Petty Charity Ride Across America would become a key supporter of Victory Junction. I never forgot what Adam said to me when we went to Daytona for Biketoberfest and toured Camp Boggy Creek. *Why don't we build a camp like this and let the Ride help pay for it?*

So that's what we did.

The Kyle Petty Charity Ride Across America had grown tremendously by then, and the Ride kept getting bigger. I like to think it got bigger in some part because we had such a good cause to ride for, but a lot of making it a better ride was Don Tilley's doing. Don came up with a fresh route for us every year, always something interesting. But he was so much more than our route maker. He was our inspiration and one of our best recruiters. My name was in the title, but Don's heart was there for every mile.

Those Rides were like memory-making machines. That's just what happens when you ride two wheels across America with two hundred of your closest friends. Unforgettable moments, mile after mile. All the kids emptying out of school to see us in Presidio, Texas. Arriving at Mount Rushmore on a day so foggy we couldn't see a single carved president from the viewing platform. Riding on the sidewalk to our hotel in downtown Chicago because every dang street seemed to run the wrong way. Those Chicagoans took us in stride, like they'd already seen just about everything. A huge contingent of Albuquerque police shutting down two major interstates—I-25 and I-40—so we could pass smoothly into their city. Cops in cars. Cops on motorcycles. Everyone this side of the SWAT team!

"It's amazing to watch you guys do this," I marveled to the commander on the scene.

"Piece of cake," he said. "We did the same thing last week for First Lady Michelle Obama."

That sealed it as far as I was concerned. "From now on," I said, "we're only going to cities where the president or the first lady has just been."

Click Baldwin, my leather-clad, Harley-dealing friend from Gastonia, was rarely far from the action. He had his own, unique way of stirring things up. There was one time we had a police escort in Kansas City, but somehow we got turned around. The officers knew a shortcut that would get us pointed the right way. It took us through a gated community of broad lawns and multimillion-dollar homes.

On a normal day, I wouldn't think this kind of neighborhood got a lot of motorcycle traffic. But at one intersection, two ladies waited patiently in an open Mercedes convertible for the roaring bikes to pass. That was too much for Click to resist.

"How y'all doin'?" he called out to the women as he pulled up beside their car. "I just bought a house around the corner, and we're having a big party. If y'all want to turn around and fall in behind the last bike, you're invited!" He was grinning ear to ear, just as friendly as could be.

I don't know whether the gated ladies believed Click's story or not. But I could just imagine the two of them, both completely stone-faced, shaking their heads no.

I love telling Ride stories. I could go on all day and night. But the best news is that the Charity Ride remains the largest continual donor to Victory Junction. And the things we experienced across America on those motorcycles pale in comparison to the stories and memories those kids make at camp week after week after week.

26

LONG RIDE

"What did you dream it was going to be like?"

We kept Petty Enterprises going through the 2008 season. But the day eventually came when my dad decided he was ready to move in a different direction and sold the company to a venture capital group called Boston Ventures. The new owners, who took over at the start of 2009, ended up merging teams with Gillett Evernham Motorsports and adjusting the name to Richard Petty Motorsports, complete with a logo that resembled the old Petty Enterprises design.

People always ask me: Was selling the company emotional for you?

It certainly was for my dad. Even though he would continue on as a part-owner, he was passing on control of the business that had defined and supported our family since the late 1940s. My grandfather started it. My dad and my uncle became partners, and then my dad and my uncle ended up with my grandfather's shares. Then, my dad bought my uncle out. The business had thrived for decades, and it carried on all those years.

I know it was an emotional decision for him and a painful one. He just felt like we were in a place where we couldn't survive as we were. We couldn't continue to go forward without a big change. It was his decision to make, and that's the decision he made. As for me, I will say it this way: Looking back on it, I have a different perspective than I did in the moment. When my dad sold the company and the Boston Ventures people were in control, I was not asked to be a part of the new team.

I didn't *decide* to quit driving. That decision was made for me. Basically,

I didn't have a job driving a race car anymore. It just took a while for my head to get around that idea.

That made the last race of my driving career the 2008 Checker O'Reilly Auto Parts 500, November 9 of that year, at Phoenix Raceway in suburban Avondale, Arizona. Jimmie Johnson had the pole. Rain delayed the start by half an hour. It was a sloppy day on the track with a nasty collision at the finish line: Matt Kenseth knocked A. J. Allmendinger into Juan Pablo Montoya. Allmendinger and Montoya got hooked together, slid across the line, and hit the inside wall, sending Montoya spinning back across traffic, collecting Tony Stewart, Robby Gordon, Bill Elliott, Ken Schrader, and others. A lot of fans were upset, as was NASCAR chairman Brian France, when ABC dropped its live coverage in the eastern and central time zones at lap 284 (of 312) so the network could air *America's Funniest Home Videos*. Viewers were able to see the finish on ESPN2.

Jimmie won that day, all but clinching his place as that year's Cup champion, his third championship in a row. I finished thirty-ninth.

So, was it emotional for me? Sure, it was. I felt some hurt of my own when I realized my driving career was over. It hurt not to have a ride. It hurt to be the guy on the outside. It hurt that the team that I had worked for and had come back to and had tried so hard to build now belonged to somebody else, and the new owner didn't want me to be a part of what was going to happen next.

Of course, that part hurt. It bruised my ego. How could it not? All I could do was turn my attention to other things I was interested in. Thankfully, I had a lot of them.

There's always the question of how long is too long to keep driving a race car. When's the right time for a driver to hang it up and go home? Some version of that question comes up in every sport, I know. And in racing, we have our own unique set of factors. Stamina. Reflexes. Competitive drive. And the continuing ability to attract sponsors. No, they don't have to worry about that last one in professional football. And some race car drivers never want to let loose of the wheel. I'd put my dad in that category. I sometimes think he'd still be driving today if he could.

Driving forever was never what I saw for myself. I didn't ever want to be one of those guys where the fans were saying, "I'm surprised he can still climb in and out of the car." I definitely missed it when I first stopped driving. There were moments I did. For me, there were times in 2009 and 2010 that I thought to myself, *Man, I'd like to try that one more time.* But there weren't too many of those moments, and they didn't last too long.

I think I'm a little different from a lot of drivers in that way. So many times, the guys who can't turn it off, who want to do it again and again and again, to them, being a race car driver—that's just who they are. They drive race cars. That defines their entire being and their entire identity.

Driving a race car was not *who* I was. It was something I did. Just like music isn't who I am. It's something I do. I guess you could say they are *part* of who I am. Being a father is also part of who I am. So is being a husband, a son, a brother, a grandpa, and a friend. There are all kinds of parts and pieces of me that come together to make up who I am, but not one of those alone defines me.

So when I had to quit driving after the 2008 season and I shook off my initial melancholy, I never had those intense emotional yearnings calling out to me: "I've got to be in a race car again" or "I'm not Kyle Petty unless I'm behind the wheel."

I do know ex-athletes—and not just race car drivers—who spend the rest of their lives battling those feelings. They've been defined by their jobs, by the company they keep, by the fresh adulation of the fans, and by so many of the other cool things that go along with these sports of ours, all those accomplishments and reactions have become who they are.

You can see it in the cars some of these guys drive on the highway and the way they drive those cars. They're still living the glory days at the track. We've all had to work so hard to turn these dreams of ours into reality. I suppose it's only natural that the dreams sometimes die hard.

I've had the opportunity to talk to a lot of race car drivers over the years. Because I knew them when I was little. Because they became friends of mine. Because I was interviewing them or they were interviewing me. Young drivers. Older drivers. All different kinds. There's one question I end up asking almost all of them: "When you were little and you wanted to be a race car driver, what did you dream it was going to be like?"

"When I was little," almost all of them say, "I dreamed of driving that car and beating Jeff Gordon." Or "I dreamed I was beating Dale Earnhardt, Sr." Or "I dreamed I was beating Richard Petty." Pick your favorite driving legend. Or "I dreamed I was driving in the Daytona 500 and I was beating David Pearson." Or maybe it was Martinsville or Talladega or some other iconic track.

But I've never had a single driver say to me, "I dreamed of making a lot of money . . . I dreamed of doing commercials . . . I dreamed of selling motor oil and paper towels . . . I dreamed of being a professional pitchman. That's what I lay up nights dreaming about."

Never heard that once.

That's not what race car drivers dream about. They dream about driving race cars.

So sure, there was a natural sadness when my dad retired. When Tony Stewart stepped out of the car. When Jeff Gordon did. To this day, I feel some sadness for all those guys. Because I know that somewhere, every one of them had to put that little boy's dream in a box, and he's not going to do that anymore. He can still be a pitchman. He can still be on TV. He can still make lots of money. But the dream that got him here, the one he had when he was five, six, or seven years old, he's not ever going to do that again.

In our sport, we are luckier than in most. Many of us have been able to carry that dream for twenty or thirty years—and that's rare in life, certainly in professional sports, getting to carry a dream for that long. But still, there will always come a day when you've got to put that dream away. How could any of us not feel some kind of loss?

Giving up the driving—not the other parts.

I'm not looking for sympathy. Most NFL players are done by their early thirties. A handful of superstars—kickers and quarterbacks, mostly—last past forty. The timetable for most basketball careers is even shorter. But in our sport, lots of guys drive into their forties. Some have gone into their fifties. We have a few ironmen who've gone even longer than that. But when you quit playing football at twenty-nine, you've got plenty of time to do something else with your life. The flip side of the longer careers we have is that by the time we step out of the car, a lot of guys have no idea what else to do and not as much time to figure it out. Thankfully, I didn't have that problem. I already had a lot of things going on in my life and in my head, but I was always open to something new.

I had always wanted to learn to fly. I'd just never taken the time away from driving and running the business to learn. There was this one night when a group of us were flying home from the race in Fontana on my dad's jet. We had to stop in Nashville to fuel. At the Nashville airport, I noticed a small plane sitting with some of the other planes. It caught my eye because it was silver, and it looked like a 1950 Mercury with a chopped top. It just looked fast sitting there. I got my dad's pilot, Mickey, and we walked over to take a closer look. It was really a cool-looking plane.

We fueled and took off for Greensboro. But the rest of the trip, all I could think about was that little plane.

When we landed, I asked Mickey to call the people he knew in the aviation business and find out how much that plane cost. A few days later, Mickey called me with the price. Did I mention I really liked that plane? So, I asked Mickey, "Can we get a silver one?"

He made a couple more phone calls and got back to me with the news. It was a commemorative anniversary edition of the Columbia 400. The company made only ten of them, and all ten were spoken for.

"OK," I said. "Never mind."

Two or three weeks later, Mickey called me and said his friend had called him. Someone had backed out on purchasing one of the silver anniversary planes. It was going to be in Lakeland, Florida, at the SUN 'n FUN Aerospace Expo if I wanted to look at it.

I didn't want to look at it. I wanted to buy it. Mickey told the guy we would take it.

A month later, I had a brand-new Columbia 400 anniversary edition delivered to the Lexington airport in North Carolina. I only had one problem: I didn't know how to fly. Mickey found an instructor for me named Mikey Matthews who had experience in Columbias. He was also an aerobatics instructor and could fly anything with an engine and wings. A few days later, Mikey showed up at the airport, and I started my lessons.

Now, some people might say that's not the best plane to learn how to fly in, and they might have a point. The Columbia 400 is considered a high-performance aircraft and, per FFA rules, you aren't allowed to learn in a high-performance aircraft. Then again, I didn't learn to drive a race car on a short track. My dad took me down to Daytona and put me in the driver's seat. That made perfect sense to me, and Daytona is where I won my first race.

So I learned to fly in the Columbia 400.

At the same time, Mikey was giving me lessons in a Cessna 172. We flew every week to the races. But as soon as I got my pilot's license, I never sat in that 172 again.

Flying was everything I dreamed it would be and more. I loved everything about it. From preflight to postflight to filing flight plans and talking on the radio. I'm not saying flying could ever replace racing, but I noticed that my spirits were lifted every time I was in the air. The best part was being up there on a partly cloudy day, dodging clouds and watching the world pass beneath me. When I was flying, I got the feeling I could truly go anywhere and do anything.

I loved my flying. I loved my music, which I'd never given up on. I was doing a lot more in TV land. But I have to be honest: Even with everything I had going on, getting out of the race car was tough for me. It was tough emotionally. And I had some other tough emotional issues that I had yet to face.

There were bits and pieces of Adam and his accident that I had never really dealt with. He was never out of my mind. He was always there with me, someplace nearby. Sometimes, I would be somewhere, and I would think I could hear him call my name. He visited me in my dreams. I would wake at three in the morning, crying. I would tell myself as long as I hurt, he was still near. I knew he was there because it hurt every day.

Grief is a lonely place to be.

When you're grieving, a crowded room can be the loneliest place in the world. I always felt alone. I think that was part of the reason, after the accident, I got back in the car as fast as I could. In hindsight, maybe too fast. But at the time, that's where I felt closest to Adam. That's where I felt most at peace.

I also didn't feel like I had much of a choice. People depended on that race car, and the company depended on me. Whatever I was feeling, I had to shove in a box and put it away. I tried, but I always knew it was there. It took a long time for me to open that box again. And when I did, I was more lost, more confused, and more hurt than I'd ever been.

Even though I kept moving forward, I wasn't going anywhere. That's not living. That's not life. It felt like everything was catching up to me all at once.

Losing my job driving was part of it. I thought I'd be at Petty Enterprises forever. Adam's accident was part of it. Everything in the world that I had always known and assumed would always stay the same, all of it was changing. I felt like I was drowning and no one could save me. No one. Not even Pattie.

She tried. We tried. But in the end, our marriage had changed too. There was nothing left to do but divorce.

Montgomery Lee and Austin were grown by then and had families and lives of their own. But I know it was also hard for them.

In Adam's name, Pattie and I and our kids helped bring to life Adam's dream of a camp that would and could change the lives of kids for many years to come. I'd like to think we ended our marriage accomplishing something special and wishing each other nothing but the best in the years ahead.

27

TALKING HEAD

"We need you to do some of this TV stuff."

I never really imagined I'd end up on television, though the idea had been floating around in the background as far back as 2001. That's when I first got to be friends with Dick Ebersol and his guys at NBC. Dick's a brilliant television producer who'd risen to president and then chairman of NBC Sports. He'd been in charge of Olympics coverage, and he was the one who led the network into NASCAR—for their first go-round.

"We need you to do some of this TV stuff," he said to me several times. "You have the knowledge. You have the personality. I think you'd be good at it."

That was nice of him to say, but I just wasn't ready yet. Adam had just been gone a year. I was still too busy driving race cars and trying to run a company. Those two together, as I kept discovering, were more than a full-time job—especially when you added in taking care of the sponsors.

Then, Benny Parsons was diagnosed with lung cancer. Benny was NASCAR champion in 1973 and had been broadcasting races for ESPN, TBS, NBC, and TNT full-time since 1989. The fans and the drivers loved Benny's folksy manner and straight-shooting style. Everybody liked how he could dish up nuggets of racing history with total ease. He kept working through his medical treatments. But when he passed away on January 16, 2007, at the much-too-young age of sixty-five, it left a giant hole in NASCAR broadcasting.

Before he died, Benny told someone: "You guys really need to talk to Kyle." And so the topic arose again. TBS came to me and said, "Would you be interested in doing this?" By then, I was a lot more open to the idea. I thought, *Yeah, I can do this. I'll get out of the car for six races in the middle of the season,* which was the Turner portion of the season. *Then, I'll jump back into the car for the rest of the year.* And that became my gradual transition from the driver's seat to the broadcast booth. From my perspective, it couldn't have been more natural or more fun.

What I discovered was that Dick Ebersol had been right. Television was a fairly natural fit for me. Actually, it wasn't all that different from the rest of my life. I got to be with racing people. I got to talk about racing. I got to use my knowledge and my experience and the fact that I'd been around the sport since before I could tie my own shoelaces. I loved talking. I never got nervous in front of a camera or a microphone. Why should I? I was just sitting with a bunch of guys, swapping stories and sharing our opinions on the latest craziness at the track, which I'd probably be doing anyway whether I called it work or not.

My transition from driving to TV was different from almost anybody else's because it went back and forth, and it didn't happen overnight. I was still an active driver when I went into the broadcast booth. It went just how we planned it. I would get out of the car and not drive for six races. Those weeks, I'd do TV. Then, I'd jump back in the car and race again. When we got to the end of the 2008 season and the company was sold and my driving days were done, my place in TV was already established. And I realize now that staying so busy helped with a lot of the heartache I was feeling at the time.

I don't want to give the impression that my weeks in the booth weren't fun. They were a blast. Especially some of the unscripted moments with my cohosts and with the fans. I got a whole new view of racing that I never had from the seat of a race car. Then, Twitter and Instagram and the other social platforms brought us even closer, making it possible for us to interact in real time with so many passionate race fans. I know, some people complain about the way social media has invaded our lives, and I get it. It would be nice to pull the plug once in a while, then I remind myself—wait, everything is wireless now! There are no plugs to pull! Plus, the truth is I'd probably miss the contact and suffer terrible pangs of withdrawal. I'm constantly amazed at our fans. Though I've been around this sport since forever—since before I was born—I'm still frequently impressed by the depths of knowledge some fans have.

And sometimes by the lack of.

Wally Dallenbach, Jr., and Bill Weber and I were in the booth together, doing the race for TNT at the road course in Sonoma. Though Twitter was newer at the time, race fans took to it quickly. Wally and Bill and I were talking away, discussing different drivers, and people were live-tweeting us. Make that live-criticizing us. Which is OK. That's part of the deal. It's a free Twitter-verse.

I made a comment about Dale Jr., saying he was having "a pretty good day." The race had just started, and he'd already moved up twelve or thirteen positions from where he started, passing a bunch of other cars. The second I said it, a tweet popped up on my phone.

You are stupid. Dale Jr. is the greatest road racer ever.

I wasn't looking for a fight, but I felt like that called for an answer. I don't know about the greatest, but he's having a pretty good day.

You are an idiot, the man typed back. He's the greatest NASCAR road racer ever.

Give me an example, I replied.

Chicago.

Oval, I tweeted back. Not a road course.

As we traded these tweets, I was still doing my job calling the race. I can do more than one thing at once. That's one of the advantages of having the attention span of a gnat.

The guy tweeted again. Milwaukee.

Oval, I tweeted back.

He won the Busch race at Watkins Glen in '99.

Ten-year rule, I answered. And Little League stats don't count in the majors.

I was proud of that comeback. I thought it might quiet the blowhard. No such luck.

California.

Northern or Southern? Sonoma, where we were, is Northern California, outside San Francisco. Would I have to remind my new critic that California Speedway east of Los Angeles, which would eventually become Auto Club Speedway, was a low-banked, D-shaped oval? Apparently so.

Southern California, he wrote.

Oval, I responded.

Then, nothing. Radio silence. I checked my phone. I checked it again. Battery power was strong. A good ten minutes went by. Then it was fifteen. Still not a peep from my Dale Jr. fan. Maybe I'd finally made some headway with him.

That's when another tweet arrived.

I'm sorry, Mr. Petty. My husband is drunk. He's been drinking since 10:00 this morning. I am very sorry.

Was that really the man's wife? Had he just found a slippery way out of our little debate? Had he passed out drunk? Any of that was possible. Maybe he just got tired of arguing with me.

I started following the guy so I could see when he replied, but I'm still waiting. That's just how it works sometimes. On social media, they come and they go. I never heard another word from him again.

Going forward from there, my real job would be to talk, not to race anymore. And everyone always knew, even when I was racing, how much I loved to talk. I was just fortunate that the racing and the talking really did overlap. I never had to stop being around the people I've enjoyed being around my whole life. Race people. People who have one goal, one love, one desire: to be the best they can be on a Sunday afternoon. I've also been fortunate to work with some of the best in TV, people who really understand the medium and how powerful it can be.

Over the years that followed, I'd work a lot of places and do a lot of different shows—for NBC Sports, FS1, Speed, TNT, and ESPN. I got to work with people far more experienced than I was, good people who always tried to guide me in the right direction. They didn't just throw me into the deep end and expect me to swim. They gave me advice: "You might want to try this . . . You might want to try that." Any criticism was always constructive. No one ever tried to turn me into something I wasn't. No one tried to take the Kyle out of me.

At every network I ever worked for, the producers said they hired me for me, and that's what I always tried to share with the viewers and the people I worked with, the best me I could deliver every week. Thankfully, people still seem interested in what I have to say.

So I find myself in a unique position at this point in life. No matter what we're talking about on television, I see it in the larger context of the sport. I will give you an example. In the spring of 2021, when NASCAR ran a dirt Cup race at Bristol, I could say, truthfully, that I was there the last time a Cup race was run on dirt. It was 1970. I was ten years old. I was there with my dad. I remember what happened that day. And, yes, it was a thrill all over again.

It's not that I'm any smarter than anybody else. It's just that I've been around for a lot, and it's almost like my memories of the sport should really belong to someone older than me. In some strange way, I'm a connector from the past to the present because I remember so much of this stuff. I remember going to Greenville, South Carolina, when it was dirt. I remember going to Islip, New York, for the northern tour when I was ten, eleven, twelve years old, to racetracks that we don't even race anymore.

I'm not the walking history book that my dad is, but I'm a smaller version of that. I remember being around Bobby Isaac and David Pearson and Cale Yarborough. I remember being around Dale Earnhardt, Sr., and Tim Richmond and guys like that. I've been around Jimmie Johnson and Jeff Gordon. And now with Joey Logano and Daniel Suárez and the new generation, I'm around them too with a different perspective than just the TV side.

I know this is crazy. But I can sit and talk to you about being at Talladega in 1972 or 1973 or being at Talladega in 1982 or 1983 or being at Talladega in 1992 or 1993 or being at Talladega in 2002 or 2003 or being at Talladega in 2012 or 2013 because that's where I've been. I'm going to be there in 2022 and 2023 and maybe even a couple of more decades after that.

Yes, it's strange to realize that all that racing lives somewhere inside my crowded head.

That's not to say that all the broadcasting surprises happen inside the booth. Fourth of July weekend, 2010 give or take. A storm had just blown through Daytona. When you're racing on the coast in the middle of the summer, rain's just part of the deal. In Florida, it's just about a guarantee. This time, it was going to take two and a half, maybe three hours for the track to dry out enough for practice to resume. We were sitting in the TNT trailer—Jeff Behnke, Rutledge Wood, Wally Dallenbach, Jr., a few others, and me. We had nothing but time to kill.

Out of nowhere, an idea popped into my head. "Hey, y'all wanna go skydiving?"

"What?" Jeff said.

"Yeah, let's drive over to DeLand and jump out of a plane."

Everybody looked at me like . . . where did that come from? "No, I'm serious," I said. "I bet we could drive over there, go skydiving, and be back before practice starts up again. Easy." I'd seen people skydiving at DeLand Municipal Airport. And that was—what?—twenty minutes from where we were sitting, a straight shot down International Speedway Boulevard. I'd never been skydiving before, but how hard could it be? They give you a parachute!

"Let's do it," Jeff agreed.

We called over to the little airport to make sure they were flying. "Storm's passed," the man said. "Come on over."

So, we jumped in a car. Jeff, Rutledge, and me, plus a couple of camera guys and some of their gear. We were at the airport in no time. "We have an hour and fifteen minutes, and we want to jump out of an airplane," I said to the people in the office. "Can that be done?"

The instructors and pilots glanced at each other and then back at us. "Tandem, right?" one of them asked.

"Any way you got," I answered. "We just wanna jump out of a plane."

"Tandem," the man repeated, his question mark now a period.

They took us into a room for a fast-track skydiving course, so fast-track all I remember is that we watched a ten-minute video. In the video, a bearded gentleman was sitting at a desk in a wood-paneled office. Maybe he said something about skydiving techniques. I don't remember that part. The gist of what he said was, "If you die, you or your heirs can't sue anybody. If something goes wrong, you're on your own."

"Let's go," Jeff said.

They fitted us up with harnesses and the other gear we needed. They introduced us to the guys we were going to jump with, tandem-style. And then they walked us out to the plane.

Rutledge decided he'd stay on the ground and be our commentator.

"Wise move," Jeff said.

Jeff and I got in the plane, along with some other students who carried themselves like they'd actually shown up for the real course. The other people looked sharp in their skydiving outfits. They knew all the lingo, and a couple of them had cool goggles. Altogether, there were probably eight of us in the back of the plane. My plan was just to do what I was told.

The plane took off. We climbed to what someone said was 10,000 or 12,000 feet, but I couldn't really tell how high we were. When I looked out the open hatch, I would have believed it if someone had told me 50,000 feet. Soon enough, the time came.

My instructor began strapping me to him. Jeff's did the same with him. My instructor asked, "You want to go forward or backwards?" my guy asked me.

"Makes no difference to me," I said. "Just tell me when to go."

"On the count of three."

Jeff went first. Then, it was *one, two, three,* and suddenly we were falling out over the great state of Florida. I could see Daytona International Speedway. I could see the beach. This being Daytona, I could see people *driving their cars* on the beach. I swear I could almost see to Tampa. That's how high we were, and the state of Florida really isn't all that wide.

As we kept falling, I thought to myself this was no different from riding a motorcycle at high speed. My jaws were pinned back. The wind was slapping my face. As I looked around, I thought how incredibly peaceful it was up there. My guy was talking to me in a very normal voice. "Hold your arms out," he said. *Do this* and *do that*. He just talked me through it like we had all the time in the world.

Now, I did know something about gravity, and I understood our free fall could only last so long. But we kept dropping, and he kept talking, and then he said, "Get ready," and he gave a good, stiff yank to the rip cord. The parachute popped, and the next thing I knew, we were gently floating down to earth, just like we were hang gliding, which is something I'd never done either, but this was just like I imagined hang gliding would be.

Just a few miles down the boulevard, there were all those people packed together at the racetrack, waiting for the asphalt to dry. And I was floating from heaven to earth with the wind blowing through my hair.

My guy handled the final steering. Swinging to the left. Swinging to the right. "Right before we get to the ground," he told me, "lift your feet up and hold them up. I'll get us on the ground."

I did exactly as he told me to. Next thing I knew, we were both standing on solid ground, and I was thanking everybody at Skydive DeLand and paying our bill and not planning to sue anybody and heading back to Daytona in plenty of time before practice began. I'm not sure anyone even missed us.

I'd do it again in a heartbeat. Maybe the next time we're at Daytona, I'll parachute right onto the track.

28

TRUE LOVE

"I'm not the son-in-law you dreamed of."

I breezed into our Charity Ride office one morning just like I usually did, running my mouth about something I had just heard on the radio or starting in on some crazy story that had happened to me since the last time I was there. But the office looked empty. I didn't see anyone. Then, from the small conference room, I heard a voice I didn't recognize.

"Hello, can I help you?"

I stepped into the room just as a young woman pressed the button to start the laminating machine. She turned and looked at me and, over the hum of lamination, asked again, "Can I help you?"

I still remember thinking how beautiful she was. "Maybe," I said. "Where is everyone?"

"They've stepped out," she said. "I'm just trying to get a little bit ahead."

"What's your name?" I asked her.

"Morgan," she said. "I've just started here."

There was a slight pause as if she were trying not to be rude, and then she asked again. "Can I help you?"

"I'm Kyle," I said. "The Ride's named after me, and I've been here a long time."

My life changed that day. I just wouldn't know it for a few more years. But it had changed.

Morgan Castano was her name, and she attended the University of South Carolina and studied public relations. As part of her degree, she needed to complete an internship. She chose the Kyle Petty Charity Ride, though not for the reasons you might imagine someone would choose a motorcycle charity. At one time, she had almost switched her major to special education. She wanted to help and work with kids, kids with special needs. Victory Junction was the perfect fit for that and the Ride was her connection to our camp.

I have to assume that she enjoyed her internship as she got to know the riders and everyone else associated with the Ride. Because just a few years later, she was back, coming to work on the Ride full-time.

Now, organizing a two- to three-thousand-mile, seven-day motorcycle ride is just as complicated as you might imagine. It takes a huge amount of effort every year to coordinate hotels, permits, and all the support we need from local cities and towns, not to mention keeping all the riders headed in the right direction, looking after all the money, and paying all the bills. But we have a system. It requires someone who can take charge and deal with every single thing that happens—ideally, with a kind word and a smile. Organization is key. You have to be buttoned up to run this Ride.

Did I mention you have to be organized? It takes someone a lot smarter and a lot more together than I am. As our full-time director, Morgan Castano took the Ride to a whole new level.

She could charm the police officers and sheriff's deputies across our routes while navigating the government bureaucracies. She could cajole a hotel manager to shave $5 off the nightly rate. That may not sound like a lot of money. But when it's a charity and you're talking $5 a room for 150 rooms over the course of a week, the next thing you know it adds up. Just like any charity event, you have to find a place to hold it, hire a caterer to feed the guests, book some kind of entertainment, and put the word out far and wide so people will come and donate. But our charity was on the move morning to night. So imagine doing all that three-plus times a day, seven days in a row, and in at least twenty-one different cities!

Everyone loved Morgan. She got it done!

It didn't happen overnight. But looking back now, I knew something was happening, at least for me, and it went all the way back to that first day we met. I began to look forward to stopping by the Ride office, meeting with Morgan and our other board members, just to see how things were going. I found more reasons to call and ask questions about T-shirts, hotels, routes, anything I could think of. Sometimes, I'd pick up lunch, and we'd all eat at the office and talk. Or I'd ask Morgan to meet me at Sonic, and we'd share an order of mozzarella sticks before she headed home from work. We talked a lot about the Ride at first and later about books, movies, and music, the kinds of things you talk about when you're getting to know someone. We had a lot more in common than I would or could have ever imagined.

We became friends, but I also knew I was falling in love. It's hard to say just when we first started officially "dating." I had moved to Charlotte to be closer to my job. I didn't really know a lot about Charlotte. I knew where the racetrack was, where Felix lived, and where the airport was. That was about it. Morgan was born and raised in Charlotte, as her mom and dad were. If you know anything about Charlotte, that makes Morgan and her family unicorns! Rare! Charlotte has become a city where people move through on their way to or from somewhere else.

She invited me a few times to have dinner with her parents, John and Valerie. Her brothers, Jordan and Zack, were there, as was her grandfather, whom they all call PaPete. I was amazed at the closeness of their family, the respect they showed for their grandfather, and the dinner conversations they had. I always learned something new when I visited. One of the things I learned early on was even though they knew about racing and had all grown up in the city that was arguably the capital of NASCAR, they really weren't race fans.

One day, I had an opportunity to play a round of golf with PaPete. I really looked forward to spending some time with him and, I hoped, discovering a little about Morgan that I didn't know. We'd played a few holes when the subject of racing came up. I guess I knew it would at some point because it follows me everywhere.

We talked about drivers and tracks, just small talk really. But there came a point in the conversation that I asked her grandfather, "You ever been to any races?"

"I went to Macon a few times when I was in the service," he said. "Almost froze to death at Darlington one year. That happened in the fifties." And then he added, almost as an afterthought, "And I knew Curtis Turner."

Really? Morgan's grandfather knew Curtis Turner? I would not have predicted that.

Curtis is a NASCAR legend, as much for his big talent on the track as for his large personality off of it. He won the 1956 Southern 500. He was a major player in the development of Charlotte Motor Speedway. He was even voted one of NASCAR's fifty greatest drivers ever and inducted into the NASCAR Hall of Fame in 2016.

"You knew Curtis Turner?" I asked him. "How?"

"Well," he said, "Morgan's grandmother's parents lived next door to Curtis. So, she and her family knew him and his wife. We used to go out to dinner with them sometimes."

I was still a little bit in shock. I had assumed from our dinner table conversations that Morgan's family's knowledge of NASCAR was only what they read in the paper or saw on the evening news. Her grandfather had just changed the game.

"Tell me about Curtis," I said.

"Not much to tell, really," PaPete said. "He was a nice guy. His wife was nice too, and we always had fun when we went out together."

I knew there had to be more to it than that. Then, he added another afterthought: "There *was* this one time . . ."

He paused for a moment. *Tell me, tell me!* my inside voice was screaming. Then, I got the story I was waiting for.

It was Curtis and his wife, Morgan's grandmother and me, and another couple. We'd all gone out to a nice restaurant close to the airport. It was just a regular dinner, a good steak and a couple of drinks, that's all. But as we sat talking after dinner, Curtis said, "Let's ride over to the airport and let me show y'all my new plane."

Everyone thought that sounded fine. So we loaded up and headed over to the airport. Well, somewhere between the restaurant and the airport, the plans changed. Curtis said, "Hey, why don't we take the new plane and fly down to Tampa or we can jump in the other plane and fly up to my house in Roanoke?"

We probably should have all said, "Yeah, that sounds like fun, but it's already a little late. Let's call it a night and do it next time." That's probably what we should have said, but we didn't. What we said was, "Tampa sounds fun, but it'll take too long to get there. Let's go to Roanoke!"

So that's what we did. We piled into Curtis's plane and took off for Virginia. It was a beautiful night. The moon wasn't full but it was bright. It didn't take very long to get there. But when we landed, the little airport was closed, and we didn't have a car to get to Curtis's house. Somehow a taxi showed up. I don't remember if we called it or if it just happened to be in the area and saw the plane land. We all squeezed in. The driver recognized Curtis and knew where his house was. We were there before we knew it. That's when the first problem of the night arose.

We'd just had a steak dinner and flown in a private plane from Charlotte to Roanoke. But we couldn't scrape up enough money between the six of us to pay the cab fare. We gave the guy all we had, and Curtis said he would catch up with him the next time he was up that way. We went inside, took a little tour of the house. Everyone got a drink, and we settled into the living room. We had been there only a short time when someone said they were hungry. Curtis's wife went into the kitchen, and that's when the second problem of the night appeared. There wasn't anything in the house to eat. It had been a while since they had been there, and they had cleaned out all the food before they left the last time so it wouldn't go bad.

"No problem," Curtis said. "I'll just run get something and be right back."

Remember the first problem of the night. No car. "Let me think," Curtis said.

Finally, he looked at the other gentleman who was with us and asked, "You know how to drive a tractor?" I don't know if the other gentleman nodded because he did know how or if he was just so surprised by the question. "Good," Curtis said. "You take the tractor and head back the way we came. I'll call the neighbors and tell them what we need and that you're on your way. It's three or four miles. House is on the left. I'll tell them to turn the porch light on."

This story was getting good, not so different from some of the funny tales I'd heard from my dad and his friends.

The two of them stepped outside. After a few minutes, I heard the tractor crank and head up the driveway and down the road. Curtis came back in smiling. Problem solved. That's what we all thought, anyway, until the third problem of the night showed up.

It seems the tractor had no lights. Even though you could see the road to drive by the light of the moon, the patrolman that brought the gentleman back to Curtis's house didn't think it was a wise decision to be riding around on a mountain road in the middle of the night in the dark. Curtis and the patrolman went outside. We could hear their muffled voices, but we couldn't make out what they were saying. A few minutes went by before we heard a car start and saw the taillights driving away.

Curtis came back smiling again. "It's all taken care of" was all he said.

We settled into the living room again, laughing about the evening and everything that had happened since we'd met for dinner at the restaurant. Suddenly, we saw headlights coming down the drive.

"Who could that be?" Curtis's wife said. There was a knock at the door. Curtis opened the door, and there stood the patrolman with the food and drinks from the neighbors down the road! Curtis was right. It was all taken care of. We flew back to Charlotte the next morning, and as best that I remember we all made it to work on time.

I told PaPete how much I enjoyed his story and how surprised I was to hear it. As we got back to the golf game, I was still picturing that no-headlights tractor getting stopped on the side of the road by the police.

"Did you ever tell that story to Morgan or to her mom?" I asked.

He let out a laugh. "They never asked," he said.

We were over at Morgan's parents' house having dinner a few weeks later, and as always, PaPete was also there. There was a lull in the conversation. I looked at Morgan's grandfather and winked. Then, I looked around the table at the others and said, "Oh, I meant to tell you guys. When your grandpa and I played golf, he told me one of the most amazing racing stories I'd ever heard."

Everyone seemed a little confused. Finally, Morgan's mom said, "Dad, you have a racing story?"

"I went to a few races," he said. "I went to Darlington. Macon when I was in the service. But Kyle wants me to tell you about Curtis Turner."

Morgan's grandpa proceeded to tell her family the exact story he had shared with me on the golf course. They, like me, hung on his every word. When he was finished, he had a smile on his face and a glimmer in his eyes as he recalled the memories. And his family learned a story about him that they may have never known if it wasn't for our round of golf.

I was always a little nervous when I was with Morgan and her family. I was afraid that they would see how much I cared for her, how much I loved her. I thought I did a pretty good job of hiding it. But honestly, the way I felt when I was near her, I wasn't sure it could be hidden.

I knew it was time to talk to her parents.

I asked them to dinner at a place close to where they lived. I didn't want it to be inconvenient for them, and I didn't want them to have to drive very far if our dinner upset them.

That was certainly a possibility.

We sat down and ordered our food. I don't remember how I started the conversation. I'm sure I was talking a thousand miles a minute about a hundred different things. Finally, I do know I said, "I need to tell you both something."

I paused for a breath and continued.

"I love your daughter," I said. "I love her more than anything in this world." Her mom nodded a little. At least I think she did. I know I was looking for even the tiniest sign of approval.

"I want to marry her," I said.

There. I said it. It was out now. "I'm asking your permission," I said. "But before you say anything, I'd like to say a couple of things to you. I know when Morgan was born and you dreamed of this day happening, I'm not the son-in-law you dreamed of. As you might have noticed, there's a few years between us. I know there's a million reasons running through your minds right now why I'm not the right one for Morgan. But please, let me give you one reason why I believe I am."

I took a sip of water. Her parents didn't say anything. I took that as a sign to go on.

"I know in my heart, no one will ever love Morgan more than I do," I said. "I know I believe that she is the most amazing woman in the world. She's kind. She's caring. She's giving. She's everything I've ever dreamed of. I hold her up *here*."

I held my hand above my head.

"I'll always keep her on a pedestal," I said. "Because to me, that's where she belongs. I've never felt the way she makes me feel when I'm with her. I promise you both I will protect and cherish her every moment we have for the rest of our lives, and I will love her more every day."

When I finished, her parents looked at each other and then back at me.

Her mom spoke first. "We know how much you love her," she said. "We see it when you're with her. And we know how much she loves you. You both just light up when you're together."

She looked at Morgan's dad. "We just want for Morgan what we've had," he said. "Happiness. That's all any parent wants for their child. She makes you happy. You make her happy. And that makes us happy."

"Yes," they both seemed to say at the same time. "You have our permission to marry our daughter."

I had one more person to ask permission from: Morgan's grandfather. I was nervous, but not as nervous as when I asked her parents. After all, we had racing in common.

PaPete said yes.

29

GOOD LIFE

"Find happiness in all that you do."

The Ride kept getting better every year. No more fried chicken out of boxes on the interstate shoulder. No more wrong exits and five-hour delays. Now, trucks carried our luggage for us, and hot meals were waiting when we arrived. Our fuel stops had all the precision of a NASCAR pit stop, and we started staying in much nicer hotels. The Greenbrier near White Sulphur Springs, West Virginia. The Grove Park in Asheville, North Carolina. The Homestead in Hot Springs, Virginia. These days, we even bring along our own orthopedic surgeon, registered nurses, paramedics, and half a dozen retired North Carolina highway patrolmen. That way, if we ever have an issue—just about any kind you could think of—we have a team in place ready to assist. Many people even say it's the most organized motorcycle ride they've ever seen. It runs like a well-oiled Harley.

Some well-known people, in and out of NASCAR, have ridden with us. Michael Waltrip. Geoff Bodine. Mike Helton. My dad. Harry Gant. Tony Stewart. Donnie Allison. Matt Kenseth. NFL great (and sprinter and mixed martial artist) Herschel Walker. World Golf Hall of Famer Davis Love III. Model Niki Taylor. Paul Teutul, Sr. and Jr., stars of the *American Chopper* TV franchise. Doctors. Lawyers. Business titans. Race car mechanics. Some husband-and-wife teams and then their children too. It truly is a family ride. And most important of all, we've raised a lot of money and helped a lot of children over the decades. By 2019, we had raised more than $19 million for Victory Junction and other children's charities, including sending more than 8,200 kids to camp at no cost to their families.

So there we were, more than a quarter century after we first started, and the Kyle Petty Charity Ride Across America was still going strong as a major supporter of Victory Junction and other causes. When the COVID-19 pandemic hit in March 2020, for the first time ever, we had to postpone our annual Ride. We moved it a full year to spring of 2021, never imagining COVID would still be an issue. Yet 2021 came, and we had to postpone again. But with the COVID vaccine rollout and the restrictions being lifted, we were eager to do something to get the Riders back together in a safe way. So we came up with Charity Ride Revival. After all, the word *revival* means to bring something back to life, and in our case, it meant reactivating after being dormant for more than two years. So in September 2021, we held an epic, three-day mini-version of our larger Ride. A one-time-only thing. Half the time. Half the size. But still all the fun.

We've built up a real sense of family, and the Ride has never stopped being fun. There are nine of us who've ridden every single year and another thirty or forty who've made it twenty-plus times.

We did suffer a major loss in 2014.

Don Tilley was returning home from a Harley-Davidson dealers conference that August, riding the Blue Ridge Parkway near mile post 394. His longtime business partner and loving wife of fifty-three years, Robinette Tilley, was on the seat behind him. Something happened. No one knows for sure what. But the bike left the parkway. Don was killed, and Robinette was critically injured.

Our hearts were broken. We couldn't believe our fearless leader, our very own Rand McNally, was gone. Over the years, Don had become another father to me. We rode more miles and shared more stories than I can count now. He taught me how to ride long distance and so much more.

A large ride was held in his honor in Statesville. His memorial service filled the football stadium at West Iredell High School. Everyone wanted to pay their respects to Don, including more than a hundred of his closest friends from the Ride.

People talked about his deeply charitable nature and his undying gift for cool. Almost no one failed to mention that he had died doing what he loved. And everyone agreed there was something we had to do in his memory. We had to ride on.

That year was just hard.

On March 25, my mom passed away after a long battle with cancer. We all knew it was coming. She was surrounded at home by the people who loved her. But I still felt totally unprepared. With Adam, his passing was unexpected. It came out of the blue. With my mom, everyone had a chance to say their goodbyes. But when the day arrived, it was just as hard on all of us. It hit me with the same intensity I'd felt losing Adam.

She was my first teacher, my Cub Scout leader, and my biggest cheerleader when I played sports in school. She was always there while my dad was racing. She was my number-one fan when I drove a race car. Then, she was gone. The loss of a child is the hardest experience for anyone. The loss of a mother or a father has got to be a close second. I felt for all three of my sisters. I felt for the grandkids and great-grandkids. But I hurt the most for my dad.

They had been together almost their whole lives, and I couldn't imagine what losing her must feel like for him or what the days ahead were going to mean. All of us, especially myself and my sisters, would have to try to fill that void in different ways. But I also knew we could only fill a small part of it. Because my mom *was* our family.

She knew thousands of people. Even more knew her. They all recalled "Mrs. Lynda" as a loving wife, mother, grandmother, great-grandmother, sister, aunt, and friend. She was often referred to as one of the first women of NASCAR. They remembered her as kind and caring, a generous neighbor and a tireless community volunteer. She helped to start the Racing Wives Auxiliary and served for sixteen years on the Randolph County School Board.

All that was true. But what I remembered was an amazing mother who, no matter what, was always there for me.

We kept her service very small, a private memorial on my parents' property in Randleman. My mama, Lynda Gayle Owens Petty, was seventy-two years old. Another big part of my world was gone.

All along, I never gave up on my music, and it never gave up on me. It's been years, decades really, since I quit looking at my songwriting, my singing, and my guitar playing as an actual career option, but my passion for my music stuck with me through everything. Music has always been fun for me. It's always been something I enjoyed sharing. At times, it's been the only way I could fully express myself.

When Adam's accident happened, I poured my heart out to that guitar. It listened, and it never argued with me. It played whatever I wanted it to, and the music gave me solace. When I couldn't find any other way to say what I was feeling, I wrote a song for Adam. "Without You," the song is called. It still rings true to me.

I thought that time would heal the hurt
But time's just not that strong.
This hurt never goes away
It keeps hanging on
Without you, without you
Without you nothing ever changes
And nothing is the same . . . without you.

Looking back, I can see: My music was a big part of my therapy.

When I fell in love with Morgan, it was the same way. The love I had for her came out through the guitar. It came out through the songs I was writing. I could say things that way that I'd never say just talking. I could express myself on a whole new level in song.

The music and the guitar will always be a part of me. No doubt about that. It's an important emotional piece of who I am. I don't play a lot of other people's music. I play my music because my music comes from inside me. When I play my music, I am sharing part of me. To me, it's a lot more meaningful than me saying, "Look, I can play 'House of the Rising Sun.'"

I can't imagine stopping. Ever.

Like her parents and grandfather, Morgan answered, "Yes."

She and I were married on December 12, 2015, a beautiful winter day in Charlotte that felt more like spring. It was 75 degrees and sunny. Just perfect. We had a small wedding with our families and closest friends. As I stood there beside my dad and the pastor and watched Morgan walk down the aisle, I wanted to cry. I was overwhelmed with happiness and with the love I had for her.

Walking toward me was all my dreams come true. She was a beautiful bride. When you least expect it, sometimes love will find you.

If you're blessed like I have been, it's a love that's deeper and stronger than anything you've ever felt before. A love of light and joy. And Morgan had only begun to change my life.

She's the muse for my music.

She's my very best friend.

She lifts me up when I need support and holds me close when I need to be comforted. She knows what I'm thinking and how I feel even before I do. She completes me and makes me whole. I pray I do the same for her. I know I try. All I want is for her to feel the same way she makes me feel.

I wrote three songs for Morgan when we were getting married. The first song was about our time together. I sang it to her when I asked her to marry me. The second song was about the dreams I had for our life together. I sang that one at our rehearsal dinner. The third song was all the promises I made to her on our wedding day. I sang it to her at our reception. Each year I write a song for her on our anniversary.

Sometimes, I feel like I can best express my love for her through my songs. This is part of the one I wrote for her after five wonderful years.

All I want every day
Is to be near you somewhere.

I don't have to be by your side.
I just need to know that you're near.

All I want every day
Is to see you smile.
To know something I do or say
Makes you happy for a while.
All I want is you.

And the love had only begun. After we were married, we bought a house that was close enough to PaPete's house that we could walk over there for dinner sometimes. My life with Morgan was blessed and made even richer with the birth of our two amazing little boys, Overton Owens on June 3, 2018, and Cotten Cable on August 2, 2020.

I love watching Morgan be a mama. It makes my heart almost burst with love for her and them. I love being a new dad again. I'm just in a different place in my life right now. A place I've never been before. A place that gives me greater appreciation for what really matters in life. When you're younger and have kids, you're spending all your time trying to get ahead and trying to make a living, trying to make a life. I've already done all of that.

Now, the most important thing I can give to Overton and Cotten is time. We spend our days playing on the floor with race cars and construction equipment, reading books and discovering the world. I love singing to them and tucking them in at night. I have been blessed in so many ways, but being a daddy is the greatest blessing of all.

I wrote a song for Overton when he was about six months old. We were on one of our many walks through our neighborhood when the song came to me. As we walked, I just thought about all the things I hoped and dreamed for him. Once again, my love and emotions came out in song.

I hope you say what you mean and mean what you say
And know who you are every day.
Don't always work, take time to play.
Stop and smell the roses along life's way.

Find happiness in all that you do,
And always try to make others happy too.
Give kindness away, it'll come back to you
And believe in true love.
True love will find you.

A couple years later, I was doing that same loop through our streets, this time pushing a new little boy in the stroller. This song for Cotten came to me.

Sometimes in your eyes I see
When you look up at me
All my hopes and dreams I have for you
But those dreams they're my own
I know someday when you're grown
You'll have your own dreams
Those dreams will be mine too.

'Cause you make me wanna be
The best daddy I can be.
'Cause you make me wanna be
The best daddy for you I can be.

When I fell in love with Morgan, I knew my life was forever changed. But I could have never dreamed of the life, the love, and the two little boys that she has given me. By the time you read this, another blessing will have come into our lives with our third child together, due summer of 2022. I'm already dreaming of the days that we'll spend together and the songs that I'll write as I push the stroller with our new baby through the neighborhood. Love will always be inspiring.

Somewhere along the way, not because I wanted to be the next big thing in Nashville, I started playing in front of audiences again, doing some open-mic nights around Charlotte, which led to me playing several times with the Salisbury Symphony. And I started working even more on my song writing.

I got into a habit: I'd get up at five thirty in the morning and spend an hour or so with my guitar. Writing lyrics. Coming up with melodies. Forging them into songs. I was surprised by how creative and productive I could be that early in the morning. Then, I'd get on with the rest of my day.

I don't think I'm a great guitar player. I'm a proficient guitar player. I'm not a great songwriter. I'm a proficient songwriter. But I bring every bit as much love and enjoyment to my music as anybody out there. If you stood me onstage with fifty other musicians, maybe you wouldn't pick me out. But I have a passion for it that has never faded in my heart. And I'd like to think I write some poignant lines and hit some true notes.

I met a man—a lot of things in my life start with "I met a man . . ." This particular man was Dolphus Ramseur. He comes from Concord, North Carolina, and everyone calls him Dolph. He owns Ramseur Records and manages a roster of artists that includes the alt-bluegrass Avett Brothers, whose hybrid of folk, country, bluegrass, punk, rock, and honky-tonk has made them beloved North Carolina originals.

Dolph also loves NASCAR. He is a huge Wood Brothers and David Pearson fan. We met and started talking. We stayed in touch. And one day out of the blue, I called him and said, "Hey, I've been writing songs. Do you have anybody who can listen to my songs and tell me if there's some potential here or tell me, 'Put 'em in a box and bury 'em in your backyard?'"

Dolph introduced me to David Childers, who's an amazing songwriter and lives twenty minutes from me in Mount Holly, North Carolina. I walked in that first day and felt like I'd known David my whole life, and it wasn't just because he had some kind things to say about my songs. We just clicked. He's been a mentor and a teacher, helping me get more comfortable performing in front of people.

He and I started playing shows together. Nothing huge. A hundred, a couple of hundred people, crowds like that. Singer-songwriter shows in bars and other places where people come to actually listen to the words and the music. After a couple of shows together, we started to sell out the listening rooms and other venues. David will give you an upbeat song, then I'll bring you down. Then, we'll flip it. I'll bring you up, and David will take you back down. We complement each other really well. He's got his own group of fans who follow him. I've got people who come out to hear me. Once David and I get going, you can hear a pin drop.

When the COVID pandemic hit in 2020, we had to suspend our live shows. But as soon as the virus eased, I knew we'd be right back at it again. I really missed playing with David. During the pandemic, when there were no live audiences and there wasn't much racing, I had to find creative ways to keep the music going. COVID had us all cut off from each other. It was so important at a time like that for me to continue sharing my music with others.

So I kept doing what I was doing, as much of it as I could, still getting up before the sun, writing for an hour or two in the morning, and seeing what I had. Next, I had to find new ways to get the songs out there.

One of them was my "Quarantunes." Every week for more than a year, I recorded a new video of me playing guitar and singing one of my songs, then put it out on Facebook and Instagram and Twitter. I was shocked how many people tuned in and how much reaction I received. People started looking forward to hearing the music as much as I looked forward to playing for them. The sharing felt to me like it went both ways. I guess people were looking for something—some kind of connection, especially when so many of us had to stay so close to home. I wrote about whatever was in my heart and on my mind.

Some of it had to do with the pandemic that everyone was living through. A lot of it was about my role as a father. Some of the songs were just stories. And every now and again, when the feeling hit me, I'd pull out an older song about my dad or about Adam. All that music meant something to me, and I was honored to share it.

In the years since I stopped driving a race car, I have never once stepped away from racing. I am so grateful for that, and I have my role as a media commentator to thank. Who knew I could be on television all these years, talking about a subject that was such a part of me? Who knew social media would rise like it has? I certainly never would have predicted it.

Television is an ever-changing business, as fast-moving in its own way as driving race cars. The networks keep being reshuffled and sometimes renamed. The good news as far as I'm concerned is that they always found a place for me and all my unique insights about racing. I was thrilled to join NASCAR on NBC in 2015, and the media landscape is continually evolving. Broadcast. Cable. Satellite. Streaming. Mobile. Podcasts. Things keep changing. I'm always willing to try new approaches. I don't think anybody knows where any of this is heading next. But as long as people are interested in racing, we'll find new and exciting ways to deliver the sport into people's lives, ways no one has even thought of yet.

For instance, I love doing stuff for NBC's streaming service, Peacock TV, and the Motorsports on NBC YouTube channel, including my *Coffee with Kyle* digital series, where I get to ask drivers, owners, broadcasters, pioneers, and legends of the sport questions I personally want to know the answers to. No script. No agenda. No heavy production. Just an intimate conversation that we invite you to eavesdrop on. It's a cool way to learn more about the history and people of the sport.

I'm also fortunate to have cocreated a TV series called *Dinner Drive with Kyle Petty* for the Circle Network. It combines my love for cool cars, good food, and incredible stories, all weaved into hometown visits with some of the biggest names in entertainment. Darius Rucker, Ric Flair, Pitbull, just to name a few. The show goes way beyond NASCAR and allows me to continue asking questions that I want to know the answers to from the worlds of music, sports, food, cars . . . almost anything. It's awesome.

And they let me call all this *work*!

I'll say this much: I'm not driving, but I am never, ever not busy.

There are always a million different things going on. I'm never bored. I'm as involved as ever in what I grew up dreaming about—the sport of racing.

30

CHANGE MACHINE

"Why dream when you can live it?"

It's an awesome run this sport has had when you think about it. A bunch of guys had a meeting in the bar of the Streamline Hotel, and three-quarters of a century later, the National Association of Stock Car Auto Racing is still roaring into the future.

Still owned by the France family. Still largely run by the descendants of Bill France, Sr. Still headquartered in Daytona Beach, Florida. And still arguably the gold standard for racing around the world. NASCAR remains a major force in American culture and politics. The sport has millions and millions of dedicated fans. It generates billions of dollars in economic activity—ticket sales, sponsorship payments, broadcast revenues, merchandising, licensing, and all the rest. It's a huge engine for charitable giving and philanthropy. Most outsiders have no clue just how sprawling an empire NASCAR is. Each year, the organization sanctions something like 1,500 races at one hundred racetracks in forty-eight U.S. states and Canada, Mexico, and Europe. I don't know how you measure all the excitement, adrenaline, and smiles, but NASCAR has certainly delivered plenty of those, along with an endless supply of passionate debates about the sport, its past, and its future. (Who's the greatest driver ever? How *stock* should a stock car be? Which kid on the Modified tour has the brightest future and which Cup driver is totally overrated?) Just state an opinion about anything connected to NASCAR. Believe me, someone will disagree.

But here's the thing that a lot of fans today don't always grasp in this tradition-loving sport of ours: Though we constantly honor our deep and rich heritage, NASCAR has always been about change and the future. Really, the sport is a chameleon. It has always changed into whatever it needed to be. That's how it's survived all these years and how it will ride into the future.

The very basics of racing won't change any time soon. We start at a white line. We run around in circles, and we end at the same white line. I suspect that will always be the case. But everything else—and I mean *everything*—is up for grabs.

Who the sponsors are. What kinds of cars we drive. How we attract new fans without alienating the old ones. The latest adjustments in the race schedule and the newest rules. The role of our media partners. Going younger. Going digital. Going green. As long as society keeps changing, NASCAR will keep changing too. That's just part of what it means to operate a sport and a business in this ever-changing world of ours.

Having lived through so many of those changes and still having the privilege to greet the next ones, here's what I know for certain: Some of the changes will be popular with both the drivers and the fans. Some won't be. Many will spark intense discussion. But let's just admit it: Debating the latest NASCAR controversy is a big part of NASCAR. If we didn't care so much, we wouldn't argue so freely. And, come on, wouldn't that be boring?

Just look at how the sport's money has changed. Not the ticket money or the money from TV revenues or the money that some drivers make winning races or writing books. I'm talking about the dollars the outside businesses pump in that keep all those cars in motion every Sunday— racing's real fuel. Nothing is more vital to the business of racing.

I was talking with my dad about this. Eighty or 90 percent of the guys who showed up in Charlotte on June 19, 1949, for the very first sanctioned NASCAR race had ties to the liquor business, its legal and especially illegal sides. That's just the way it was. Who else had access to so many drivers and mechanics and so much money to burn? The liquor boys managed to hang on for a while. But in the mid-1950s, a millionaire businessman from Wisconsin named Carl Kiekhaefer, the founder of Mercury Marine, saw something that would eventually be obvious to everyone: Race cars could promote other brands, including Kiekhaefer's outboard motor company. He paid Tim Flock $40,000 to come out of retirement and drive a Chrysler 300 to eighteen wins and the 1955 NASCAR championship. Of course, the car had KIEKHAEFER OUTBOARDS painted on the side. And the whole economics of stock car racing were forever changed.

Next up, Detroit's auto manufacturers moved in, becoming NASCAR's chief economic engine until the fuel crisis of the 1970s drove them out. Then, R.J. Reynolds tobacco company showed up, flush with marketing dollars after their cigarette commercials were tossed off TV. They dominated the sport for a couple of decades, not just with their money, but also with their marketing know-how. But when the health controversies around tobacco became too hot to handle, a wide variety of big corporate brands filled the void. And so the brand names you see today at the racetrack aren't so different from the brands on the shelves of your local supermarket or home-improvement store or in the commercials you see on TV.

Change. NASCAR changed to survive.

The France family deserves a lot of credit for being open to all this change. Far more than any other professional sport, NASCAR has always been flexible. The sport hasn't always responded as quickly as it should or could have. But eventually, the change that's been needed is the change that's arrived.

The vision and passion of Bill France, Sr., set that tradition. Bill France, Jr., made it his own. He passed it on to his son, former CEO and chairman Brian France. And the same has proven true for the next generation, led by current CEO and Chairman Jim France, Vice Chair Lesa France Kennedy, and up-and-coming Senior Vice President Ben Kennedy. They've always been able to lead NASCAR through the storms and to come out on the other side with a new direction. It's through that lens that we can view everything that's happening now.

I can guarantee you one thing: Any issue that shows up in America will find its way eventually into NASCAR. That's how intertwined this sport and this country are. So, of course, as America began to face a new round of racial reckoning, so did NASCAR.

It's just a fact: Stock car racing grew up as a largely white sport in the southeastern United States. Most of the fans were white. So were the vast majority of the drivers, the owners, and the crews. For a long time, the Confederate flag flew at the track not far from two other high-flying symbols near and dear to race fans—the American flag and the checkered one. There's no sense in denying it: There is ugliness in the past. Wendell Scott, the first African American driver to win at the sport's top level, was often greeted with racial taunts and unfairness in a career that ran from 1961 to 1973.

Race hasn't been the only cause for soul-searching in NASCAR. In the 1980s, when driver Tim Richmond was diagnosed with AIDS, the sport in many ways turned its back on him. When Danica Patrick showed up two decades later, the sponsors loved her, but some fans not so much. Heck, even I made comments that were taken out of context and blown out of proportion. But things may be changing again. As athletes in other sports began taking a knee during the national anthem, NASCAR was also confronting some difficult issues from the past.

It took Bubba Wallace to spark this confrontation. And who better? Bubba is, after all, the most successful African American driver in NAS-CAR. He had the credibility. And he was driving the legendary no. 43 car for Richard Petty Motorsports. In June 2020, after the police killing of George Floyd and the Black Lives Matter protests that followed, Bubba became NASCAR's public face for racial justice. His stand led NASCAR to ban the Confederate flag at the racetracks and opened the door for the sport to find new ways of inclusion.

And here's what surprised a lot of outsiders, I think: He did it with solid support from his fellow drivers and NASCAR. I was proud to see my dad standing at Bubba's side, helping to lead the sport they both loved into the next chapter.

Were all the fans happy about it? No. Did some feel like they were being unfairly accused of racism? I'm sure some did. But NASCAR was also responding to a business reality in today's diverse world. A lot of those big corporate sponsors were also putting the pressure on. They could not have their logos in the same TV shots as a symbol tied to slavery and discrimination. If you're Procter & Gamble, do you really want your Tide car driving past a grandstand dotted with Confederate flags? Probably not. Again, NASCAR is changing to move forward.

Here's how I like to explain it: For three and a half hours every Sunday, NASCAR is a sport, cars running around in circles, racing toward the start-finish line. The rest of the week, NASCAR is a business, though every part of that business is affected by whatever happens at the race-track on Sunday afternoon. You can't understand one without the other.

Sometimes in the past, when people have tried to address these questions of diversity and inclusion, the efforts were incomplete. It's like when a white person says, "I'm not racist. I've got a Black friend." Well, good for you, but how far does that go? In the past, it meant we included people in the sport who weren't white males. But how many and at what levels?

It's been nearly two decades since NASCAR's first diversity program began. And we're just beginning to see its results. Bubba, Daniel Suárez, and Kyle Larson (and no women in Cup) can't carry this torch all alone. Where are your diverse owners? Where are your new Black, Latino, and female superstars? All of that is key to attracting new fans.

I get it. Change comes slowly most of the time. This sport took an incredible amount of hate from its fan base when Toyota first ran a car. *That's a Japanese car!* There were drivers in the sport during that time who made derogatory comments about Toyota. All I wanted to know was, *Can the car go fast?* From the driver's seat you couldn't see the nameplate at all. And here's the lesson from that one: Change might come slowly, but it almost always comes, as it should in this instance too. When you think about it, the racing competition at its very core is about having an individual in the car who can truly wheel it and a wide variety of folks behind that driver who are contributing to the car going as fast as possible. Engineers. Fabricators. Crew. Salespeople. And on and on. But very little, if any of that, has anything to do with anyone's race, gender, ethnicity, or size. Nor does it matter who any of those people pray to, who they love, or where they're from. At the end of the day, the heart of a racer is the heart of a racer. Why wouldn't we want everyone who loves racing to feel included and part of our NASCAR family? The best part of NASCAR is family, and my hope is everyone who loves this sport as much as I do sees the great opportunity in front of the sport we all love so much.

Doesn't that make sense?

We have fresh reason for optimism now on the diversity front. That's why basketball legend Michael Jordan coming into the sport as an owner is so important. He joins former NBA superstar Brad Daugherty and becomes the second African American car owner at NASCAR's top level, just as NFL great Emmitt Smith announced his intention to start an Xfinity team. And Pitbull, the Cuban American musician, entrepreneur, and global ambassador, is very much in the mix. These are people with a history of success, not just in their initial, chosen professions but also in the larger business world. And all of them are longtime race fans, which helps. As Michael told NBC Sports: "I love, love NASCAR. I don't go into it with the idea and concept that I'm trying to change and shape NAS-CAR. I go in with my passion." Same with Pitbull. "Why dream when you can live it?" as he told the *Charlotte Observer*.

We all hope they can be successful in NASCAR. I'm pulling for all of them. A lot of people are. I'm especially pulling for Michael and Denny Hamlin's team, 23xi. Denny called me in the latter of the 2021 season to ask personally if my family would allow them to run the no. 45 with Kurt Busch behind the wheel. NASCAR, as I've said before, owns the numbers. But out of respect for our family, they've never let anyone else run the 45. As far as NASCAR was concerned, the decision was up to us. It had been Michael's baseball number, so it meant something to Michael and Denny's team. They also knew how much it meant to us. I always knew this day would come, but it still didn't make it easier. I called Austin and Montgomery Lee to get their feelings. They both felt the same way, that when people see the 45, they'll think of Adam. Kurt has always been a huge supporter of Victory Junction, and I know he can win races. It will be a happy day for our family when Kurt puts the 45 in Victory Lane. We recognize that the future of NASCAR depends in part on our ability to broaden the sport. We have a great product here. There is no reason it can't be a draw for everyone. They just need to feel welcome and have a reason to stick around. There's no way around it: That includes a diverse lineup of owners, drivers, crews, officials, and, most of all, fans.

So who can Michael and Pitbull bring along with them? That'll be fascinating to see. Can they bring people into the grandstands who followed Michael's dominance in the NBA, people who've been inspired and entertained by Pitbull's talent and charisma? These two are already delivering fresh eyes to the sport. Now, we have to put on a show that's good enough to keep those eyeballs here.

There is a lot of pressure on Bubba and also on Daniel Suárez, the sport's top Latino driver. And in some ways that isn't fair. "I've already got ten thousand more eyes on me because I am of color," Bubba said. These guys live under a spotlight that's different from what other drivers are expected to bear, just like Danica Patrick did when she arrived in the male-dominated world of racing.

NASCAR has always been a family sport. Not just the Pettys. Lots of fathers and sons. The Earnhardts. The Allisons. The Jarretts. The Blaneys. The Elliotts. The father-and-son list goes on and on. Truex. Keslowski. Nemechek. Baker. Ragan. So when will we have the first father-daughter racing family? Someday, we may even have a daughter following her mother into NASCAR.

None of these fresh faces need to be the next Jimmie Johnson or Dale Earnhardt. Most drivers never will achieve that level of success. They don't have to be superstars. But they do need to be able to be competitive and win races, no matter their skin color or gender.

And this new wave of diversity needs to become a part of what the sport is. It has to be embedded in NASCAR's DNA, a part of the fabric, part of the long-term success. The sport has to be a patchwork quilt, and this is the latest piece that we're adding.

That change is coming. We must embrace it and do it right. Our future, the sport's future, depends on it.

As all these social issues swirl around us, NASCAR is reimagining its future in all kinds of ways. How we watch races is already changing, and

I promise you the changes have only begun. It's not just in racing. Big changes are also happening in football, basketball, baseball, and all kinds of other live events. Already, I can take my phone and, whenever I want to, stream Dale Jr.'s latest *Lost Speedways* episode or binge-watch a season's worth of *Yellowstone*. I can also say, "The race comes on this afternoon at two thirty, and I'll watch it tonight at ten." But hold on a second. By ten, the race results will be on my phone. Do I still want to watch if I already know who won? That's a crucial question and one that will go a long way to shaping the race-watching future. The honest answer, I guess, is . . . *it depends*. But information is so fluid now, I know I can watch on my phone, on my computer, on my iPad . . . and, soon, maybe on the inside of my glasses too while I am having dinner with my family. I'm sure they won't notice that I'm following a race out of the corner of my eye. Ha!

We know there will be a million ways to watch anything. What we don't know is which ones will be great. To me, live sports will always be better live. I like not knowing who won. But the questions are flying at all of us: In 2040, how will we be watching races? What comes after streaming? How does the sport adjust to the changing social-media environment? How big a role will be played by iRacing and other digital-competition platforms, where you're on your computer in New York and I'm on mine in North Carolina and we can race our butts off all day long? There are no fatalities in iRacing. Which brings up another set of questions. Will people watch racing without the element of danger? It's the same question people ask about hockey. Do you go to a hockey game to see the fight or to see the hat trick?

NASCAR attendance has dropped in recent years. So have the TV ratings. Some people believe the sport needs to up the danger quotient. It's such a hard sport to figure out. There was a time when the racing was more dangerous than it is today. The deaths of my son Adam, Dale Earnhardt, Tony Roper, and Kenny Irwin helped to change that with the HANS head-restraint device and other safety improvements in the cars and on the tracks. The SAFER barriers—for Steel And Foam Energy Reduction—softened the concrete, a little. They aren't quite as soft as some fans imagine, but they are an amazing invention. They've saved numerous lives. Think about the near head-on collisions with walls in recent years. Without these safety changes, who knows how many drivers we might have lost.

The safety progress is real, so real some people tend to forget that the danger is always there. You're still putting human beings into vehicles that are capable of running 200 miles an hour. As long as there is racing, there will be tragedy. We have all focused so much lately on other issues in the sport, it's easy to get complacent about the dangers. *It doesn't happen. It's not gonna happen. It'll never happen again.* A lot of people have started believing that. And then when something happens, like Ryan Newman's heart-stopping crash in a sea of sparks and fire on the last lap of the 2020 Daytona 500, people seemed surprised. "That can still happen?"

Yes, it can.

If diversity and inclusion have been the recent hot-button issues in NAS-CAR, green is coming next. Why wouldn't it? The environment and the future of the planet are huge topics in the world we now live in. NASCAR launched its NASCAR Green platform in 2009, introducing American-made ethanol into the fuel, recycling the tires and fluids from competition, and engaging in a nationwide tree-planting campaign to offset carbon emissions. But that was just a start for where this entire issue is going. And if NASCAR doesn't step up with some additional, significant change beyond the on-track product, it'll soon be a major issue for NAS-CAR. In fact, that debate has already begun.

If a NASCAR Cup race draws sixty-five thousand people to a track, how did all those people get there? They drove, most of them. How many cars are in the parking lot? Too many to count. Not to mention all the campers and RVs parked in the infield. And just wait until everyone tries to leave at once! How much carbon did those vehicles put into the atmosphere? How much fuel did that burn up? Someone can figure that out, just not me. And they all came to watch forty race cars run four hundred or five hundred miles, burning fossil fuels. And those race cars had to be transported in eighteen-wheel haulers from track to track, from

Pennsylvania to Michigan then out west to California, south to Florida, and as far north as New Hampshire. Following those haulers are motor coaches for drivers and owners to stay in on race weekends. And how did the drivers and teams get to the track?

By private plane.

When you start calculating, it all adds up. I'm not saying other sports don't have environmental impact, but the perception of motorsports is different. Formula One already has an E-Series, racing electric cars. Mark my words: From top to bottom, NASCAR is about to have a big green debate. How we dispose of our tires, where all the oil goes, how the mountains of trash at the racetrack get recycled—it'll all be on the table if it isn't already.

iRacing or whatever it morphs into will be part of the discussion, as will, believe it or not, electric cars. And let's be honest: There's no law that says internal-combustion engines are the only kind that you can race. The problem here, don't forget: A large part of racing's appeal is the roar of the engines. Even on television the producers are pumping up the volume. They call it "giving the folks at home the track experience." Will fans cheer just as loudly for a silent flash of color racing across their TV screen?

As someone who has been around this sport my entire life, I will always crave the sound of the engine. That sound tells me the car is running. But Overton and Cotten may end up loving electric cars just as much as I love the gasoline-powered kind, and I can't tell them they're wrong. I grew up on 427-cubic-inch engines and spent my entire career driving 350-cubic-inch engines. With the people who helped build the sport into what we now know. I remain deeply humbled by that legacy. But we all need open minds to keep moving forward. Our kids and grandkids may start talking just as passionately about lithium batteries and electric motor output. And here's one advantage on their side: It might be nice to go to a track where no one had to shout . . . or read lips!

Who knows? Maybe all this will help the sport continue to grow, bringing in new generations of people while giving lifelong fans like myself something new to cheer about. That's a whole other kind of diversity, and I say, "I'm ready. Bring it on."

I'm not sure we'll ever reach the automobile equivalent of Elon Musk's driverless cars. I hope not! But as I say, change has always been part of NASCAR. Why should we stop now?

ACKNOWLEDGMENTS

First, I'd like to thank God for giving me the courage and the strength in life to push through and carry on when there were days I didn't want to. Thank you for giving me the ability to find blessings in the middle of tragedy.

To my mom, my Uncle Randy, and Adam. I am who I am because of all of you. I hope that every day I make you proud.

Thank you to my wife, Morgan, for making this book possible. You jogged my memory when it needed to be jogged and pushed me to tell stories I'd only told to you. You held me when the stories hurt, and you laughed with me when the stories were funny. You gave me the strength and the belief that somewhere in me, there was a story that someone needed to hear. Because of you, if this book touches one life, then it's all worth it. I love you.

Thank you to my dad, to my three sisters, Sharon, Lisa, and Rebecca, and to Austin, Montgomery Lee, Overton, and Cotten for your unconditional love and support. I love you all just as much.

I want to thank Ellis Henican, my cowriter, for allowing me to ramble on and bring my thoughts into cohesive sentences. It's a good thing you're originally from New Orleans and can tap into your memory to speak southern. Thank you for asking the hard questions I didn't want to answer and for not giving up until I finally answered. I know that starting this memoir in the middle of the COVID-19 pandemic might not have been the best timing, but through all the phone calls and the time together, I enjoyed every minute and a friendship blossomed. And to Roberta Teer, for your meticulous editing and passion for my project. I owe you dinner and race tickets. To Michael Homler and the team at St. Martin's Press and Macmillan for giving my manuscript a home and letting me tell my story.

To Russell Weinrich and Jimmy Hicks of Racing Insights (aka Bert and Ernie) for fact-checking all my dates, years, and racing statistics. You guys know more than anybody. I never let the facts stand in the way of a good story!

Thank you to Eric Nyquist, senior vice president of strategic development at NASCAR, for reading my manuscript and encouraging me throughout the process. This would not have been possible without your friendship and support.

Thank you Ginny Talley, communications specialist at the Kyle Petty Charity Ride, for reading and editing my manuscript. Your edits, punctuations, and insights helped me to see the book in a different way. Bet you never thought a kid from Level Cross who can't spell could write a book!

Thank you to everyone I ever worked with in racing, especially the Wood family and Felix Sabates. Everybody I worked with at every shop, on every car I drove, and every sponsor I ever had. I never felt like I worked for anybody, and I never felt like anybody worked for me. I always felt like we worked together.

Thank you also to every fan who has ever watched a NASCAR race on TV or sat in the stands. Without you, there are no stories. Without you, there is no NASCAR.

Lastly, thank you to everyone who has ever ridden on the Kyle Petty Charity Ride and helped us raise money and awareness for Victory Junction. You are my family. Thank you to every parent and child who has ever crossed through the gates at Victory Junction. You changed my life, and you are my heroes. In each of you, when I see your smile, I know Adam is still here.

KYLE PETTY is a former American stock car racer and current racing commentator on NBC Sports. He is the son of racing icon Richard Petty, the grandson of NASCAR pioneer Lee Petty, and the father of rising racer Adam Petty, who was killed in a crash in May 2000. Outside of the sport, he is a musician, philanthropist, motivational speaker, and TV host.

ELLIS HENICAN is a Pulitzer Prize–winning journalist, a popular TV pundit, and a multi–*New York Times* bestselling author.